Jewelry
International

THE WORLD'S FINEST JEWELRY BOOK®

BY CAROLINE CHILDERS

Jewelry *International*

THE WORLD'S FINEST JEWELRY BOOK®

First published in the United States in 2014 by:
**CAROLINE CHILDERS AND
TOURBILLON INTERNATIONAL
A Modern Luxury Company**

11 West 25th Street, 8th floor
New York, NY 10010
Tel: +1 212 627 7732

CHIEF EXECUTIVE OFFICER Lew Dickey
PRESIDENT Michael Dickey
PUBLISHER Caroline Childers
EDITOR IN CHIEF Elise Nussbaum
ART DIRECTOR Franca Vitali
ASSOCIATE EDITOR Julie Singer
JUNIOR ASSISTANT EDITOR Amber Ruiz
VICE PRESIDENT OF OPERATIONS Sean Bertram
DIRECTOR OF PRODUCTION & CREATIVE SERVICES Erin Quinn
PRODUCTION COORDINATORS Tim Maxwell & Kari Grota Compean
NATIONAL CIRCULATION MANAGER Mike Petre
DIRECTOR OF INFORMATION TECHNOLOGY Scott Brookman

In association with ***RIZZOLI*** International Publications Inc.

300 Park Avenue South, New York, NY 10010

ISBN: 978-0-8478-4303-9

Printed in Italy

COVER Sharon Stone wears de GRISOGONO jewels at amfAR's Cinema Against AIDS event at the 2013 International Film Festival at Cannes. The earrings are crafted in pink gold and set with 1,144 diamonds (33.61 carats). The starfish cuff bracelet is crafted in white and pink gold and set with 721 red spinels (210.80 carats), 7 white diamonds (0.60 carats) and 247 white diamonds (5.40 carats). She wears 2 pink-gold rings: one is set with 235 white diamonds (7.27 carats) and the other with 167 white diamonds (2.86 carats) and 59 Icy diamonds (3.93 carats). PREVIOUS PAGE de GRISOGONO necklace in white gold set with 1,252 white diamonds (62.092 carats) and 1,367 emeralds (53.306 carats), with white-gold earrings set with 239 emeralds (4.80 carats) and 1,547 white diamonds (19.34 carats). INSIDE FRONT FLAP Hammerman Brothers emerald necklace. INSIDE BACK FLAP Jacob & Co. emerald earrings. BACK COVER TAKAT pendant set with tanzanite (279.20 carats).

ULTIMATE FEMININITY

LIMELIGHT GALA

18K white gold watch
Case set with brilliant-cut diamonds

www.piaget.fr

PIAGET

TABLE OF CONTENTS

TOP: Assael earrings.

ASSAEL

THE MOST MAGNIFICENT PEARLS IN THE WORLD

SINCE 1919

ASSAEL.COM   212 819 0060

GUY ELLIA

PARIS
16 PLACE VENDÔME

FOREWORD

JEWELS ARE A FANTASY

As a child, I used to love to admire pictures of royalty, splendid in their regalia from head to toe. Diamonds and pearls shone from every inch of the court, and I could hardly distinguish where one gem ended and the next began. The opulence blurred together in an exquisite fantasy that left an overall impression of luxury and ease, but the specifics fled from the grasp of my imagination.

As I grew older and learned more about the histories of these men and women, about life, about love and about jewels, everything came into clearer focus—for better or for worse. However, jewels have always retained their magic and mystery for me, with the realization that millennia of artistic development and cultural forces have brought us to a point where jewelry is so charged with meaning that each of us ultimately determines what it symbolizes to us.

The sapphire ring with which Prince Charles proposed to Diana Spencer was given new life and new meaning when Prince William offered it to Kate Middleton, and the rings I wear remind me not only of important people in my life, but also the joy that comes from being able to indulge one's aesthetic tastes. My jewelry collection comprises brooches inherited from my grandmother, bracelets that belonged to my mother, rings given as love tokens from men whose names I've forgotten, necklaces given to me by my sweet granddaughter, earrings that twinkled irresistibly at me from a jeweler's tray and watches to remind me that our time on Earth is short, so we should indulge our fantasies while we can.

Every piece of jewelry contains within it a fragment of a dream. As we realize our dreams, or as they fade, new ones come to take their place. I see them in my grandmother's brooch, my mother's bracelet and most especially my granddaughter's necklace. Where do you see yours?

Caroline Childers

Bayco earrings.

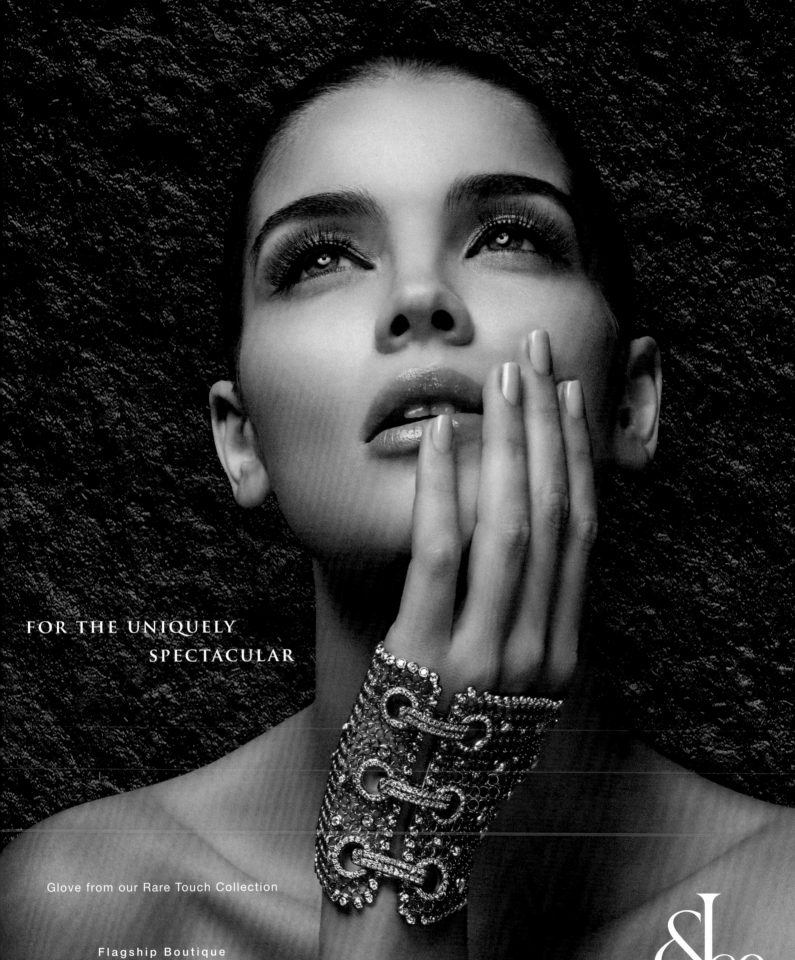

FOR THE UNIQUELY
SPECTACULAR

Glove from our Rare Touch Collection

&co
JACOB&CO

☩ TAKAT

email: rtakat@takat.com
www.takat.com

BOUCHERON

PARIS

FIRST JEWELER OF THE PLACE VENDÔME*

A COLLECTION OF ANIMALS

LETTER FROM THE EDITOR

FROM HEAD TO TOE

Many women build their jewelry collections as carefully as they do their wardrobe, layering a look that combines distinct elements—opal brooch, moonstone earrings, pearl choker—or sticking with one material for a visual impact that makes up in self-assurance what it lacks in subtlety. This approach has roots that go back to antiquity, as we have seen in tombs full of regalia that includes precious jewelry to adorn every part of the body.

The jewelers in our pages are well in tune with the myriad aspects jewelry can take on, has taken on and will take on. They understand the implications of a ring, from the technical side—one outstanding diamond often shines best in this form—to the emotions such a spectacular piece produces at the other end of the process. They understand the sensuality of a bracelet wrapping around the wrist, sharing a root with the word "embrace" as it envelops the wearer in a sparkling reverie. They understand how earrings reflect light onto a woman's face, and how a statement necklace can be louder than words. They understand that a tiara can make a woman feel like a queen, that a wristwatch's function is no more important than its exquisite form and that a brooch is no less than a portable canvas.

In the past, we've traveled around the world together, but this time we invite you on a tour of the human body, examining the different histories of each major kind of jewelry—each genre, if you will—and the layers of significance and power each one has accreted over the centuries. Every time you gesture a little more emphatically to ensure the ring on your finger catches the light, you are participating in a conversation about the meaning and power of jewelry. When your beloved surprises you with gold bangles, you can feel connected to the women of ancient Byzantium, who wore them in pairs. When you buy yourself a chunky ring to show off your individuality, you are participating in a tradition that includes the signets of ages past, carved with a seal that belonged only to the wearer. Learn the language from A to Z… so you can use it to write poetry.

Elise Nussbaum

Sutra earrings.

de GRISOGONO

GENEVE

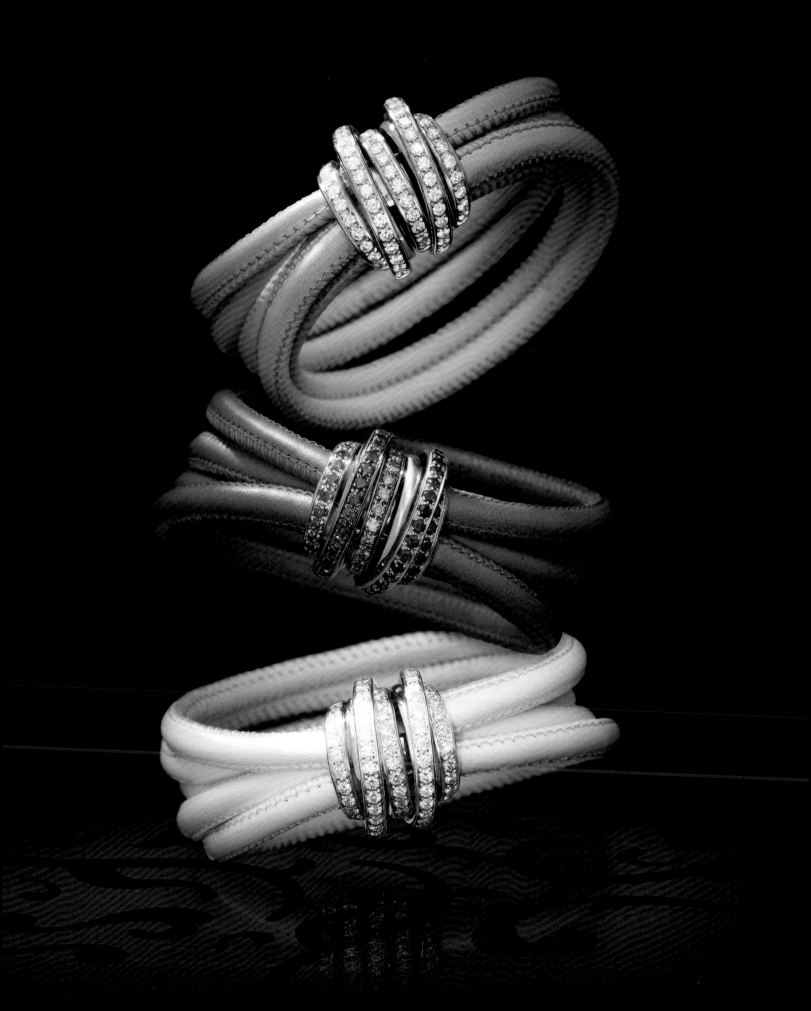

de GRISOGONO

GENEVE

ABU DHABI · COURCHEVEL · DUBAI · GENEVA · GSTAAD · KUWAIT · LONDON · MIAMI · MOSCOW
NEW YORK · PARIS · PORTO CERVO · ROME · S^T BARTHELEMY · S^T MORITZ

www.degrisogono.com

ACKNOWLEDGMENTS

We wish to express our profound appreciation and gratitude to everyone who helped make this book a reality: Jack Hadjibay, Leonora Hadjibay, Caroline Hadjibay, Danielle Hadjibay, Nicole Semah, Brian Moghadam from **Andreoli**; Christina Lang Assael, Lawrence Lewis, Michael MacKenzie from **Assael International**; Moris Hadjibay, Giacomo Hadjibay, Marco Hadjibay, Manuel Hadjibay from **Bayco**; Pierre Bouissou, Alban Pesneau, Mathieu Poirier-Lauvin, Patrick Rogliardo, Alexandra Sfez from **Boucheron**; Sandrine Jard, Isabelle Lallouette, Michel Aliaga, Véronique Sacuto from **Cartier**; Thierry Fritsch, Alexandre Vaysse, Stéphanie Coutens, Céline Levistre, Gersende Scour, Juliette Tourtet from **Chaumet**; Caroline Scheufele, Annick Benoit-Godet, Prerna Balani, Brian Cheng from **Chopard**; Fawaz Gruosi, Michèle Reichenbach, Laure Monney, Marina Coelho from **de Grisogono Switzerland**; Giovanni Mattera, Denise De Luca from **de Grisogono New York**; Myriam Gumuchian Schreiber, Patricia Gumuchian Grayson, Anita Gumuchian, Andre Gumuchian, Jr., Jodi Heald, Cynthia Lobacz from **Gumuchian**; Guy Ellia, Claire-Marie Thiennot, Aurélie Bangsithideth from **Guy Ellia**; Brett Hammerman, Darcy Hammerman, Angela Sarris from **Hammerman Brothers**; Angela Arabo, Jacob Arabov, Susan Finkelstein from **Jacob & Co.**; Jacques Branellec, Gaëlle Branellec, Janthina Fong, Joan del Rosario from **Jewelmer Joaillerie**; Valérie Messika, André Messika, Emilie Muller, Estelle Khebour, Charlotte Dumoux from **Messika**; Marie-Pierre Anselot, Frédéric Parisot, Sophia Bouaouni, Sabrina Escana from **Piaget**; Manuel Mallen, Karen Bacos from **Poiray**; Robert Wan, Heitiare Tribondeau from **Robert Wan**; Arpita Parikh, Divyanshu Navlakha, Callye Peyrovi from **Sutra Jewels**; Rayaz Takat, Sanaa Chafai, Russell Starr from **Takat**. This book would not be possible without the skill and dedication of all the artisans who assemble fine jewelry with expertise and flair. A hearty thank you to Sean Bertram, Erin Quinn and Scott Brookman at Modern Luxury Media, associate editor Julie Singer, junior assistant editor Amber Ruiz and of course my deepest gratitude goes out to my writer and editor Elise Nussbaum, and my art director Franca Vitali. An extra-special note of gratitude to Annick Benoit-Godet for her invaluable support and assistance. We couldn't have done it without each and every one of you!

Caroline Childers

Andreoli earrings.

CHAUMET
PARIS

Attrape-moi… si tu m'aimes Watch

70 RUE DU FAUBOURG SAINT-HONORÉ, PARIS
WWW.POIRAY.COM

Poiray
PARIS

Ravishing Ruby & Diamond Rings

New York   1-800-376-7200   www.bayco.com

THIS PAGE
Bayco's talents shine from every fact of this full set of Colombian emerald and diamond jewelry, which includes a ring set with a 22-carat cushion-cut emerald, earrings set with a pair of pear-shaped emeralds (30 carats total), a necklace set with 18 emeralds (54 carats total) and a bracelet set with 9 emerald-cut emeralds (19 carats total).

FACING PAGE
The Imperial Emerald: a 206-carat, unenhanced, cushion-cut Colombian emerald.

BAYCO

ONCE UPON A TIME: THE IMPERIAL EMERALD

Gems have always seemed to hold mystical
qualities—maybe that is why the truly
exceptional gemstones seem to come to us right
out of a fairy tale. This fantastical effect was in the air
one morning in April 2013, as a crowd began gathering
at the BaselWorld Watch & Jewelry Show. They had
heard hints and rumors about Bayco and its promise to
reveal "one of the most precious gemstones to ever exist."

The Imperial
Emerald.

Pure geometry brings
pure delight on this pair
of Colombian emerald and
diamond earrings.

As with all celebrated precious stones, the Imperial Emerald's past contains notes of both history and mystery. Forty years ago, Amir Hadjibay, the founder of Bayco, first encountered the gemstone in the collection of a European gem enthusiast, and immediately lost his heart to it. The collector said he would never sell the piece, but at last agreed that if the time ever came, the first phone call he made would be to Amir. Four decades later, the owner felt that he had derived all the enjoyment he could from the exquisite stone, and it was time to pass it along. His family did not share his fervent passion for jewels, so he turned to the only man who did: Amir.

The stone's owner came by Bayco's offices and, in a transaction that Amir's son (and Bayco's co-CEO, with his brother Giacomo) Moris describes as "old school," left the

From left: Manuel, Moris, Giacomo and Marco Hadjibay with The Imperial Emerald at the unveiling of the stone.

emerald with the family overnight, with a verbal agreement that if they liked the stone, they would buy it. After forty years of waiting, the family didn't need another 24 hours to decide, enthusiastically renewing their offer. Amir asked the collector if he was happy with the agreed-upon price, and when the collector said he was, Amir added another five percent to the offer, explaining, "I want this stone to have nothing but happiness around it."

Though the gem has haunted the dreams of the Hadjibays for decades, they know very little about its past. In fact, its story before it fell into the hands of the European collector is a tabula rasa, similar to many famous gemstones, which often show up out of nowhere or feature long blank periods in their stories.

This emerald and diamond ring features a 20-carat Mogul hand-carved emerald, set in an intricate design with rose-cut diamonds and diamond micropavé.

A 20-carat emerald-cut Colombian emerald takes center stage on this emerald and diamond ring.

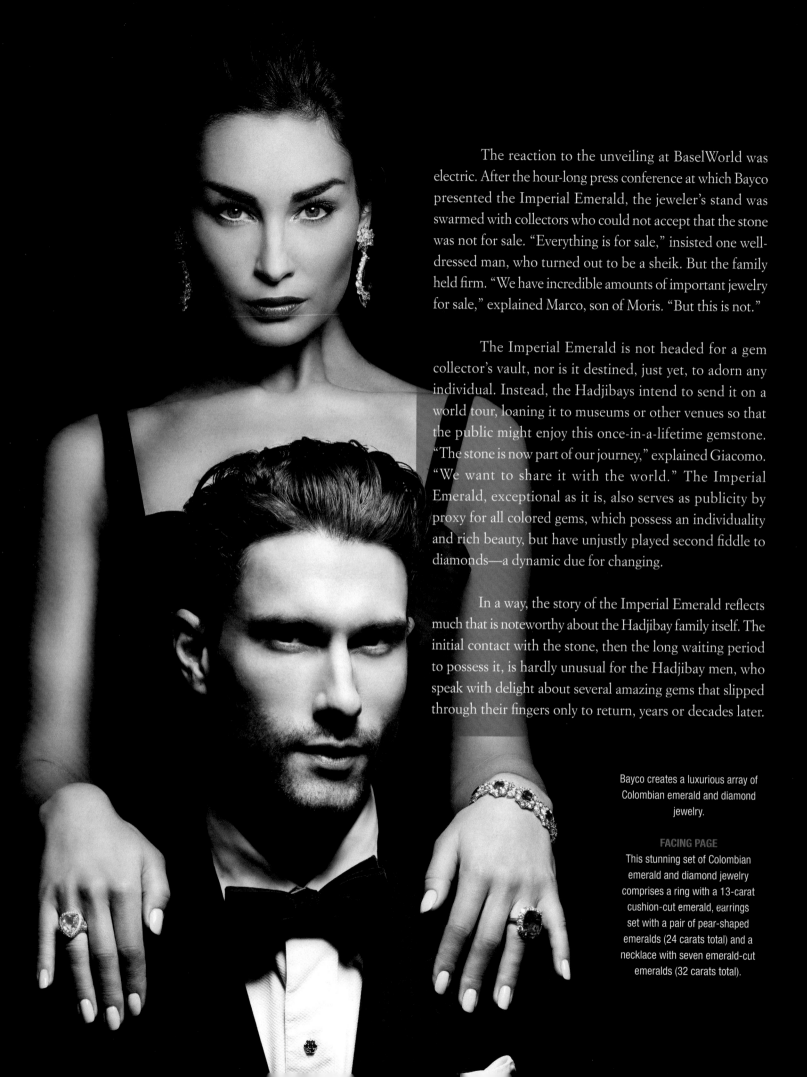

The reaction to the unveiling at BaselWorld was electric. After the hour-long press conference at which Bayco presented the Imperial Emerald, the jeweler's stand was swarmed with collectors who could not accept that the stone was not for sale. "Everything is for sale," insisted one well-dressed man, who turned out to be a sheik. But the family held firm. "We have incredible amounts of important jewelry for sale," explained Marco, son of Moris. "But this is not."

The Imperial Emerald is not headed for a gem collector's vault, nor is it destined, just yet, to adorn any individual. Instead, the Hadjibays intend to send it on a world tour, loaning it to museums or other venues so that the public might enjoy this once-in-a-lifetime gemstone. "The stone is now part of our journey," explained Giacomo. "We want to share it with the world." The Imperial Emerald, exceptional as it is, also serves as publicity by proxy for all colored gems, which possess an individuality and rich beauty, but have unjustly played second fiddle to diamonds—a dynamic due for changing.

In a way, the story of the Imperial Emerald reflects much that is noteworthy about the Hadjibay family itself. The initial contact with the stone, then the long waiting period to possess it, is hardly unusual for the Hadjibay men, who speak with delight about several amazing gems that slipped through their fingers only to return, years or decades later.

Bayco creates a luxurious array of Colombian emerald and diamond jewelry.

FACING PAGE
This stunning set of Colombian emerald and diamond jewelry comprises a ring with a 13-carat cushion-cut emerald, earrings set with a pair of pear-shaped emeralds (24 carats total) and a necklace with seven emerald-cut emeralds (32 carats total).

The affection and trust shown by the collector is also a familiar motif, in an industry where Bayco is one of the most trusted and revered names. Amir's insistence on a generous price would be no surprise to anyone who knew him. The name of the emerald, therefore, is entirely fitting:

Amir means "emperor" in Persian, and the Imperial Emerald would have adorned an emperor, in the days when gemstones were reserved for royalty. "We honor our father's legacy with this stone," confirms Moris, and the family reaffirms its commitment to Amir's ideals.

Bayco crafts a variety of Colombian emerald and diamond jewelry, as well as rose-cut diamond jewelry.

The delicious-looking emerald cabochons and drops on these emerald and diamond earrings weigh a total of 25 carats.

The central stone of this emerald and diamond ring is a 20-carat cushion-cut old-mine Colombian emerald.

Quite literally, there is nothing like the Imperial Emerald anywhere in the world. Larger emeralds do exist, but they lack the impeccable quality of the Imperial, and many have been treated—the Imperial is completely untreated, and has no cracks or fissures to mar its intense green hue. The most respected authorities in the industry—Gübelin, GIA and AGL—have not only issued the highest grade certificates for the stone, they have created monographs devoted to its remarkable characteristics, a highly unusual honor for any gem, let alone a colored one. Gübelin, for example, has issued only seven monographs, and this is the first emerald it has so honored—out of millions of stones that pass through its lab. Even without the public recognition, the Imperial Emerald speaks for itself: one look suffices to let the observer know that this is a gem without peer.

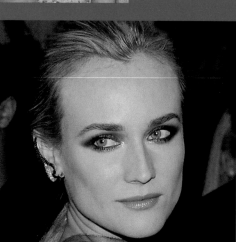

36

WRITTEN ON THE BODY: HOUSES OF PRESTIGE

Though jewelry is an art form, it is different from any other. Though we may see jewelry in museums, it is never created with that in mind—on the contrary, jewels are meant to go out in the world, to attract admirers, to enhance a woman's beauty and help express her individual sense of style. The Houses in these pages are successful by any metric, but particularly that one. Staking claim to each part of the body as they come across it, these jewelers understand that their art is inextricably bound with sensuality, with transforming metal and minerals into a treasured accessory that absorbs and retains the warmth of the skin.

Andreoli.

Bringing an Italian design sensibility to every piece, **Andreoli** welcomes a wide range of materials to its jewelry, creating jewels in everything from diamonds, sapphires, rubies and emeralds to coral, turquoise and enamel. With fresh, unconventional styles realized in materials both traditional and up-to-the-minute, Andreoli stakes a claim to the many ways in which we envision, collect and wear jewelry. Its sets, which include a necklace, a ring, a bracelet and earrings, undertake a jeweled exploration of the human body, claiming territory at each crucial spot by the sheer force of color, line and beauty.

Continuing a tradition begun by its founder Salvador Assael, **ASSAEL** uses only magnificent pearls in designs that emphasize the classic timelessness of nature. The wonders of the sea live on in extraordinary jewels that take the nacreous beauties as both a starting point and a final destination. ASSAEL was founded on a passion for pearls, and four decades later, that passion still burns bright. Though some jewelers delight in elaborate designs, ASSAEL's pieces hew close to the inimitable natural allure of "the queen of gems." Whether set in earrings, a necklace or a bracelet, the gems are always the star of the show—the pearls may be baroque, but the designs never are.

Assael.

Bayco.

Astonishing precious colored gemstones have created an entirely new language at **Bayco**, a language that the jeweler speaks fluently. With diamonds of brilliant clarity, fiery rubies, rejuvenating emeralds and sapphires as expansive and compelling as the ocean, Bayco's pieces sing extravagant poems that belong to the ages. The jeweler recently presented the Imperial Emerald, a breathtaking gemstone that is superlative even by Bayco's standards. For now content to share the company of Bayco's other imposing emeralds, which show up in forms ranging from drop-shaped, to cabochons, to square-cut, to carved in the Mughal tradition, the Imperial Emerald is not for sale.

A long, rich history guides the venerable **Boucheron**, with tradition, expertise and unique motifs as watchwords that crop up throughout the jeweler's collections. The House's artisans bring into focus, and into the present, themes first elaborated by its founder, Frédéric Boucheron, in the nineteenth century. Using the latest savoir-faire as well as traditional jewelmaking expertise, Boucheron creates exceptional pieces that use light itself as a subject, with more earthy works focused on the drape of a cloth, twisting vines of ivy, or colorful blossoms. A charming menagerie prowls, climbs, flits and slithers throughout.

Boucheron.

Cartier.

With a back catalogue that covers over a century and every imaginable theme, using every imaginable material, **Cartier** boasts an artistic sensibility that extends in all directions. With its Odyssée d'un Parcours collection, the "king of jewelers" emphasizes its historical geographical scope, with warm topaz and orange tourmaline to evoke the African palette, carved rubellite and diamond-set dragons to capture a Chinese sensibility, luscious emeralds and sapphires to suggest the splendor of the Indian royal courts and a minimalist, Art Deco-inspired work in white diamonds that recalls the twentieth-century birth of the modern city. Its pieces at the Biennale des Antiquaires also offered a historical perspective on this essential jeweler.

Flaunting a passion for the impetuousness and beauty found in summer flowers, **Chaumet** brings its 234-year expertise and artistic sensibility to bear on the hydrangea in its stunning Hortensia collection. Using the blossom's range of colors as an entry point for a frank aesthetic discourse on love, the Parisian jeweler develops bloom-bedecked pieces that tell a love story from first glance to heedless passion. Sapphires, tourmalines, pink opals and white diamonds come together to create a secret garden in which every aspect of affection, infatuation and true love receives its time in the sun.

Chaumet.

43

Chopard.

The world's most beautiful women turn to **Chopard** on the most important nights of their lives. Whether it is a night at the Oscars or the famous ritual of "mounting the steps" at the Cannes Film Festival, actresses clamor to walk the red carpet in Chopard's collections, whether Red Carpet or Haute Jewelry. The jeweler's intimate relationship with the Cannes Film Festival itself is just one facet of the love affair between the jewels, crafted in gold or platinum, and the silver screen. The imagination and skill required to create these works of art echoes that demanded of the people who live out our dreams on screens twenty feet high.

Boundless creativity meets a voracious appetite for precious materials in the jewels created by **de GRISOGONO**. The jeweler's maxim is maximalistic, with pieces that sprawl over clavicles, dangle from earlobe to shoulder and stretch across fingers and forearms. Never afraid to try out off-the-wall inspiration in bold colors that capture the ephemeral rainbow in timeless gemstones, jewelry visionary Fawaz Gruosi has built an empire over the last two decades, creating an instantly recognizable visual language that often punctuates its statement pieces with exclamation points.

de Grisogono.

Gumuchian.

What is a jewel if it cannot be worn? The women at **Gumuchian** take a personal interest in haute jewelry, as the sisters at the head—and the heart—of the company design pieces not just for their clients, but themselves. Drawing inspiration from equestrianism, spices and happiness itself, among other places, Gumuchian's collections evince a joy in the act of creation and the wearing of each piece. The jewelry slides on like a caress, with an ease born from artistry so deeply engrained that it has become instinct. A personal touch is key, as is personal experience that guides the lines of 18-karat gold and diamond-setting.

An exuberant spirit with jewelry to match, **Guy Ellia** takes on exceptional diamonds to create the perfect homes for them. Whether the pieces are founded in the jeweler's love of architecture, a flawless starry night or an outstanding diamond in search of just the right setting, they win hearts through an expert use of precious materials, seasoned with a dash of moxie. The jeweler's watch collection also bears witness to this daring spirit, as it mixes gem setting with a focus on haute horology that displays the highly complicated movements for all the world to see.

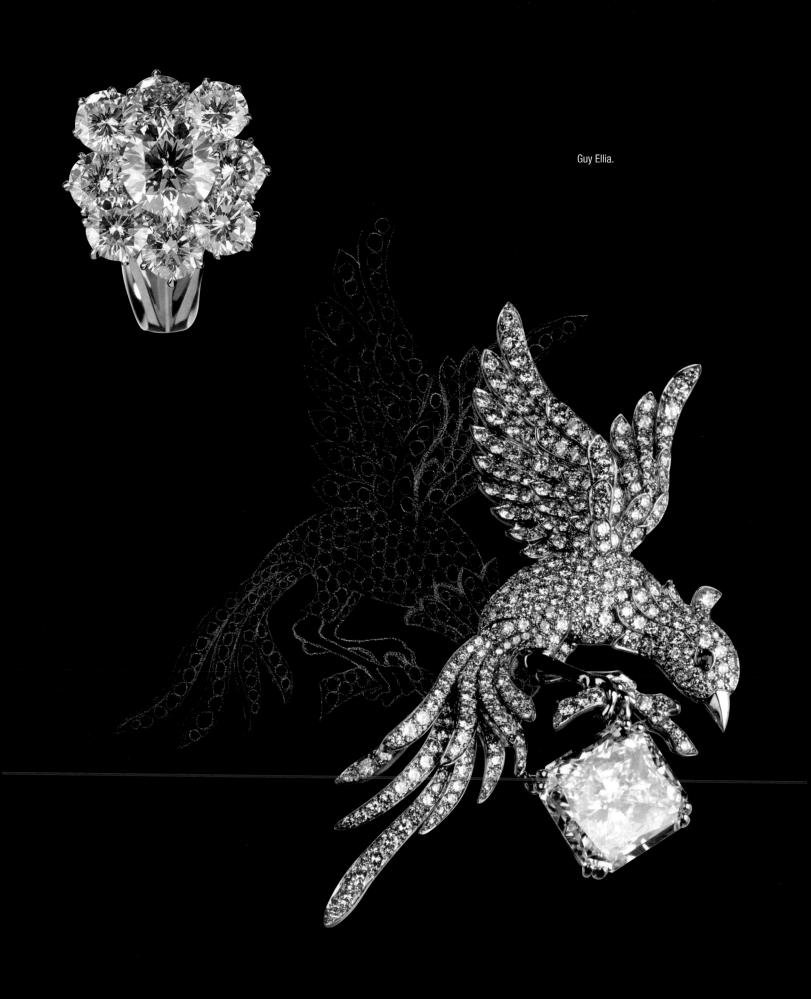

Guy Ellia.

Hammerman
Brothers.

With every jewel created in an atelier in New York City, **Hammerman Brothers** holds true to a philosophy that has served it well for decades: Hammerman Made – American Made. An abiding affection and familiarity with precious materials serves as the foundation for an intense focus on quality and craftsmanship, with gorgeous gemstones cropping up to breathe vivacity into shimmery moonstone earrings, mysterious black opal rings and breathtaking sapphire necklaces. With a unique take on current jewelry trends and eternal classics of the haute jewelry imagination, Hammerman creates pieces that will look fresh and sharp for decades to come.

Known for its dramatic diamonds, **Jacob & Co.** shows a great deal of range, using rubies, sapphires, emeralds, tourmalines and many other gemstones in its various collections. With sources of inspiration such as butterflies, Spanish fans, Biblical temptresses and delicate lace, the jeweler's designs occupy a uniquely feminine terrain that might be described as flirtatious yet demure. The unique pieces that the jeweler chooses to highlight its exceptional colored diamonds, however, are anything but modest, with exceedingly rare diamonds in candy-colored shades that look good enough to eat. Jacob & Co. also creates custom pieces in intimate collaborations with clients.

Jacob & Co.

Jewelmer Joaillerie.

With a keen focus on the artistic possibilities provided by the South Sea pearl, **Jewelmer Joaillerie** creates an entire world for the "queen of gems," one in which it is easy to get lost and dream for hours. Carefully selecting diamonds and gold to compliment the exquisite luster and subtle gradations of color of the star gem, Jewelmer Joaillerie's designers highlight the pearl's beauty with impeccable flair. Collections that focus on the natural world remind us of the need to protect the oysters' habitat, while jewels that refer to art or culture suggest that the modern pearl is as much a creation of humans as it is of mollusks.

A fun, fierce femininity dominates the collections by **Messika**, which plays with texture and tone within its lines and sometimes within a single piece. Using thin lines or unbroken paved expanses of diamonds, the jewels shimmer with daintiness or ferocity. Framed by an entirely modern aesthetic and philosophy, these pieces are suited to the woman who knows exactly what she wants, and isn't afraid to go out and get it. Designer Valérie Messika understands and explores the paradoxes of what it means to be a woman today, with diamond pieces soft as silk or harder-edged—but always self-confident and bold.

Messika.

Piaget.

Blushing roses are in bloom at **Piaget**, which takes the much-loved flower and builds a new collection among its blossoms. Inspired by the Yves Piaget rose, which is distinguished by its delectable petals and cheerful hot pink shade, the collection interprets the rose in gold, diamonds, tourmalines and pink opal. The brand's rich history is also reflected in its Couture Précieuse haute jewelry collections, which paint exquisite pictures with diamonds and other gemstones. The eternal, global feminine, as interpreted by this jeweler, is confirmed by the brand ambassadors, who number among the world's most beautiful women.

Hearts are art at **POIRAY**, a jeweler that turned heads on the Place Vendôme when it first arrived there in the 1970s—and still turns heads today. Its famous heart motif skips a beat throughout the jeweler's collections, whether its shape is solid, hollowed out, silhouetted, intertwined, mirrored or layered and abstracted. The jeweler also pays close attention to rings, with chunky central stones that announce their presence and demand attention. POIRAY's breakthrough in the field of watches was to include the option of creating a customizable timepiece by the addition of the interchangeable strap that followed the every whim of its owner.

Poiray.

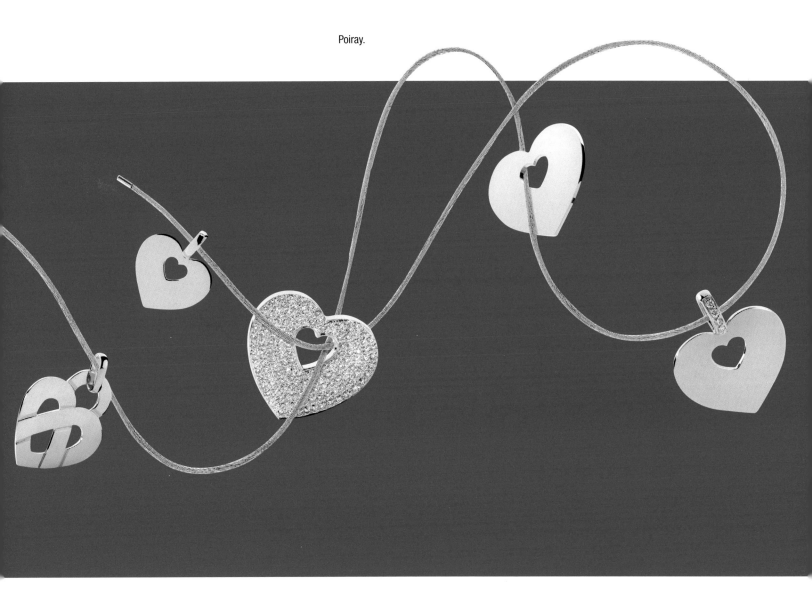

TOP AND LEFT
Robert Wan.

RIGHT
Sutra.

The cultured Tahitian pearl reigns at **Robert Wan**, with its dusky mysteries exalted if not explicated. The jeweler begins with stunning Tahitian pearls in a range of colors, then uses them in ways that build upon that beauty with a process of addition and layering. Whether the jeweler paints directly on the pearl with gold powder, uses precious gems to create a fanciful frame or piles dozens of Tahitian pearls in a cascade, Robert Wan builds a dreamscape in which anything is possible. The names of the pieces recognize this sense of limitless potential, with titles such as Desert Rose and Fairy Tale.

The funky yet elegant jewelry of **Sutra** is immediately recognizable, yet unclassifiable. The pieces seem to pluck inspiration from thin air, giving voice to a design philosophy that treats gemstones with respect yet does not yet hesitate to use them in service to a greater vision. With earrings that are modeled on the delicacy, flexibility and strength of feathers, bracelets whose forms follow those of Gothic architecture and necklaces that showcase the inimitable beauty of an unbroken chain of precious colored gems, Sutra announces the arrival of a crucial new vision in the jewelry world.

Hewing closely to a traditional color palette, **TAKAT** lets its rare gems speak for themselves. A single necklace might contain dozens of carats of pure Colombian emeralds, framed and supported by even more diamonds. The deep blue of tanzanite dominates many pieces, with pendants, rings and earrings given over to that intense cerulean shade. With a huge selection of impressive stones, TAKAT lets the gemstones shine with their own light, using only white diamonds as accents on these superb pieces.

Sutra.

RIGHT AND BOTTOM
Takat.

LES PARURES:
JEWELS FROM
HEAD TO TOE

Antique gold
and coral brooch.

(Photograph Courtesy
of Sotheby's, Inc. (c)2010)

Coffin of the pharaoh Amenemope.

TOP
Cartier necklace, 1932.

BOTTOM
Cartier clock, 1927.

Sutra earrings.

T

Though there are times when understatement
is called for, when a simple ring or pair of earrings
communicates all the wearer wants to convey,
jewelry, at its heart, is all about display. Strictly
speaking, any jewel is superfluous, designed,
styled and worn to create an aesthetic effect.

This approach leads, naturally, to an accumulation
of jewels—if a diamond catches the light and sparkles in a
fetching way, how much greater the result of adding a pair of
diamond earrings? A set of jewelry layers together precious
materials, creating a powerful mood with each place the eye
lands, enhancing the force of each motif as it is repeated
upon different parts of the body. An accent becomes a theme
and then a declaration, making the jewelry set much
greater than the sum of its parts.

After the French Revolution, which
was disastrous for fine jewelry and those who
wore it, the country's supremacy in jewelry
design and construction was in tatters. Enter

Chaumet Liens ring.

59

LEFT
Portrait of Mycenaen
woman in a wall painting.

TOP
Sutra earrings.

Andreoli ring.

Andreoli necklace and earring set.

TOP
Detail, portrait of Sangram Singh,
maharana of Udaipur, circa 1725.

BOTTOM
Andreoli earrings.

LEFT
Painting of Raja Savant Singh
and Batni Thani as the deities Krishna
and Radha, circa 1780.

RIGHT
Sutra bracelet.

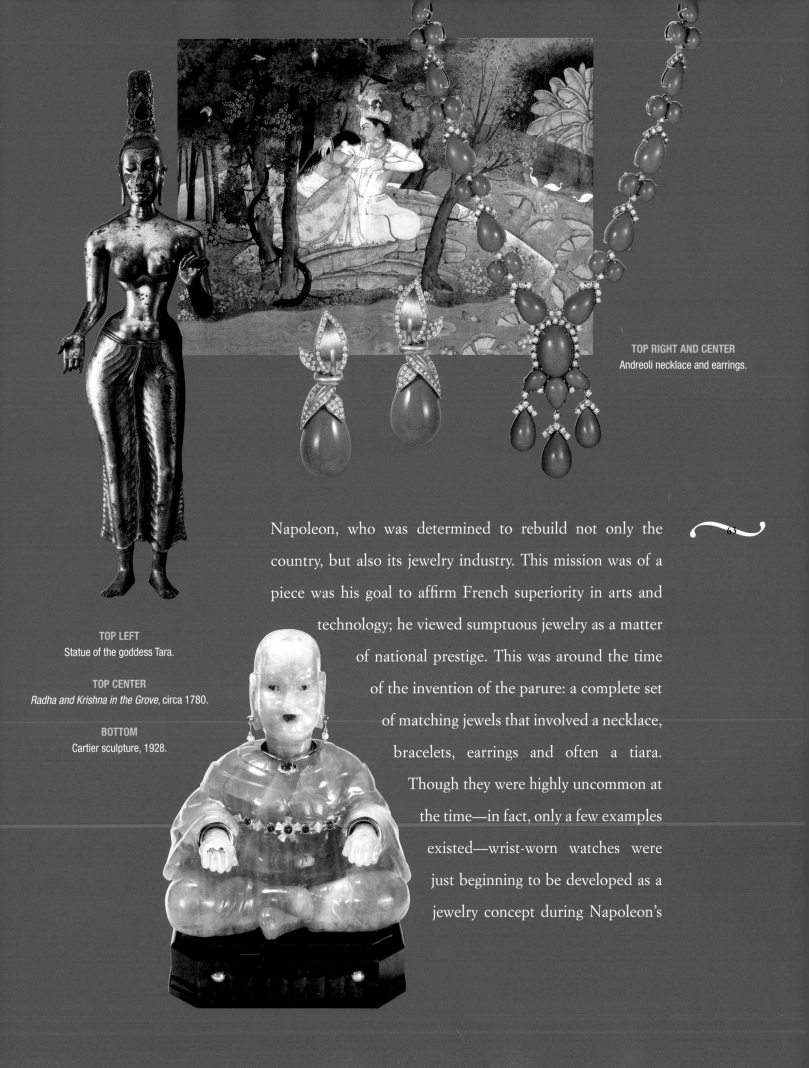

63

TOP RIGHT AND CENTER
Andreoli necklace and earrings.

TOP LEFT
Statue of the goddess Tara.

TOP CENTER
Radha and Krishna in the Grove, circa 1780.

BOTTOM
Cartier sculpture, 1928.

Napoleon, who was determined to rebuild not only the country, but also its jewelry industry. This mission was of a piece was his goal to affirm French superiority in arts and technology; he viewed sumptuous jewelry as a matter of national prestige. This was around the time of the invention of the parure: a complete set of matching jewels that involved a necklace, bracelets, earrings and often a tiara. Though they were highly uncommon at the time—in fact, only a few examples existed—wrist-worn watches were just beginning to be developed as a jewelry concept during Napoleon's

The Tyche of Antioch,
Roman copy of a bronze by Eutychides.

(Galleria dei Candelabri, Vatican Museums)

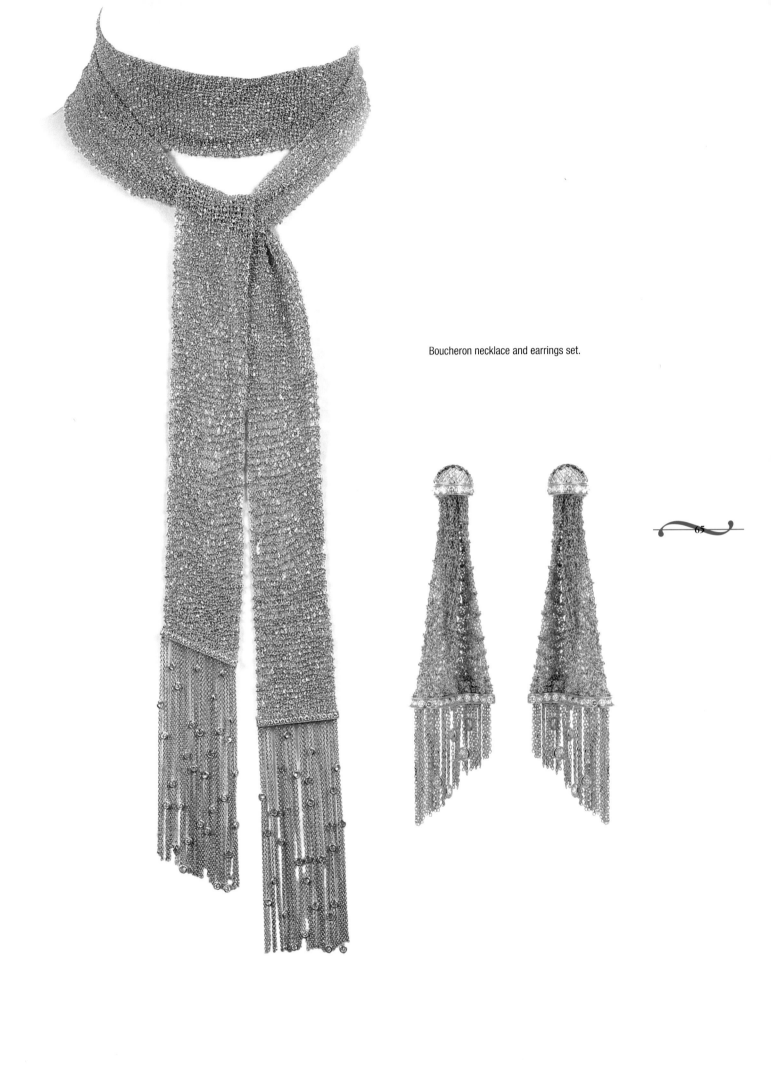

Boucheron necklace and earrings set.

Vintage Boucheron necklace.

Boucheron jewelry.

TOP LEFT
Sarah Bernhardt wearing Boucheron jewelry.

TOP RIGHT
Vintage Boucheron bracelet.

BOTTOM
Boucheron archival designs.

LEFT
Gumuchian necklace.

RIGHT
Portrait of Charlotte of Mecklenburg-Strelitz
by studio of Allan Ramsay, 1762.

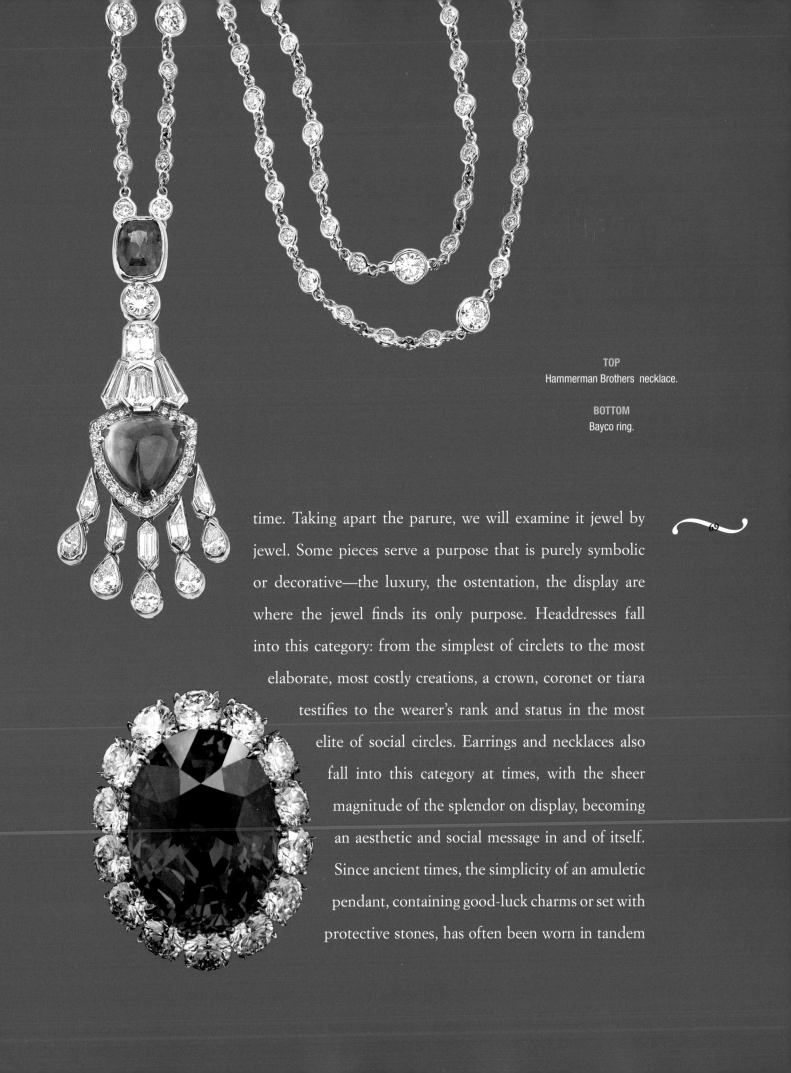

time. Taking apart the parure, we will examine it jewel by jewel. Some pieces serve a purpose that is purely symbolic or decorative—the luxury, the ostentation, the display are where the jewel finds its only purpose. Headdresses fall into this category: from the simplest of circlets to the most elaborate, most costly creations, a crown, coronet or tiara testifies to the wearer's rank and status in the most elite of social circles. Earrings and necklaces also fall into this category at times, with the sheer magnitude of the splendor on display, becoming an aesthetic and social message in and of itself. Since ancient times, the simplicity of an amuletic pendant, containing good-luck charms or set with protective stones, has often been worn in tandem

TOP LEFT
Detail, *Portrait of Simonetta Vespucci* by Piero di Cosimo, about 1480 or 1490.

TOP RIGHT
Portrait of *Marie-Antoinette* by Jacques-Fabien Gautier d'Agoty.

Boucheron necklace and earrings..

with ear decorations, whose preferred milieu—the pierced ear—remains a sign of the seriousness of the proposition of self-adornment. Bracelets have often stood outside the weighty symbolism of other jewels, at least in the Western world, where bangles, cuffs and chains tend towards the playful and the fashion-forward. On the other hand, bangles take on a much weightier significance in India and other Asian cultures, where they are an essential symbol of a woman's marital status and bare arms are a sartorial faux pas.

Finally, there are "genres" of jewelry that, as elaborate as they have become, were once considered chiefly for their practical

TOP LEFT
Rober Wan pearl.

TOP RIGHT
Bayco ring.

LEFT
Cartier bracelet.

BOTTOM
de Grisogono cuff.

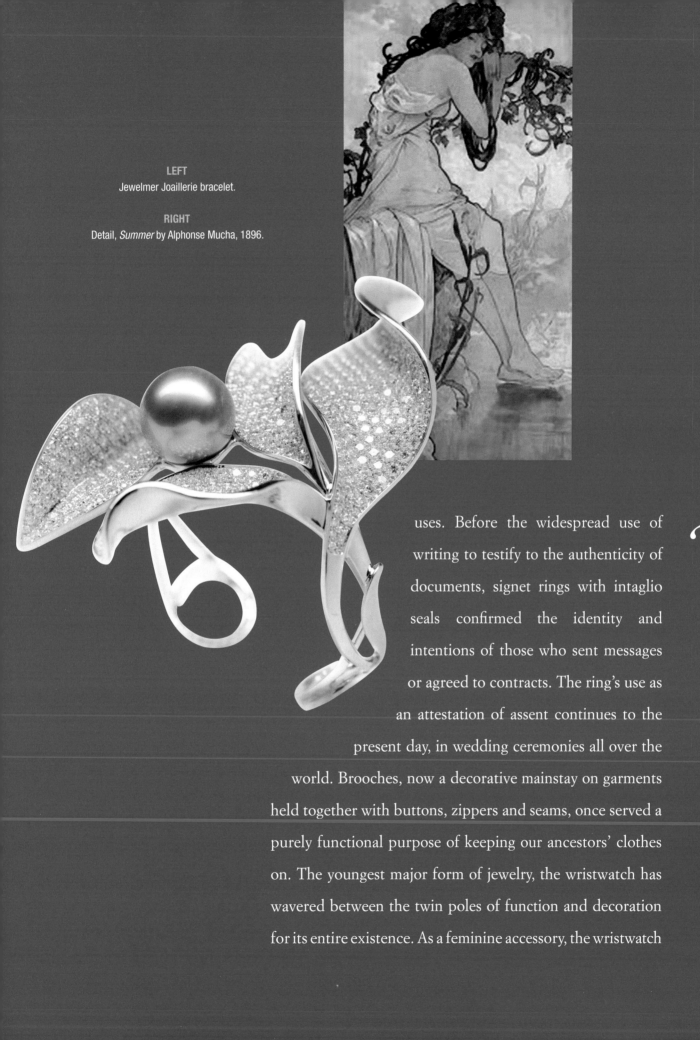

uses. Before the widespread use of writing to testify to the authenticity of documents, signet rings with intaglio seals confirmed the identity and intentions of those who sent messages or agreed to contracts. The ring's use as an attestation of assent continues to the present day, in wedding ceremonies all over the world. Brooches, now a decorative mainstay on garments held together with buttons, zippers and seams, once served a purely functional purpose of keeping our ancestors' clothes on. The youngest major form of jewelry, the wristwatch has wavered between the twin poles of function and decoration for its entire existence. As a feminine accessory, the wristwatch

Judith I by Gustav Klimt. 1901.
Galerie Vytvarneho Umeni, Ostrava,
Czech Republic

came to prominence in the nineteenth century, when ladies didn't have pocket watches to tell time because… they had no pockets. This dainty approach ran into a strictly utilitarian one when military commanders realized a hands-free method of telling time would be incredibly useful for soldiers in the field. The modern pervasiveness of time-telling devices on everything from microwaves to cell phones has somewhat obviated the need for wristwatches, strictly speaking, liberating the instrument to become a jewel once more.

Throughout it all—as the fortunes of individual jewelry forms rise and fall, and rise again—jewels continue to be a mainstay in

Beatrice by Fyodor Krichevsky, 1911.

(National Art Museum of Ukraine, Kiev, Ukraine)

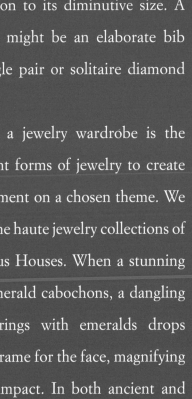

our wardrobes. Each piece carries emotions, memories and significance out of all proportion to its diminutive size. A woman's most cherished piece might be an elaborate bib necklace, or it might be a single pair or solitaire diamond stud earrings.

Part of building a jewelry wardrobe is the combination of different forms of jewelry to create a coherent visual statement on a chosen theme. We see this all the time in the haute jewelry collections of today's most prestigious Houses. When a stunning necklace drips with emerald cabochons, a dangling pair of pendant earrings with emeralds drops completes a precious frame for the face, magnifying the stone's aesthetic impact. In both ancient and

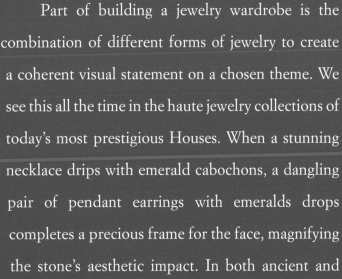

Cartier clock.

TOP LEFT
Sutra rings.

TOP RIGHT
Cartier necklace.

CENTER
de Grisogono earrings.

BOTTOM
Takat ring.

Naomi Campbell
wearing de Grisogono jewelry.

Gong Li wearing Piaget jewelry.

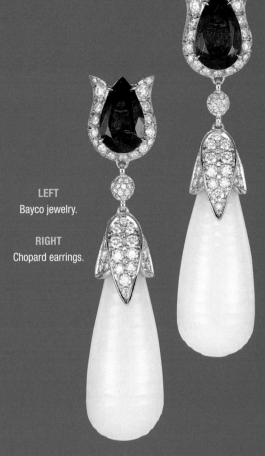

modern times, jewelers have sought to combine jewelry forms, ending up with a hybrid jewel that blends lovely elements of each form into a piece that charms on its own terms. An inordinate, often inconvenient, love of heavy earrings, led ancient women to experiment with threading supports for ear adornments through headdresses, which would be better able to support the weight than delicate earlobes. Another blending of forms, with a long history that extends to the present day, is a whole hand jewel that embraces elements of both the bracelet and the ring in its construction. Beloved in traditional Indian jewelry, it is a form

Chopard ring.

Takat jewelry.

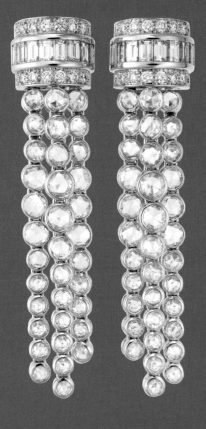

83

Messika ring.

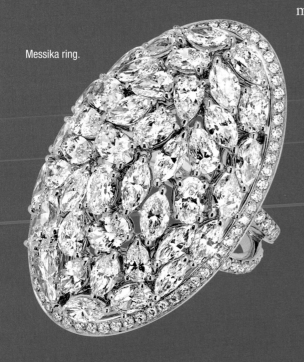

that Western haute jewelers such as Jacob & Co. have drawn upon for creative pieces that use the back of the hand as an unexpected canvas for the jeweler's art.

We are currently in the midst of an explosive creative movement in jewelry, with the vanguard emerging from an unlikely place. Body jewelry opens up new vistas of experimentation and aesthetic impact: Beyoncé's body chain is merely one of the most recent salvos in a campaign that includes multiple ear piercings for the defiant, navel rings for the exhibitionistic, and toe rings for the Earth Mothers among us. Anklets, whose charms tinkled softly throughout the ancient world, now grace the feet of young

Gong Li wearing
Piaget jewelry.

Boucheron necklace.

Aaron Basha jewelry.

TOP LEFT
Jewelmer Joaillerie jewelry.

TOP CENTER
Boucheron earrings.

TOP RIGHT
Jewelmer Joaillerie earrings.

87

LEFT
de Grisogono ring.

RIGHT
Jewelmer Joaillerie cuff.

Assael necklace.

89

women all over. These trends are bubbling up to the world of haute jewelry as well, with a so-called "slave bracelet"—a bracelet that attaches to a ring—making a showing in elite circles.

The more traditional forms of jewelry are no less popular for all that, however. Though modern fashion has taken a turn for the body-conscious, the most exquisite pieces are still made to adorn the ears, neck, wrists, fingers and the outside of our clothes, with tiaras bringing a regal touch to any woman who wants to be princess for a day.

A full parure is an unparalleled vehicle for expressing a jewelry designer's particular artistic vision. Materials, motifs or color combinations that might seem unlikely or awkward on their own develop a narrative that makes more sense with each

LEFT
Bayco jewelry.

RIGHT
Gumuchian necklace.

CENTER
Jacob & Co. bracelet.

BOTTOM LEFT
Jacob & Co. ring.

BOTTOM RIGHT
Messika ring.

Penelope Cruz wearing
Chopard jewelry.

TOP LEFT
Olivia Wilde wearing Sutra earrings.

BOTTOM
de Grisogono earrings.

piece that is added. With time, these once-shocking aesthetic choices—such as combining amethysts and turquoise—become more accepted and even traditional in their own right. The different kind of jewels available offer varied opportunities to explore the implications of a new idea, in different dimensions and with different purposes.

Though the possibilities for personal adornment seem endless, we return to the same wells of inspiration, drinking deep every time. The elegance of crowns, the beauty of earrings, the drama of necklaces, the sensuality of bracelets, the importance of rings, the modern sensibility of wristwatches, the playfulness of brooches—each one has explored and exploded its boundaries and limitations, providing the world of haute jewelry with a limitless palette.

Boucheron necklace
and earrings set.

Poiray pendant.

LEFT
Jewelmer Joaillerie necklace.

RIGHT
de Grisogono earrings.

Gumuchian ring.

LEFT
Carmen Electra wearing Sutra earrings.

RIGHT
Katherine Heigl wearing Sutra earrings.

LEFT
Stacy Keibler wearing Sutra earrings.

RIGHT
Sutra earrings.

95

Anja Rubik wearing
Chopard jewelry.

Jacob & Co. necklace.

de Grisogono jewelry.

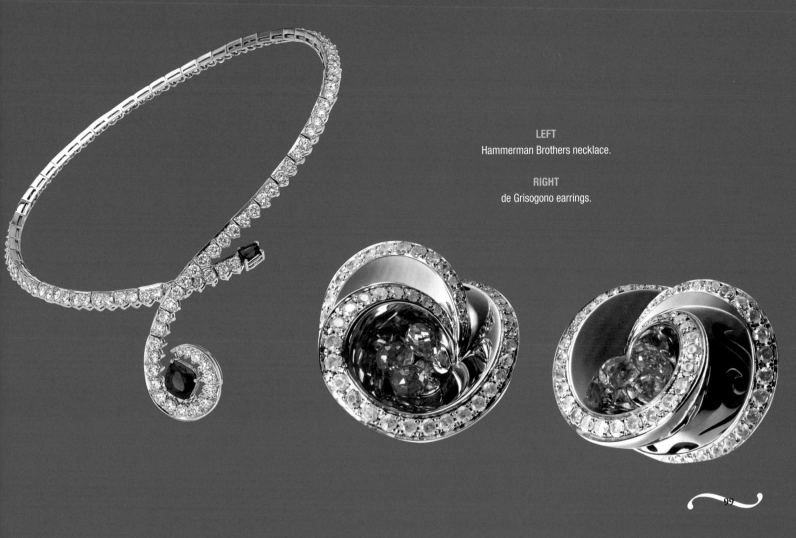

99

Bayco ring.

LEFT
Robert Wan necklace.

RIGHT
Chopard necklace.

BOTTOM
Robert Wan ring.

Messika jewelry.

de Grisogono jewelry.

TIARAS & CROWNS

The head that wears a crown may lie uneasy, but plenty of heads are nonetheless up for the challenge. The supreme significance of the human head has left fingerprints all over our language: not only are our leaders referred to as "heads of state," but "capital," from the Latin "capitalis," of the head, has a multitude of meanings, from "brilliant" (as in "capital idea") to "seat of government" to "monetary resources." Is it any wonder that in all times, all over the world, rulers make their power felt by displaying their wealth at the very top of their bodies?

The word "crown" in English—as well as in languages all over Europe—stems from the Latin word "corona," meaning "wreath." When pagan gods still held sway and they might animate the local foliage, wreaths made from branches and bushes conferred honor upon those who wore them. The ancient Greeks bestowed the laurel wreath (beloved by Apollo) as a reward for athletic or musical prowess, and the laurel wreath continued into Roman times as a symbol of leadership for emperors such as Julius Caesar. Due to the ephemeral nature of anything

FACING PAGE
Daniella Kronfle tiara.

THIS PAGE
Zhang Ziyi wearing
Boucheron jewelry.

made from organic materials, especially flowers and leaves, people eventually began recreating the sacred shapes in metal.

A similar trajectory lies behind the diadem, whose root word in Greek means "headband." Once lavish headbands, in the costly fabrics of linen or silk, began to signify rank, it was only a matter of time before precious metal and jewels would adorn, enhance and eventually usurp the more perishable cloth.

Bright, beautiful feathers can be seen as jewelry for birds, and people have used them as decorative elements for millennia. Wearing feathers in the hair as a mark of distinction is a custom that echoes and perpetuates the same human drive that led to crowns in the first place. Not just any feather will do: the same talismanic idea that led the Greeks to incorporate images of bulls in their jewelry iconography, or the use of tiger-claw necklaces, meant that the feathers used as marks of distinction must come from birds that are exceptionally strong, fierce, beautiful or rare. Feathers from extinct species can go for thousands of dollars. The appeal of the feather has led to diamond-set interpretations called aigrettes.

Gustave Moreau, *Cleopatra*, circa 1887.

Solid gold pendant
of King Tutankhamen.

TOP CENTER
Two kneeling women with lotus flowers.
Each wears a cone of unguent on her wig
which would release perfume as it melted.
New Kingdom, 18th Dynasty, circa 1500 BC.
(Aegyptisches Museum, Staatliche Museen, Berlin)

TOP RIGHT
Headdress and necklace by Lalaounis.

Egyptian tombs and wall paintings reveal a wide range of crowns, tiaras and other headdresses. Many bear fetishistic animals of the Egyptian culture. The Uraeus—a cobra, poised to strike—is often represented, whether realistically or in a more stylized manner, and features prominently on Tutankhamen's headdress. It was a natural choice for a crown, as the serpent represented royalty and divine authority. Another Egyptian symbol of divinity, the vulture, showed up as a more stylized element; the combination of cobra and vulture on the same crown signified the united realms of Lower and Upper Egypt.

The Greek word diademe refers to a headband, and its descendant "diadem" is a jeweled ornament synonymous with "tiara." That word's origins lie in ancient Persia, where it referred to a gem-studded band tied around the cidaris, a hat reserved for nobles. As happens again and again throughout the history of jewelry, what was once cloth transformed over the centuries to a metal adornment with precious stones set throughout.

Among other crowned deities in ancient Greece, including Hermes and his winged helmet, the much-feared deities of vengeance the Erinyes

The Marquise of Santa Cruz,
by Francisco Goya, 1805.

(and their Roman counterparts the Furies) wore serpent diadems. A popular motif on many forms of jewelry in ancient Greece, the Hercules knot was worn on diadems, placed at the center of the forehead. Based on the knot Hercules used to tie the paws of the skin of the Nemean lion, which he wore around his shoulders, the Hercules knot offered protection to those who wore it, and was also believed to have the power to heal.

As part of Heinrich Schliemann's so-called "Priam's Treasure," a hoard unearthed in Turkey in the 1870s, two golden diadems drew the archaeologist's eye. Convinced that he had found the historical site of the ancient city of Troy, Schliemann dubbed them the "Jewels of Helen." Each diadem was constructed of small gold ornaments, dangling on chains from a band that would be tied around the head—a Greek diadem in the truest sense of the word. Dating from 1500 BC, the precious finds of Priam's Treasure actually postdate Homer's Troy by 500 years.

The Babylonian Queen Pu-abi went to her tomb in 2500 BC wearing a complex headdress and diadem, from which dangled beads, golden and lapis

TOP
Mummy Portrait of a Woman.
Romano-Egyptian,
active 100 - 125.
(J. Paul Getty Museum)

RIGHT
Portrait of a woman, personification
of Soteria the Protectress, mosaic,
fifth century, Narlica, near Antaya, Turkey.
(Antioch Museum, Turkey)

Diadem from ancient Apulia.

lazuli discs, and overlapping gold leaves. Three gold flowers hovered overhead. Like the pharaohs, Queen Pu-abi was buried with her entire royal retinue, and among her entourage are women wearing similar headdresses, with simple golden leaves on the bands.

Cleopatra, no stranger to showmanship, chose her headdresses with an eye to creating a stunning impression, and her lover Marc Antony followed her example. While the Queen of the Nile wore a gold mesh cap from which hung all varieties of precious gems, representing the stars, Antony favored a golden gem-set crown that evoked the sun's rays. The power couple thus aligned themselves with heavenly bodies and a conception of the divine.

The Iron Crown of Lombardy, which dates back to the eighth or early ninth century, is one of the oldest European crowns. Its flat, circular shape hearkens back to the days of cloth headbands as royal insignia, and to complete the allusion, it is flexible, comprised of six enameled gold segments joined by hinges. It may have originally had two more

Portrait of the empress dowager Ts'u Hsi
of China in the 19th century.

Tibetan reliquary figure, 1700 AD.

TOP CENTER
Nadir Shah, ruler of Persia, circa 1739.

TOP RIGHT
Mahajanaka jataka,
Indian painting of the 7th century.

110

segments that were lost, and the end result is a rather small piece—so small, in fact, that when Napoleon used it to crown himself King of Italy, he had to attach it to a cloth band so it would fit his head. No fool when it came to pageantry, Napoleon was positioning himself in a centuries-long tradition: no less a figure than Charlemagne had used the crown in his coronation, and at least 33 subsequent coronations of Kings of Italy (a title given to the Holy Roman Emperor) used the Iron Crown. The crown's name derives from the belief that an inner iron circle

was made from a nail out of the True Cross. In 1993, the iron ring was analyzed, and turned out to be silver.

The wearing of a crown, already a highly symbolic act, could take on new shades of meaning, depending on who was doing the wearing, and under what circumstances. Napoléon II and his Empress Eugénie conducted a state visit to Queen Victoria in 1855, and arrived on a ship that had made its way through a blanket of thick fog. A secondary ship, the one with the opulent jewels and charming outfits

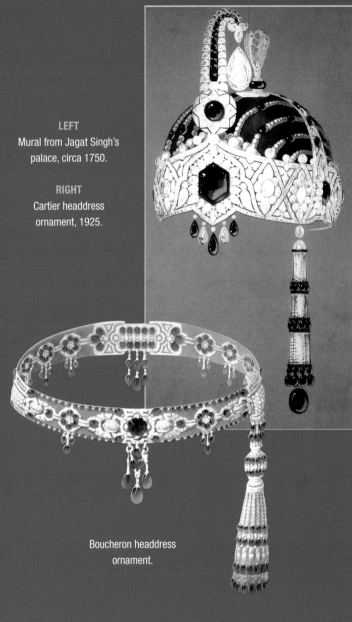

she had been planning to wear, had gotten lost in the famous English fog. Victoria knew the awkward situation in which her guest found herself, but—perhaps because of Eugénie's uncertain relationships with other courts—chose to dress to the nines for the reception, wearing full regalia and a circlet set with the incredible Koh-I-Noor, a 108.93-carat diamond that is still among the world's most famous. Two thousand smaller diamonds surrounded the centerpiece. Without any of her jewels, Eugénie took a different tack. She borrowed a simple dress from one

of her ladies-in-waiting and braided spring flowers into her hair, presenting a fresh-faced contrast to the heavily jeweled ladies of the English court. The young English queen took a liking to the younger woman, and reciprocated the state visit with one of her own a few months later. The French public, meanwhile, went gaga for the tale of their empress's floral fashion success, and jewelry designers leapt on spring flowers as the latest popular design element. On a subtler note, the evening may have led to the ever-more voracious appetite for jewels evidenced by

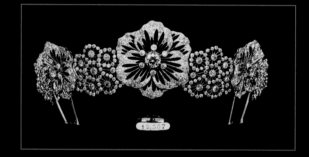

TOP
Boucheron diadem, 1868.

LEFT
Tsar Nicholas II of Russia
was a faithful client of Boucheron.

RIGHT
Vintage Boucheron tiara.

BOTTOM
Cartier tiara.

RIGHT
Sir Yadavindra Singh, Maharajah of Patiala,
wearing Cartier and Van Cleef & Arpels jewelry.

BOTTOM
Boucheron.

Napoleon III and Eugénie, as the French and English courts participated in an arms race of splendor.

Despite a Western conception of crowns looking a certain way, or containing particular elements, the truth is that what a crown can be varies widely from culture to culture. Whatever its appearance or component materials, a crown is any headdress that symbolizes the supreme importance of its wearer. In regions where cloth head coverings act as a signifier of rank, the society enacts rules to prevent the common people from wearing anything similar. Although ostentatious crowns of precious materials impress the outsider, many cloth headdresses display meanings available only to an insider, based on the way in which the cloth is folded and manipulated. Different ways of wearing the same cloth can point to distinctions of family groups or regions.

Perhaps because tiaras are associated with the head and by extension all things lofty, celestial motifs have often found their way into pieces as design

elements. Yellow gold was an obvious stand-in for the sun, and diamonds twinkle like stars. Comets passed into vogue in the eighteenth and nineteenth centuries, at around the same times as Halley's Comet (1758) and the Great Comets of 1843 and 1882. Stars and the crescent moon also became popular as motifs in the nineteenth century, as Islamic and European rulers exchanged royal visits.

The regalia of the English royal family cannot be removed from England, leading to the production of substitute crowns under certain situations. For instance, when King George V and Queen Mary traveled to India in 1911, Garrard, the Crown Jeweler of the United Kingdom, had to construct a crown to present the king—also Emperor of India—in an appropriately royal light. The proscription against removing the Crown Jewels was not always observed. In 1936, when Edward VIII abdicated the throne, he took with him the coronet used to crown the Prince of Wales. This was illegal, but Edward's family chose not to charge him with theft—perhaps they had enough on their plate.

Edward VIII's appropriation of the Prince of Wales coronet meant that when it came time to

crown Prince Charles as the Prince of Wales, a new
piece had to be commissioned. The year being 1969,
the design of the headpiece took on a futuristic tinge,
though it still had traditional elements. The designers
used a process called "electroforming," in which gold
is deposited onto a mold that is later removed, to craft
the headpiece. The small golden orb that tops the
coronet actually derives its shape from a table tennis
ball around which the gold was deposited. Far from
being encrusted with huge gemstones, the jewels on
the coronet are relatively understated, and each one
contributes to a larger significance, particular to Prince
Charles: 13 diamonds set vertically represent the stars
in the Scorpio constellation, the Prince's Zodiac sign.
Engravings on the coronet depict the prince's heraldic
symbols: feathers, sheaves of corn and the Welsh
dragon. Despite its relatively light appearance, the
Prince of Wales coronet contains nearly three pounds
of 24-karat gold.

If there is one thing that European-style crowns
have in common, it might be the extreme physical
discomfort they inflict upon their wearers. Queen Victoria
had to have a new crown made for her coronation, as

the Saint Edward's Crown was literally too heavy for her head, and George V of England complained in his diary about the weight of the crown he wore in India. One English noblewoman, Nicole, Duchess of Bedford, wrote in her memoirs that wearing tiaras always gave her a headache.

In the Himalayan Ladakh region of India, women wear the perak, a headdress whose decoration denotes the status of the wearer. Densely set with precious and semiprecious stones, especially turquoise, and sometimes even silver and gold ornaments, the jewels not only show off the wearer's wealth, but connect women to lu, protective deities, and extend that

protection to humanity. The number of rows of turquoise was once directly related to the noble rank of the wearer—nine rows for a queen, seven for an aristocrat, and so on down the line.

One spectacular crown achieved fame for its role in an exhibition the British organized in the Indian city of Jaipur, in 1883. The organizers requested that Indian states submit representative crafts of each region, and the Maharaja of Rewa went above and beyond the request, sending three impressive royal headdresses. Each one featured an abundance of jewels that completely covered the cloth base, and one of them

proudly displayed an enormous sapphire carved into the form of the Hindu god Vishnu. The use of the sapphire is highly unusual for Indian jewels, as it is believed to carry bad luck, but the beauty of this stone, and its value—20,000 rupees at the time—convinced the maharaja otherwise.

The ancient Persian royal headdress, a tall, cylindrical, tapering crown, was known as the cidaris. Though the heir to the throne and other court personages wore similar head coverings, they were obliged to wear theirs at an angle, while the ruler wore his cidaris perfectly upright. One of the oldest surviving crowns of this type is a domed headdress that the Ottoman Sultan Ahmed I gave to Transylvanian Prince István Bocskay in 1605. The crown was crafted in gold, silk, spinels, rubies, emeralds, pearls and turquoise. Ahmed saw this gift as a sign that the prince was to become his vassal, but Bocskay refused the royal honor.

The cidaris influenced the nation's most famous crown, the amazing Kiani Crown, which was constructed in 1798. Used for the coronation of Fath Ali Shah, this incredible piece was described by the French envoy to Persia as, "a sort of tiara of which a fabric of pearls, sprinkled with rubies and emeralds, formed the border." Thousands of gems adorn the red velvet

Crown of Empress Farah Diba Pahlavi,
designed by Van Cleef & Arpels.

background, including numerous diamonds and approximately 1,800 pearls, 1,800 spinels and 300 emeralds. The crown features two gem-set aigrettes, and has also been worn with three black heron plumes, symbols of royalty, which only the shah was permitted to wear.

The coronation of Iran's Empress Farah, in 1967, was a momentous occasion for the country. In two and a half millennia, no woman had ever been crowned, and m any saw Farah's coronation as a welcome step for women's rights. Mohammed Reza Shah went beyond the symbolic and granted his wife

real—if only potential—power, assigning her the status of regent should their son be required to take the throne as a minor. The Empress's coronation was also a grand event for the jeweler, Van Cleef & Arpels, who had been selected to craft her crown, a magnificent piece adorned with a total of 1,541 stones, including a carved central emerald of 150 carats. With the other gemstones set on the piece, including 1,469 diamonds, 36 emeralds, 34 rubies, two spinels and 105 pearls, the Empress's crown weighed 4.3 pounds.

TOP
Andreoli tiara.

CENTER
Boucheron tiara.

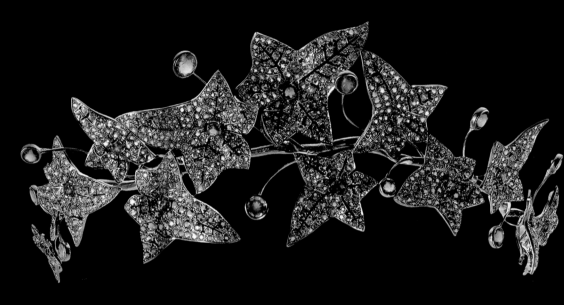

LEFT
Jacques-Louis David,
*The Coronation of Napoleon I,
December 2, 1804,*
painted in 1825.

crown upon him. When a new sultan of Ternate is crowned, he must wear the headpiece to the island's oldest settlement, both to show that the crown remains on the island and that the cassowary feathers that adorn it are still black, as they are believed to turn white during the interregnum. Every Thursday, members of the sultan's family make offerings to the crown; legend has it that if they do not, the family line—and the unbroken dynasty—will die out.

As the sovereign of one of the world's few monarchies that has survived since the fourteenth century, each sultan of Brunei has had an extravagant crown constructed for his coronation. The crown of the current sultan, Hassanal Bolkiah, was crafted in 1967. The golden headdress is full of symbolic elements, such as the 99 sapphires set on the rim, which stand for the 99 virtues of Islam, and golden rice shafts that represent Brunei's prosperity. Small, golden, three-tiered umbrellas adorn the crown as well, with each tier representing a regal virtue: supremacy, glory and bravery.

Empress Farah's wedding crown is an equally—if not more—important piece of jewelry, as it contains the pink Noor-ol-Ain diamond, one of the largest pink diamonds in the world at 60 carats. White, yellow, blue and pink diamonds surround it, creating a nearly unbroken stretch of opulent sparkle.

The Indonesian Crown of Ternate has a particularly rich mythical history, as well as a demanding maintenance ritual. As the legend goes, the first ruler of Ternate was the son of a nymph and grandson of the Lord Of Heaven, who bestowed the

The prospect of making a traditional crown is no simple task. Specialists from a range of disciplines—goldsmiths, gem-setters, engravers, furriers and others—must collaborate to ensure that the result is literally fit for a king. The materials usually come from the palace's own treasury, and though gold is obviously the most resonant choice, pure gold is impractical crown material for a variety of reasons. First of all, of course, gold is quite heavy, and crowns are heavy enough already. The metal is also too soft to be durable, and until platinum arrived on the scene as a suitable alternative in the nineteenth century, most crowns were gilded or crafted in gold alloys.

Art Deco began to coax the tiara into the mainstream, as its lighter materials and clean lines permeated not only the increasingly anachronistic royal courts, but also formal occasions such as society events and the opera. Another event of the 1920s created an entirely new venue for tiara-wearing: in 1921, the first

The actress Sarah Bernhardt.

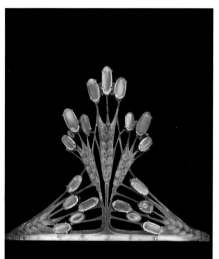

TOP RIGHT
Harry Wilson Arts and Crafts tiara, circa 1909.

RIGHT
Tiara by Fred Partridge
for Liberty & Co., circa 1900.

BOTTOM
Vintage Cartier tiara.

Messika tiara.

Miss America pageant took place in Atlantic City. A new tiara tradition was born…

A tiny fraction of the world's population will ever wear an official crown of any sort, but tiaras as a personal adornment are only growing in popularity. For a bride on her wedding day, a tiara can be the perfect grace note for that royal feeling. Wedding tiaras have a similar history to that of any other kind of headdress. Ancient peoples made nuptial wreaths of white flowers—signifying both virginity and a hopeful wish for vibrant fertility for the newly wedded pair. Just as the Roman's laurel wreath began to be crafted in gold, so too did floral

wedding crowns take on less perishable forms. Wedding tiaras in the Western world tend to be quite delicate, using slender design elements that recall flowers, leaves and other natural, delicate forms.

Natural materials were also a massively important element in Art Nouveau tiaras, which used horn and other materials that were chosen more for their aesthetic properties than their inherent value. Using horn to convey other natural elements such as ferns transformed jewelry into a celebration of the natural world and all its delicate possibilities, rather than the ostentatious display of wealth. Diamonds are

LEFT
Robert Wan crown.

RIGHT
Jewelmer Joaillerie jewelry.

relegated to extras in these character-driven pieces, showing up as dewy accents rather than central points of attention. These designs also hearken back to the tiara's origins, as wreaths crafted from laurel branches and other materials from the natural world.

Due to their complementary shapes, a tiara and a necklace sometimes find themselves built into the same piece of jewelry, like one of those pictures that is simultaneously a beautiful young woman and a crone. This versatile type of jewelry usually consists of a gem-set "fringe," and resembles the Russian kokoshnik, a kind of tiara that evolved from a headdress that a peasant woman would wear to an extravagance of the aristocracy. Because of its appearance when worn as a tiara, when the fringe radiates outward from the brow like rays of the sun, this form of jewelry also takes the name "sun tiara."

Hammerman Brothers crown.

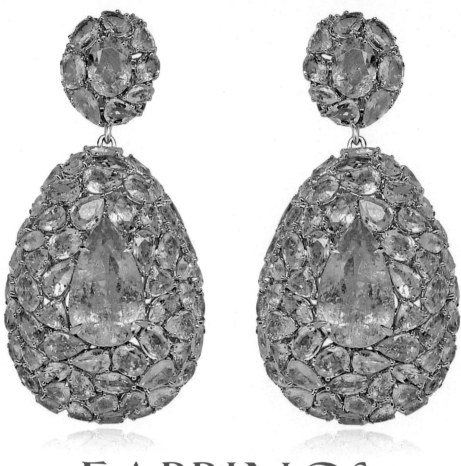

EARRINGS

Dangling or self-contained, flexible or rigid, set with diamonds, pearls or no stones at all, earrings have a special relationship to the human body. Not only do they sit closest of all to the face, imbuing it with a particular sparkle or glow—think of Vermeer's painting *Girl with a Pearl Earring*—but they are the only kind of jewelry to actually penetrate the body, leaving an indelible trace of its presence— think of the character of Griet in Tracy Chevalier's novel *Girl with a Pearl Earring*. Just like ears, earrings come in pairs, and unlike every other kind of jewelry, which may be worn in multiples, earrings must be worn in pairs (at least outside of some youth subcultures). And yet, earrings themselves are nowhere nearly as loaded with significance and symbolism as finger-rings are. This could possibly be because, while rings have had the same basic design for thousands of years, earrings have changed dramatically, bringing new styles, new techniques and new meanings to the ears century in and century old. They have even fallen

entirely out of favor for long periods, when women took to covering their ears, or decided en masse that ear piercing was not acceptable.

Though piercing the cartilage at the top of the ear has enjoyed a surge in popularity over the last few decades, the vast majority of those who decide to wear earrings do so in a hole through the fleshy lobe. Earrings thus become a way to accentuate a feminine jawline or a swanlike neck, adapting themselves perfectly to the location in which they find themselves. Piercing itself has been subject to

Joseph and Potiphar's Wife
by Guido Reni, about 1630.
(J. Paul Getty Museum)

swings in perceived acceptability. Until
the advent of ear piercing guns in the second
half of the twentieth century, to pierce one's
ears required a needle, a cork to support the lobe,
and a high pain threshold. Though a persistent
vogue for heavy earrings required pierced ears, as
a non-pronged setting would slip right off the lobe,
uneasiness persisted through the twentieth century.
The invention of the clip setting in the 1930s was a
godsend for women who wanted to wear the latest
styles with intact lobes. Today, ear piercing is by and

Sutra earrings.

large a non-issue, with the vast majority of women painlessly piercing their ears in childhood.

At various points throughout history, men have also taken to the practice of piercing their ears and wearing earrings, though not as consistently or as universally as women. In the late sixteenth and early seventeenth centuries, English courtiers of the male sex took to wearing single pearl drop earrings, but by the eighteenth century, French officers were mocked in England for their habit of wearing the jewelry. As late as the early nineteenth century, men all over France and Italy had taken up the practice, including Napoleon's brother-in-law Joachim Murat, the King of Naples. The pirates who preyed upon the seas in the seventeenth and eighteenth centuries were also known for wearing earrings, which they did for reasons both superstitious (the widely held belief that wearing gold or silver would improve one's eyesight or prevent one from drowning) and utilitarian (pirates would engrave the name of their home port on the earrings so their

bodies could be sent home for burial, and
hung bits of wax from them to use as earplugs
during deafening cannon battles). Over the last
two centuries, men's earrings all but disappeared,
until making a comeback in the 1970s. Once widely
seen as a sign that the earringed man was gay, earrings
for men spread through youth subcultures until it
was more or less mainstream in the 1990s. (One sign
of the transition: Judd Nelson's juvenile delinquent
character in beloved 1985 teen drama The Breakfast
Club wears a diamond stud earring.)

HISTORY

As early as the third century BC, people were
creating objects to decorate their ears, and the
notion of piercing the earlobe began where many
cultural memes did, in Western Asia. The royal tombs
of Ur contained examples of golden crescent earrings
from 2500 BC, as well as more complex Babylonian
examples from a thousand years later that possessed
the same basic shape, but with details created by
embossing, filigree and granulation. Like all great
ideas whose time has come, earrings spread throughout

La Favorite
by Clément-Serveau.
(Musée d'Art Moderne de la Ville de Paris, Paris)

TOP
Andreoli earrings.

RIGHT
Piaget earrings.

135

the ancient world: in the second half of the second millennium BC, the hoop earrings had made it to Greece, Western Asia, Cyprus and Syria. Archaeologists have not only found earrings in all of these places, earring-wearing statues as well, particularly in Cyprus. There, terracotta figures—probably fertility totems—have their ears pierced two or three times, with terracotta earrings as adornments. Sculpted reliefs from the ninth century BC show Assyrian king Ashurnasirpal II and his courtiers with earrings, dangling from pierced ears and ending in an acorn motif.

ANCIENT EGYPT

Enthusiasts of jewelry in all its varieties, the ancient Egyptians had a great deal of affection for earrings as well, using them to adorn not just woman but men, children and statues of gods, goddesses and sacred animals. Earrings came to Egypt via Asia around 1600 BC, and some mummies have the distended earlobes common to those who habitually wore heavy earrings. Mummies from the New Kingdom also have enlarged earlobes, from the practice of wearing large earplugs in the form of

Detail from
The Cheat with the Ace of Diamonds
(Cardsharp)
by Georges de la Tour, 1635.
(Musée du Louvre, Paris)

LEFT
Hammerman Brothers earrings.

CENTER
Sutra earrings.

RIGHT
de Grisogono earrings.

BOTTOM
Piaget earrings.

137

The cat-goddess Bastet,
Daughter of Re, wearing earrings. Egypt,
Late Period (715-343 BC).
(Ashmolean Museum, Oxford, Great Britain)

138

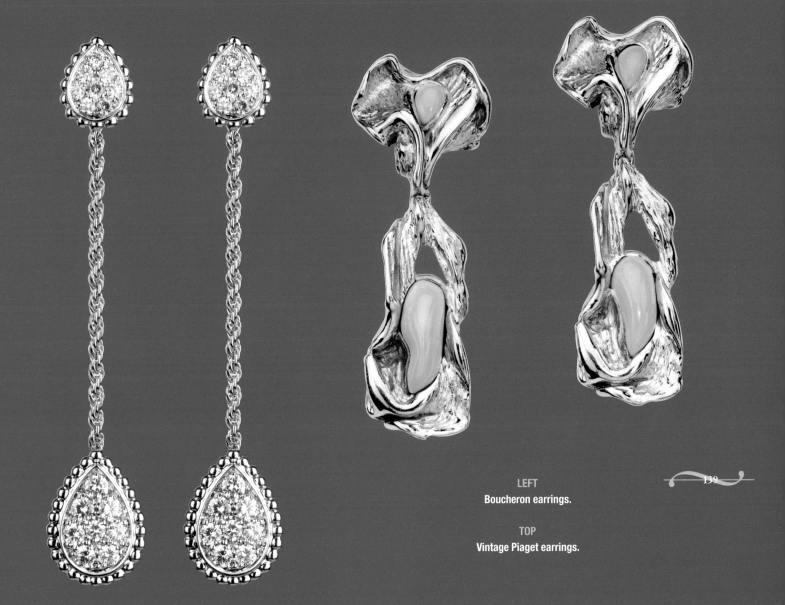

LEFT
Boucheron earrings.

TOP
Vintage Piaget earrings.

mushroom-shaped studs or faience discs, akin in shape, if not material, to those worn in some subcultures today.

The ancient Greeks were mad for earrings, both as an element of everyday dress (as depicted on vase paintings and terracotta statuettes) and as an addition to female statuary (as shown by the statues of goddesses that bear either marble earrings or pierced ears). Many of the earrings that have survived to this day are in the form of flat crescents suspended from gold chains, or smaller, spiral-shaped pieces that were worn in the earlobes. In the Iliad, when Hera beautifies herself to seduce Zeus and distract him from the war below, she puts on a pair of earrings with three clustering drops. One byproduct of Alexander the Great's conquests was an enlarged, enriched vocabulary for earrings, and the jewels grew more detailed, incorporating chains and pendants. Some of the earrings from these cultures raise the question of how they might have been worn: though clearly meant to be worn in pierced ears, animal head or helix terminals seem too large for the

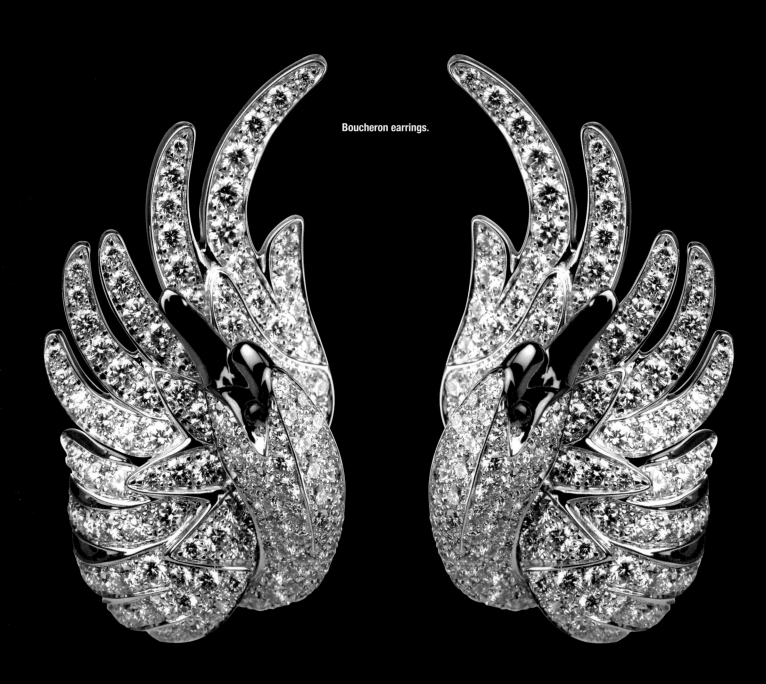

Boucheron earrings.

141

usual size of the piercing. Barring any other forthcoming explanations, it seems that women simply gritted their teeth and suffered for beauty.

In ancient Roman times, a new earring design arrived to take its place alongside the inherited styles. a gemstone and a pendant attached to an S-shaped hook. Some inherited issues, however, still persisted, giving rise to the profession of auricolae ornatrices, women who were called in to ameliorate problems caused by wearing (of course) heavy earrings. Writers Seneca, Petronius and Pliny all made numerous

references to earrings, the latter describing the finery of Caligula's wife Lollia Paulina, as well as that of less powerful women, whom he describes as wearing earrings with pearl drops that clinked together with every movement.

The European Middle Ages were the Dark Ages for earrings, which were pushed aside by high-necked outfits and ornate head coverings that concealed the ears. However, as the Renaissance spread across the continent, earrings began to regain popularity. A change in preferred hairstyles led to

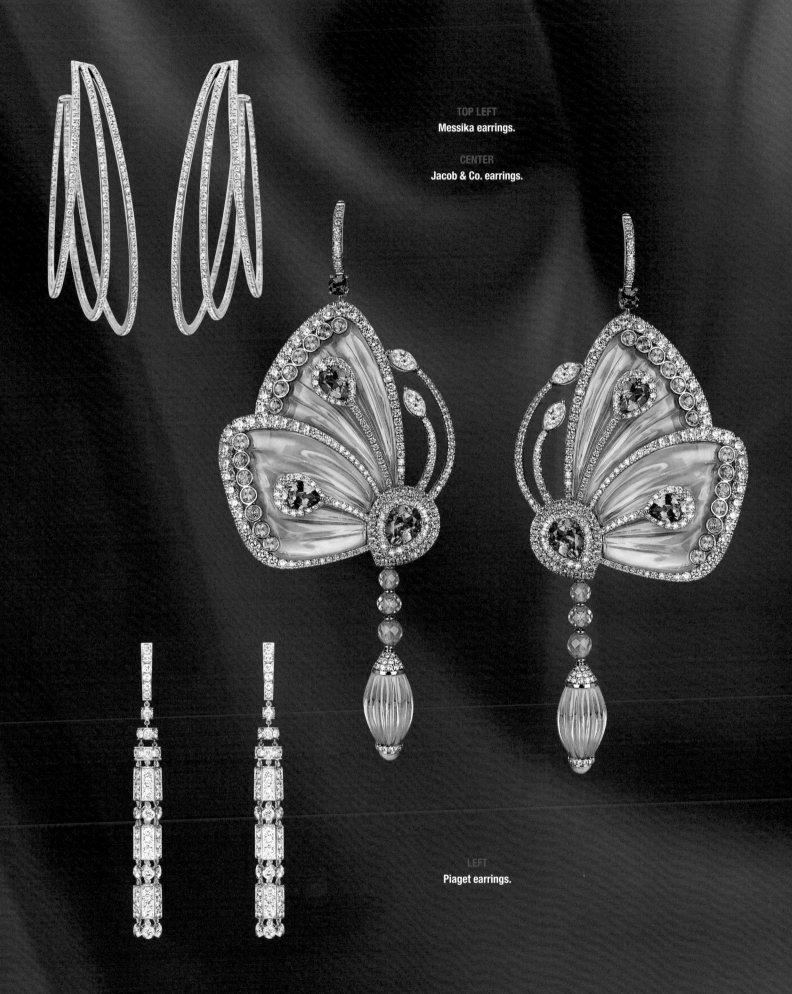

Reverie
by John William Godward, 1904.
(J. Paul Getty Museum)

TOP RIGHT
de Grisogono earrings.

BOTTOM LEFT
Andreoli earrings.

BOTTOM CENTER
Boucheron earrings.

BOTTOM RIGHT
Leon Bakst, costume design
for La Péri, 1910.

144

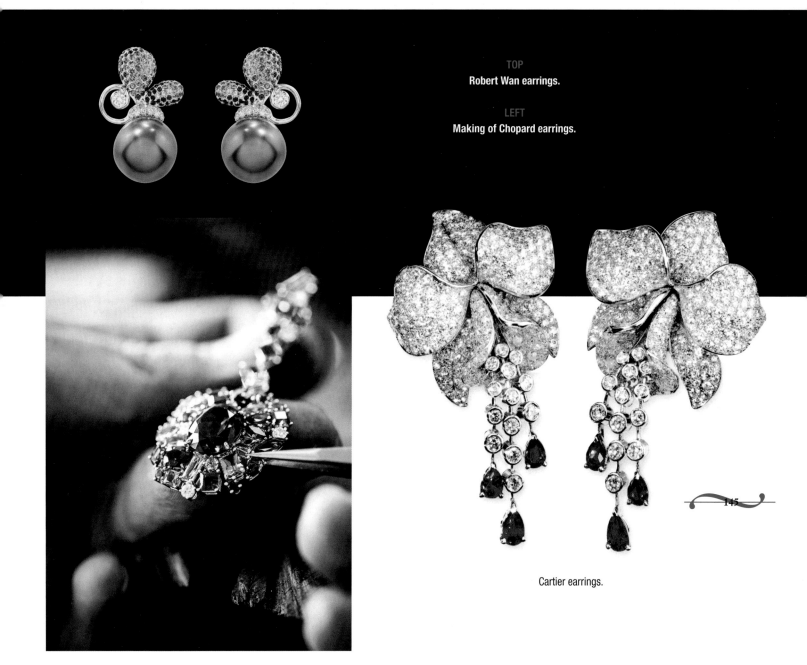

Cartier earrings.

145

the reintroduction of earrings in Italy (but not northern Europe) around the 1530s. After the return of the earring, pearl drops were an extremely popular ornament throughout the sixteenth century, a remarkably long-lived trend that persisted for a century and a half. Because the pearl is the one organic precious gem and only lasts for 300 years or so, none of these earrings still survive.

From here, the popularity of earrings only grew, aided by such proponents as Marie de Medici and the highly individualized, often whimsical motifs of the sixteenth century. Because there was nothing unusual about the practice of wearing earrings, they were the perfect medium for coded messages—Louis XIV gave a pair in diamonds and emeralds to his mistress Madame de Soubise. When she wore them, the king knew that her husband was away and his wife could play.

Beginning in the late seventeenth century, the girandole form of earring gained favor. Ignoring any desire for comfort on the part of its wearer, the girandole, which included a surmount, a bow or other

TOP LEFT
de Grisogono earrings.

TOP RIGHT
Takat earrings.

BOTTOM RIGHT
Andreoli earrings.

146

decorative element and three drops hanging
from the bow, was so heavy that women secured
it not only to their ears, but also to their hair, in
order to ease the burden. They also waited until the
last minute to don these pieces, keeping the earrings
in a pocket until it was time to make a grand entrance.
Despite these practices, girandole earrings—like other
heavy earrings—often permanently distended the tender
earlobes from which they hung. As time went by, the
design of the girandole went from mainly horizontal,
with three drops in a row, to vertical, with a longer and

Fawaz Gruosi and Eva Mendes wearing de Grisogono jewelry.

TOP LEFT
Sharon Stone wearing
de Grisogono jewelry.

BOTTOM
de Grisogono earrings.

LEFT
Piaget earrings.

BELOW
de Grisogono earrings.

Sutra earrings.

more elaborate central drop. The pendeloque was another popular form of earring in the eighteenth century, with an exaggerated length that counterbalanced the towering hairstyles that held sway among the upper crust.

The 1820s and 1830s saw a revival of the heavy girandole style, and no less a jewelry enthusiast than the future Queen Victoria wore vintage girandoles (inherited from Queen Charlotte). Even royal blood did not protect her ears against the predictable effects of such weighty ornaments. By the 1840s, hairstyles had

Piaget earrings.

changed again, covering the ears and spelling doom for earrings. Even when the hair was worn up at grand events, the fashion for face-framing tiaras obviated the need for earrings. Women did not give up entirely on the earring at this point, though—at night they wore simple studs (called "dormeuses" or "sleepers") to prevent the hole from closing up. This was a wise move, as earrings returned to fashion in the 1860s, with silly decorative motifs that included baskets of flowers or hammers, masks or vases inspired by archaeological excavations, and an entire menagerie of winning creatures. The same forces that the nineteenth century exerted on other forms of jewelry also applied to earrings, as exotic materials and various revivals (such as the Classical revival and the Renaissance revival) changed the landscape. Contemporary jewelry designers, though widely inspired, always included a few touches—a foliate detail here, a superfluous chain there—that distinguished the earrings from their inspirations.

Piaget earrings.

RIGHT
Demi Moore wearing
de Grisogono earrings.

CENTER
Gumuchian earrings.

Hammerman Brothers earrings.

153

Chopard earrings.

134

TOP RIGHT
Clothilde Courau wearing
de Grisogono jewelry.

BOTTOM RIGHT
Hammerman Brothers
earrings.

NEAR RIGHT
Hammerman Brothers
earrings.

Maria Menounos
wearing Sutra earrings.

TOP AND BOTTOM
Takat earrings.

Takat jewelry.

In the field of earrings, as in other domains, the twentieth century took a while to get under way, and the earrings of the early 1900s are quite similar to those of the previous century, using mostly clusters and small pendants as design elements. Platinum, a metal that had only recently become workable, was the new precious metal of choice, as its strength was such that only a small amount was needed to set the diamonds that continued to be the first choice for earrings. Delicate details were also much in demand; jewelry designers, and in particular those at Cartier, used architectural elements writ small.

The Roaring Twenties required a complete reimagining of the earring, which took advantage of the shockingly short coifs and simple styles to become a form of exclamation point near each ear. They grew long and dramatic, geometric rather than organic, emphasizing the vertical with bold bars of rock crystal, black onyx, red coral, green jade and all hues of enamel. These earrings became the most important item of jewelry, colonizing the suddenly empty real estate between the jawline and

LEFT
Chaumet Hortensia earrings.

TOP RIGHT
Chopard earrings.

BOTTOM
Chaumet Hortensia earrings.

RIGHT
Bianca Balti wearing
de Grisogono jewelry.

TOP AND BOTTOM
Sutra earrings.

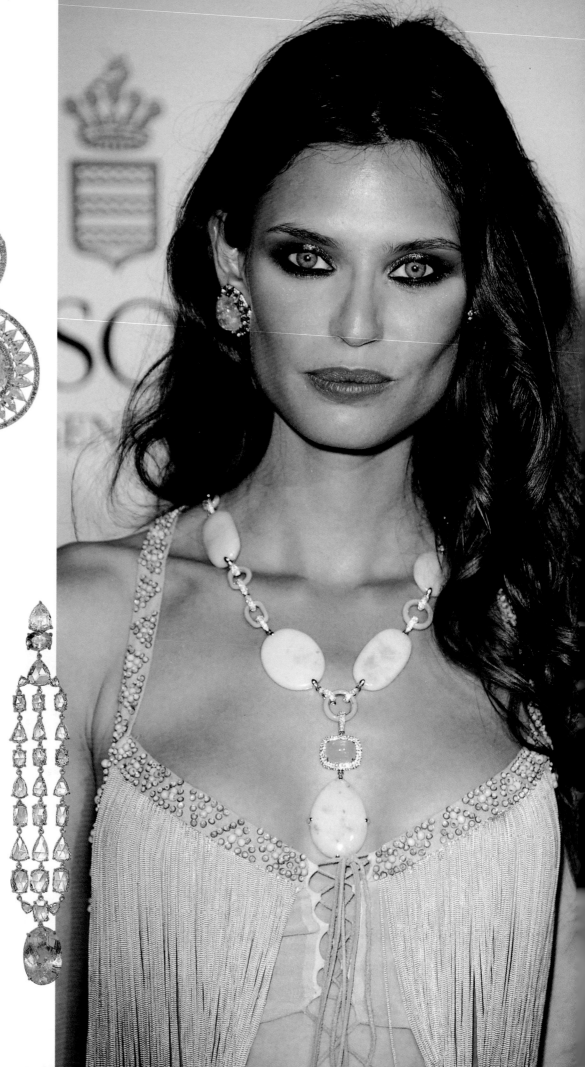

the shoulder. They were held in place by a screw fitting (which did not require piercing) or, increasingly, a stud fitting that penetrated the lobe. With women engaging in more physical activity, and the back of the ear visible to all, the stud offered an unbeatable mix of security and discretion.

Amid the sweeping changes of the 1930s was included a huge one in the world of earrings: the clip-on. Up until this point, women who loved earrings had two choices. They could pierce their ears—a practice still viewed with a bit of suspicion—or they could try the cumbersome screw-fitting, which was inelegant and unsuitable for anything heavy (and if there is one thing that earring-lovers have in common, from Egyptian mummies to Queen Victoria, it is an inordinate fondness for heavy earrings). Because the clip fastened the jewel so securely to the ear, it allowed for designs that curved upward, following the delicate sweep of cartilage and distinguishing earrings for the left and right ears for the first time.

In the prosperous years following World War II, women celebrated a return to normalcy (jewelry had been restricted during the war, as the metal was needed for munitions) by wearing relaxed jewels in classic pearls and diamonds, shown off by contemporary hairstyles that swept back from the face. Clip-ons

Bayco earrings.

Hammerman Brothers
earrings.

TOP LEFT
Bayco earrings.

CENTER
de Grisogono earrings.

161

enjoyed a period of dominance, due not to any social unacceptability of pierced ears, but because women didn't like the look of a bare pierced ear, covering the hole with, paradoxically, a gem that obviated it. The warm glow of pearl earrings flattered any face and the simplicity of the pieces—often just a pearl, with no other embellishment—appealed to women who realized they could wear the jewels with any dress, day or night.

As the 1950s became the 1960s, however—a process that took longer than one might think—all bets were off when it came to earrings. Women elided the distinction between day jewels in gold and night jewels set with precious stones, wearing large, jaunty statement earrings with disregard for the clock. Jewelers set them with raw, unfinished stones or found natural materials, erasing, or rather disguising, the work and artfulness of creating jewels. Another trend that found new life was the use of whimsical themes, exemplified in iconic designs that included enameled critters of all varieties.

This "anything goes" approach has continued since the 1970s, when the only requirement for the earring is that it be bold and large, whether hoop or pendant. The 1990s took things a step further, as multiple ear piercings dove into the mainstream, and it was not uncommon to see women or men with a row of studs or small hoops adorning the entire whorl of cartilage.

These days, earrings are as popular as ever, if not more so, as designers explore the intriguing design possibilities unique to the jewel. Because every earring has a mate, the form opens up remarkable possibilities. Traditional haute jewelers search high and low for two stones that are identical in size, color and clarity, holding on to gems for years until its perfect soulmate comes along. More iconoclastic designers however, experiment with the concepts of mismatching, asymmetry and negative images. For example, a ruby surmount and a diamond pendant might be paired with a diamond surmount and a ruby pendant. For designers who value perfect, yet natural symmetry in larger stones,

de Grisogono earrings.

Piaget earrings.

163

Gumuchian earrings.

they might use a colored gemstone slice as a pendant, bisecting a larger stone so that the two earrings are exact mirror images, down to the imperfections in the crystal. Jewelers are also trying out titanium, a metal known for its exceptionally light weight, as a way to create imposing pieces that are no longer painful to wear. Amid this ferment of imagination, some classics will never fade away. As long as women show off our ears, we will want something to adorn them with, whether it is a simple stud, a gem-set hoop, a dazzling pendant or a new trend that is still waiting in the wings.

DIFFERENT KINDS OF EARRINGS

STUD

The stud earring is the first kind of earring that most girls wear after first piercing their ears, as it is simple, light and easy on the ear. Discreet diamond studs are analogous to the "little black dress" as a fashion staple, though their high inherent value makes them less ubiquitous. Many haute jewelers offer diamonds studs in large carat sizes or unusual colors, as well as studs crafted from precious colored gemstones.

TOP LEFT
Emma Watson wearing
Boucheron jewelry.

CENTER
Messika earrings.

Actress Kristin Scott Thomas in de Grisogono at the Cannes Film Festival.

RIGHT
Hammerman Brothers earrings.

CENTER
Andreoli earrings.

BELOW LEFT
Jewelmer Joaillerie jewelry.

Robert Wan earrings.

TOP LEFT
Fan Bing Bing wearing
Chopard jewelry.

TOP RIGHT
Bayco earrings.

CENTER
Hammerman Brothers earrings.

Hammerman Brothers earrings.

167

PEARL

Pearls have been a favorite earring material for ages, for a few reasons. Before the advent of cultured pearls, the gem was much rarer and more expensive, so pearl jewelry that did not require buckets of the nacreous beauties was much easier to come by. (By the same token, the superlatively powerful and wealthy—think Queen Elizabeth I—coated themselves in pearls as a display of rank.) In addition, pearls are such delicate things that a pearl ring or bracelet could easily be damaged. The pearl drops of the Renaissance and the pearl studs of the 1950s and today thus bring a soft illumination to the face while remaining out of harm's way.

168

TOP
Jacob & Co. earrings.

BOTTOM
Hammerman Brothers earrings.

PENDANTS

The French word "pendant" means "dangling," and that is the idea behind pendant earrings, which encompass several subsets and styles. In its simplest incarnation, the pendant earring supports a gemstone or motif that hangs straight down from the ear. There are, however, endless variations, from miniature amphorae motifs (popular in antiquity and during revivalist periods) to cascades of gemstones, to clusters suspended from a jeweled surmount.

CHANDELIER

Bold, dramatic chandelier earrings recall the light fixture of the same name, with multiple strands of gems descending from the ear to catch the light and scatter it in pleasing directions. These are usually quite elaborate and at least an inch long.

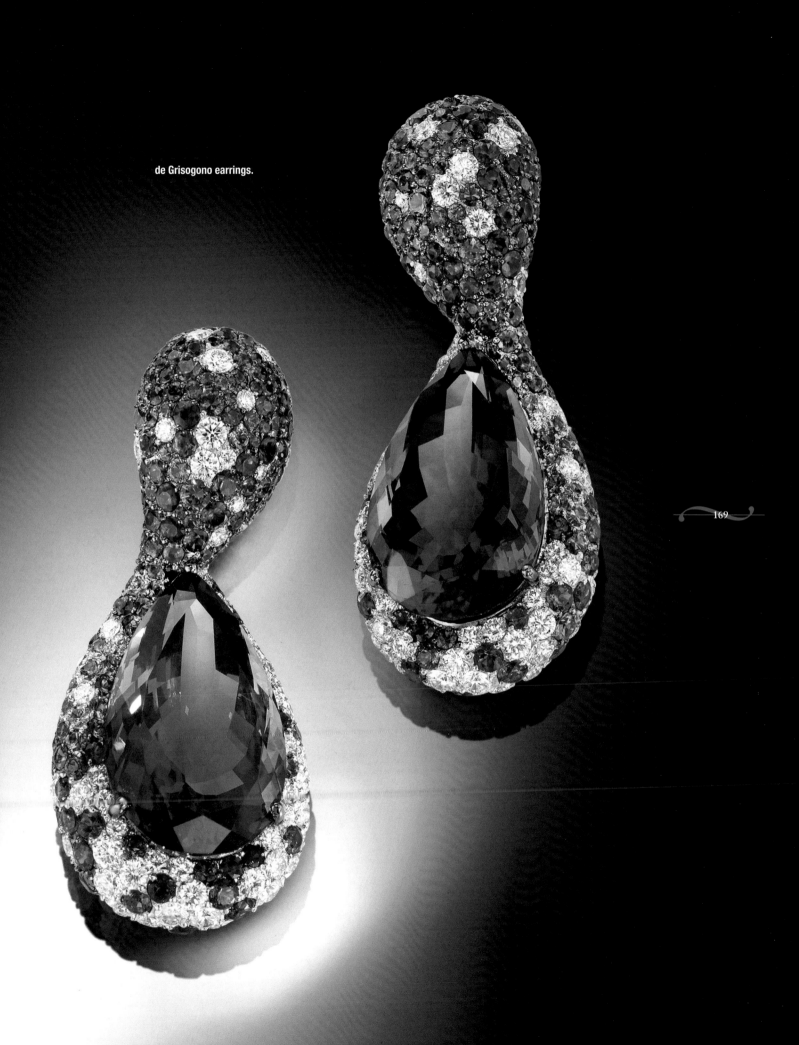

de Grisogono earrings.

169

Bayco jewelry

Gumuchian earrings.

de Grisogono earrings.

Jewelmer Joaillerie jewelry.

GIRANDOLE/PENDELOQUE

The girandole and pendeloque styles of earring were popular in the seventeenth and eighteenth century, with a revival in the nineteenth century. The girandole featured three drops arranged horizontally, dangling from a bow or other motif, while the pendeloque is arranged along more vertical lines, with a prominent, long pendant element that may be flanked by two smaller ones.

HOOPS

The hoop earring has been with us for a very long time—examples of this type have been found at the earliest archaeological sites with earrings, and their basic design has remained the same! Today's designers take this iconic form and experiment with materials, using rock crystal, turquoise, black onyx or even a thick setting of precious colored gems to provide a modern take on this ancient stalwart.

Bar Refaeli wearing
Chopard earrings.

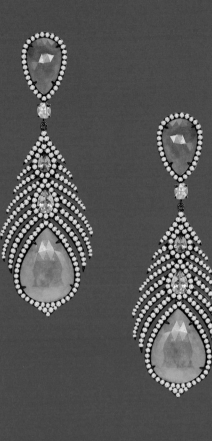

TOP LEFT
Sutra earrings.

TOP RIGHT
Sutra earrings.

BOTTOM LEFT
Bayco earrings.

BOTTOM RIGHT
de Grisogono earrings.

Bayco jewelry.

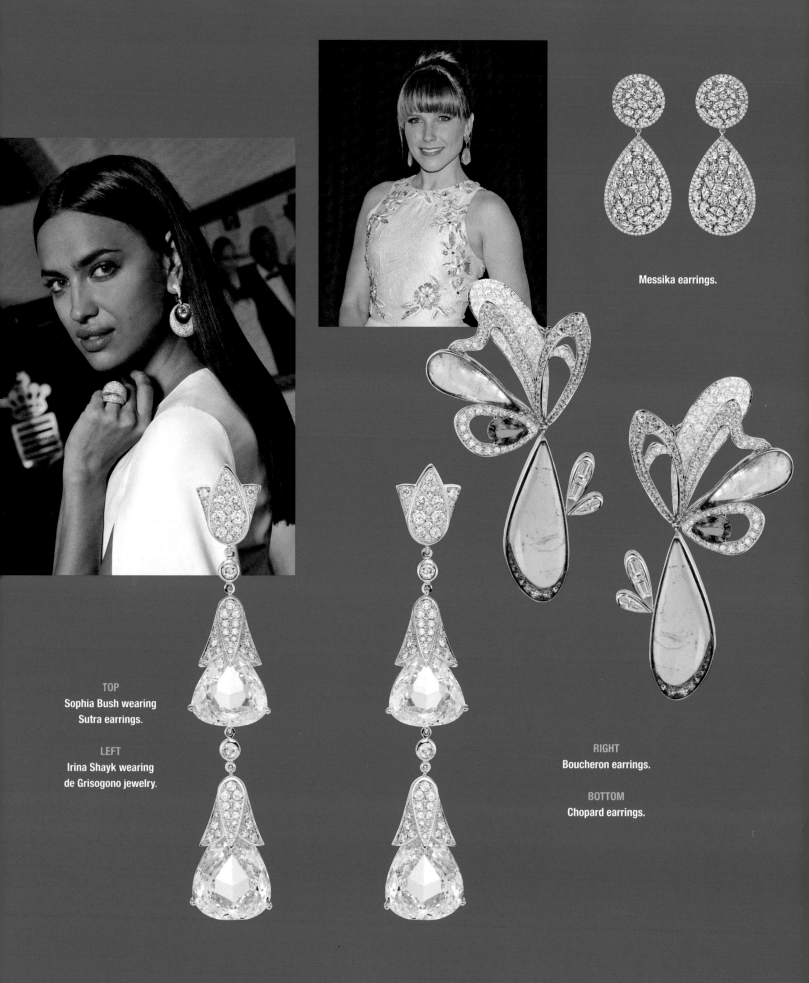

Messika earrings.

TOP
Sophia Bush wearing
Sutra earrings.

LEFT
Irina Shayk wearing
de Grisogono jewelry.

RIGHT
Boucheron earrings.

BOTTOM
Chopard earrings.

Bayco jewelry.

TOP LEFT
Amanda Righetti wearing Sutra earrings.

TOP CENTER
Katherine Heigl wearing Sutra earrings.

LEFT
Eva Herzegova
wearing Chopard jewelry.

BELOW
Bayco earrings.

CENTER
Nikki Reed wearing Sutra earrings.

RIGHT
Mila Kunis wearing Sutra earrings.

Piaget earrings.

BOTTOM LEFT
Gumuchian earrings.

BOTTOM CENTER
Jennifer Lawrence
wearing Chopard.

TOP LEFT
Andreoli earings.

TOP RIGHT
Nieves Alvarez wearing
Chopard jewelry.

LEFT
Andreoli jewelry.

BOTTOM
Bayco earrings.

NECKLACES

The base of the neck cries out to be decorated with our most precious objects. Necklaces highlight our facial features, draw attention to the elegant clavicle and creatively adorn the bust. The necklace is among the most versatile pieces of jewelry. With the strength and relative size of the torso to support it, rather than a delicate earlobe or petite finger, the necklaces enjoys a vast freedom in terms of size, going from a simple beaded strand to an elaborate festoon necklace, dripping with large gemstones set in heavy gold. Because it is so often strung with beads, it can be added to as its wearer grows—either from a child into an adult, or into someone with more power and wealth, who accordingly wears more charms or jewels around her neck. A damaged necklace is easily repaired with a few new beads to replace ones that are lost. Necklaces can even be shared—while dining with her son Reggie Vanderbilt and new daughter-in-law Gloria (parents of fashion designer Gloria Vanderbilt), socialite Alice Vanderbilt asked Gloria if she had her pearls yet. Upon hearing that the young couple could

FACING PAGE
Takat necklace.

THIS PAGE
Izabel Goulart wearing
de Grisogono jewelry.

TOP
Andreoli necklace.

BOTTOM
Illustration from
Royaume de la perle, 1920.

181

not yet afford such jewelry, Alice removed her strand of natural pearls and snipped off about $70,000 worth of pearls with a pair of scissors. She handed it to Gloria, saying simply, "All the Vanderbilt women have pearls."

The relationship between clothing fashions and the design of necklaces cannot be denied. Ancient Egyptians wore only simple white linen garments, depending on colorful necklaces for any brightness or design in their dress. Eras that insisted on high necklines, such as the Middle Ages, could wipe the necklace from the bust of fashion for centuries, only for the long-dormant jewelry form to spring back to life when its natural habitat reappeared. At the end of the nineteenth century, collars were high during the day, but low and daring by evening, when women wore multiple necklaces, perhaps overcompensating for their daytime restraint. The new emphasis on vertical lines during the 1920s, when women were expected to have practically no bust, lent itself to longer necklaces that swung freely with the newly acceptable feminine practice of physical activity in public. Today's statement necklaces are best appreciated against a backdrop of

182

Detail, *Cleopatra* by Alexandra Cabanel, 1887.
(Musée des Beaux Arts, Antwerp)

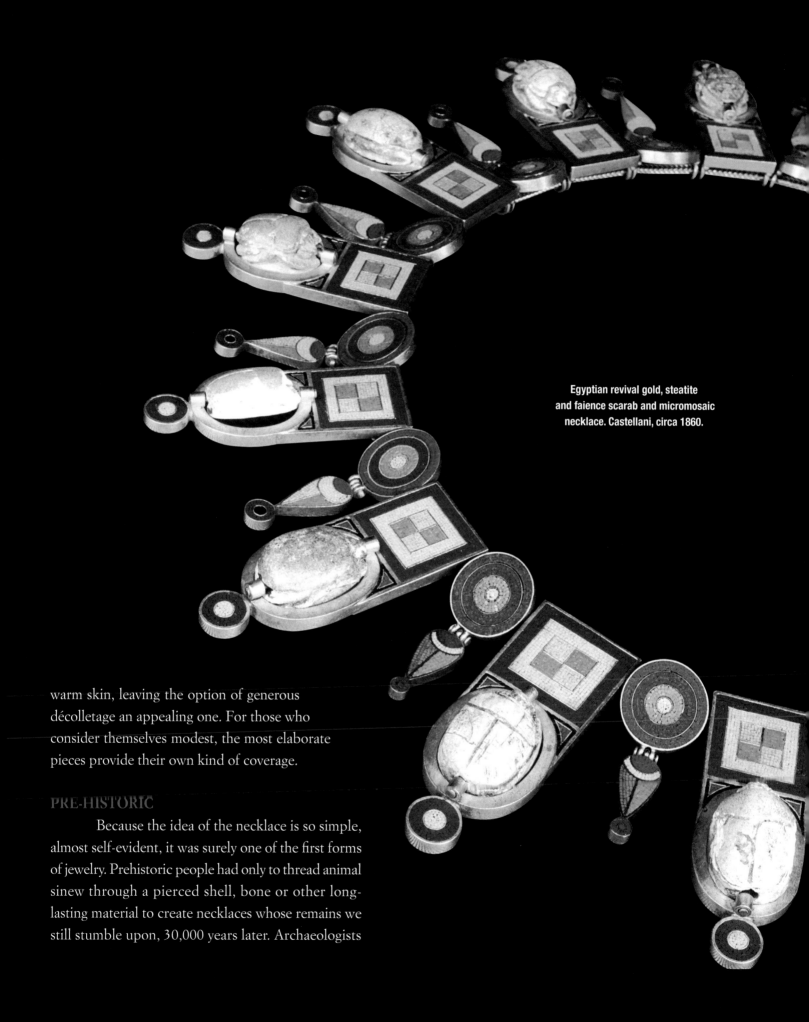

Egyptian revival gold, steatite
and faience scarab and micromosaic
necklace. Castellani, circa 1860.

warm skin, leaving the option of generous
décolletage an appealing one. For those who
consider themselves modest, the most elaborate
pieces provide their own kind of coverage.

PRE-HISTORIC

Because the idea of the necklace is so simple,
almost self-evident, it was surely one of the first forms
of jewelry. Prehistoric people had only to thread animal
sinew through a pierced shell, bone or other long-
lasting material to create necklaces whose remains we
still stumble upon, 30,000 years later. Archaeologists

Takat pendant.

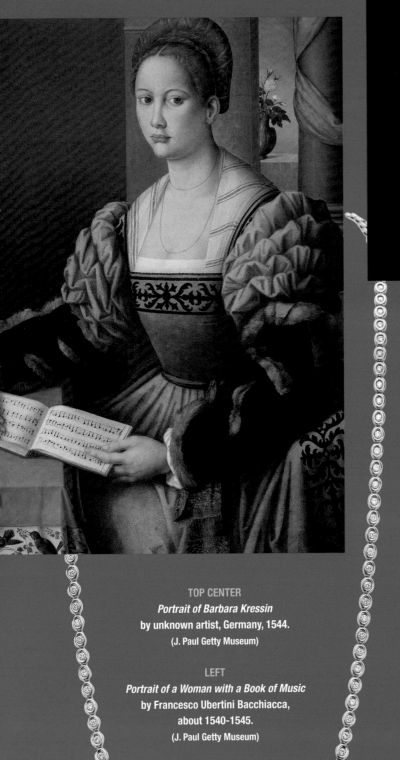

have found animal teeth, bones, shells, claws and spacer beads lying in arrangements that clearly indicate a string that had rotted away in the intervening millennia. Given the harsh environment and superstitious beliefs of nearly all of our forebears, these necklaces were most likely amuletic, meant to provide mystical protection against the world by appropriating the strength or talents of the animals who provided the materials. The basic design of many of these prehistoric pieces remains the style for countless necklaces today, proving that some forms cannot be improved upon.

ANCIENT SUMER

The earliest, simplest and most common necklaces in ancient Sumer consisted of strings threaded with clay, mother-of-pearl, obsidian or stone beads, with gold beginning to show up around 2500 BC. The Sumerian city of Ur contained royal tombs yielding necklaces with beads of lapis lazuli and carnelian, interspersed with gold pendants. As time goes on, Sumerian necklaces show increasing sophistication, with the different colors of stones and metal in alternating patterns.

185

TOP
Jacob & Co. necklace.

LEFT
Portrait of Louis XV,
after Hyacinthe Rigaud,
18th century.
(J. Paul Getty Museum)

Daniel and Cyrus before the Idol Bel
by Rembrandt van Rijn, 1633.
(J. Paul Getty Museum)

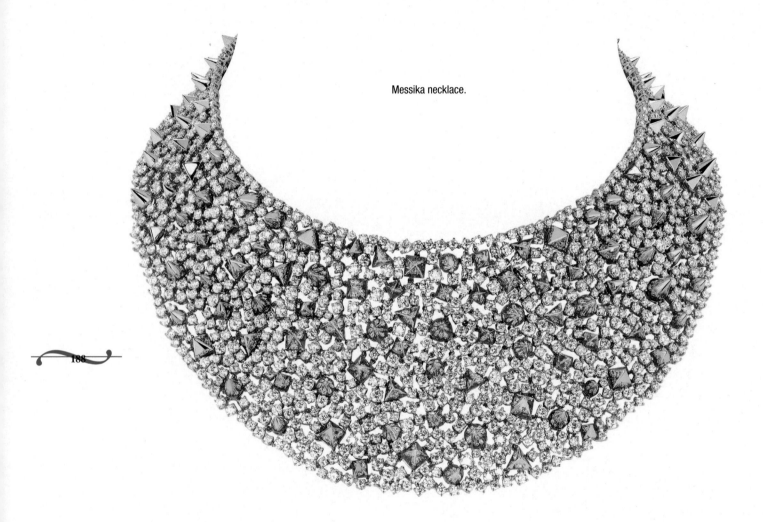

Messika necklace.

ANCIENT EGYPT

The development of necklaces in Egypt followed a trajectory that started out much like the Sumerian one, with simple strings of beads evolving into more elaborate patterns. Necklaces were highly valued in Ancient Egypt, and men and women both wore brightly colored ornaments that differ only slightly from those we wear today, while still being highly specific to their time and place. Two forms stand out as being particularly representative of the period's jewelry. The broad collar (also known as wesekh) is exactly what it sounds like: a wide jewel, set with several rows of faience beads or gemstones, that rested on the shoulders and chest. The gems encompassed all the most valuable materials of the culture: amethyst, turquoise, lapis lazuli and gold were heavily represented. The strings of beads often ended in elaborate terminals that bore their own symbolic motifs, such as lotus flowers or falcon heads. The collars were so heavy that they required a counterweight, hanging down from the back of the necklace, between the shoulder blades, to keep the elaborate jewel in place.

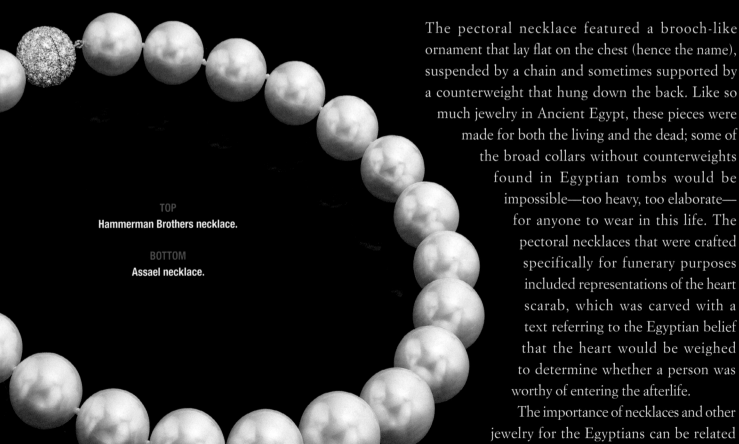

TOP
Hammerman Brothers necklace.

BOTTOM
Assael necklace.

The pectoral necklace featured a brooch-like ornament that lay flat on the chest (hence the name), suspended by a chain and sometimes supported by a counterweight that hung down the back. Like so much jewelry in Ancient Egypt, these pieces were made for both the living and the dead; some of the broad collars without counterweights found in Egyptian tombs would be impossible—too heavy, too elaborate— for anyone to wear in this life. The pectoral necklaces that were crafted specifically for funerary purposes included representations of the heart scarab, which was carved with a text referring to the Egyptian belief that the heart would be weighed to determine whether a person was worthy of entering the afterlife.

The importance of necklaces and other jewelry for the Egyptians can be related

Portrait of a Woman by Jan Mytens, 1660s. (J. Paul Getty Museum)

to their simple, almost austere style of dress. The society highly valued color and ornament, yet dressed in fitted garments of white linen that left the upper body bare. The colorful, elaborate necklaces favored by both sexes injected a dose of vibrancy and aesthetic pleasure into the sartorial landscape.

ANCIENT GREECE

The Greeks' fondness for the necklace may be surmised from the fact that they had many words to refer to different styles. (Modern English has at least as many, which is equally telling.) A peritrachelion or perideraion fit snugly around the neck like a choker, while the hypoderaion and hormos descended lower on the bust. The triopis had three ornaments hanging from it as drops. The plokion built upon a flexible woven strap that supported small gold chains from which hung three-dimensional representations of tiny heads, flower buds, acorns, seeds and similar nature-inspired pendants.

As in other parts of the world, Greek necklaces not only enhanced a woman's beauty, but also displayed her wealth and status, aside from any religious or

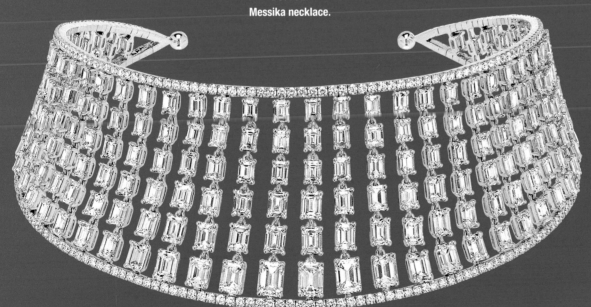

RIGHT
Vintage Boucheron Question
Mark necklace.

BOTTOM
Messika necklace.

TOP LEFT
Portrait of Queen Alexandra,
19th century.

TOP CENTER
Bayco necklace.

TOP RIGHT
Boucheron La Païva necklace,
1878.

Dance before a Fountain
by Nicolas Lancret, 1724.
(J. Paul Getty Museum)

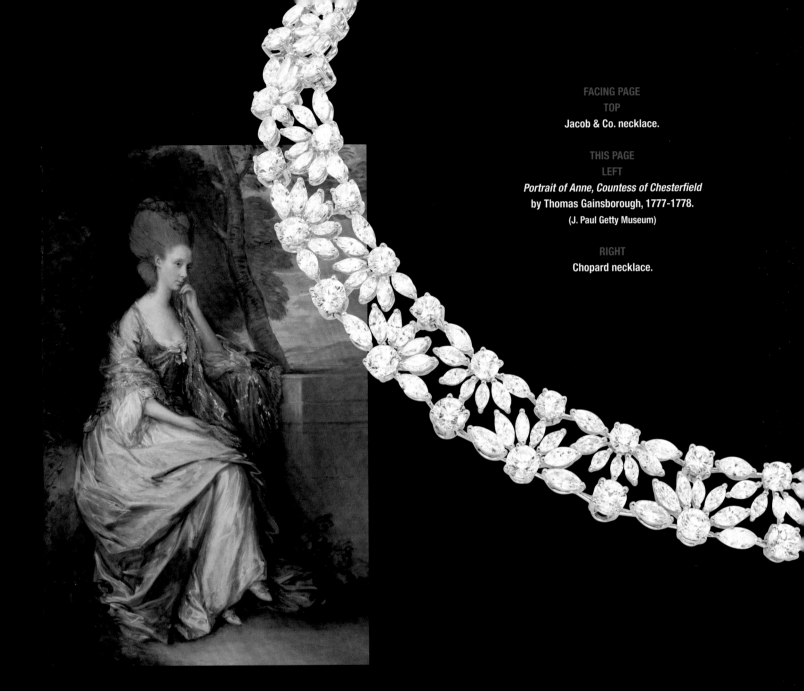

talismanic significance the jewel might have. Necklaces adorned the statues of the gods in their temples and were given as thanksgiving offerings. Women were often buried with their necklaces, but men wouldn't be caught dead in one, by the mid-sixth century BC, men generally abstained from jewelry other than finger rings or occasionally golden wreaths. Statues and painted vases show us how the Greeks generally wore their jewelry; as the favored garment was the chiton, which draped around the shoulders, necklaces stayed close around the base of the neck.

The Greeks had a complex view of the world, and saw necklaces as having the power both of protection and destruction. The story of Harmonia and her ill-fated necklace provides one example of this. Harmonia was the child of Aphrodite and her lover Ares, god of war. Hephaestus, Aphrodite's continually cuckolded husband, vowed to take his revenge on any descendants of the adulterous pair. When Harmonia herself was wed, to Cadmus of Thebes, Hephaestus showed up and presented her with a necklace he had made himself, which Harmonia accepted, strangely enough,

Cartier necklace.

LEFT
Cartier pendant.

RIGHT
Andreoli necklace.

LEFT
Vintage Cartier necklace.

RIGHT
Hammerman Brothers necklace.

de Grisogono necklace.

Vintage Boucheron necklace.

199

without suspicion. Made of gold, with inlaid gems, and crafted to resemble two serpents, with a clasp where the snakes' mouths were to meet, the jewel conferred eternal youth and beauty upon any woman who wore it. Predictably enough for the fetish object of a Greek myth, the necklace also assured its wearer's destruction. Harmonia and Cadmus watched their children undergo various torments (madness and untimely death chief among them), until they could take it no longer and begged the gods to turn them into snakes. Their daughter Semele wore the necklace when

a jealous Hera came to her and insinuated that Zeus was not the father of her child, an act that eventually led to Semele's incineration by Zeus. A few generations later, the necklace passed to Queen Jocasta, whose necklace-induced youth and beauty were probably a factor in her son Oedipus's willingness to accidentally commit incest with his mother. After several more disastrous stories of this type, the owners of the necklace eventually dedicated the necklace to the Temple of Delphi. However, that was not enough to stem its destructive power, as Phayllus, the ruler of Phocis,

FACING PAGE
BACKGROUND
Albert Cahen d'Anvers
by Pierre-Auguste Renoir, 1881.
(J. Paul Getty Museum)

LEFT
Messika necklace.

Chopard necklace.

stole it for his mistress. Her son went mad and burned down her house, engulfing his mother and all her other possessions—including Harmonia's cursed necklace—in flames. The Romans also greatly enjoyed necklaces, often wearing them in multiples. A woman might wear up to five necklaces at a time, covering the torso from the neck to the waist.

BRONZE AGE

The most common neck ornament in the European Bronze Age was the torc, a ring that encircled the neck and most likely had more significance than we understand today. Usually made in gold or bronze, and slightly less often in silver or iron, torcs were often crafted from ropes of twisted wire. Because of the difficulty in donning or removing a rigid neck ring of this type, torcs were meant to be worn constantly. Among the Celts of the Iron Age, a gold torc was a sign of high rank, and gods and warriors were often depicted wearing torcs, as in the famous sculpture *The Dying Gaul*, a Roman marble copy of a lost Greek work in bronze.

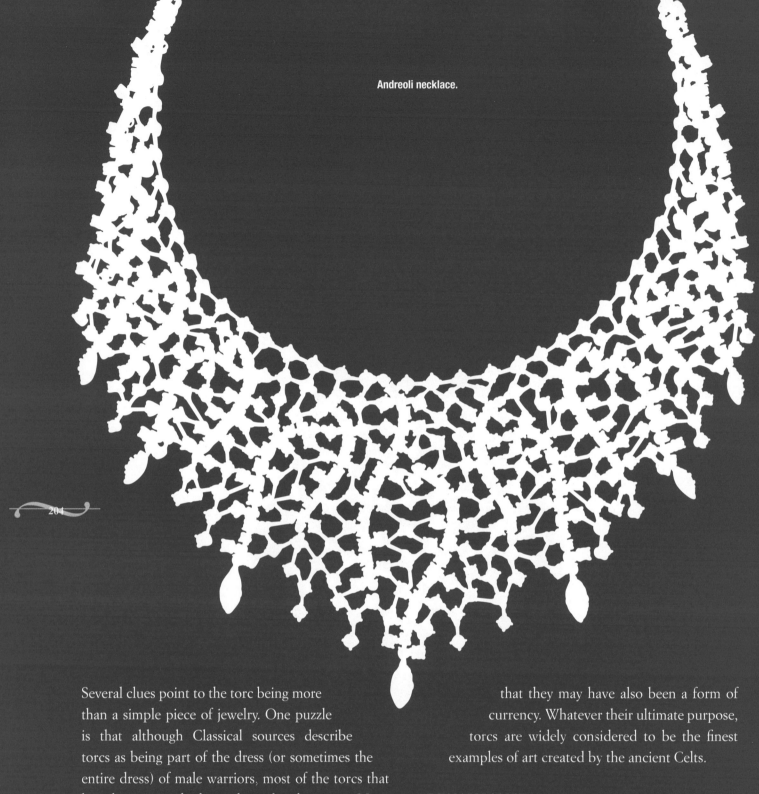

Andreoli necklace.

Several clues point to the torc being more than a simple piece of jewelry. One puzzle is that although Classical sources describe torcs as being part of the dress (or sometimes the entire dress) of male warriors, most of the torcs that have been unearthed were buried with women. Many torcs show up in hoards that include other valuables, but no bodies, which suggests that they were hidden away in the Bronze Age equivalent of a safety deposit box. Gold torcs found on the Iberian peninsula always weigh a multiple of a specific weight, which corresponds to the Phoenician shekel, suggesting that they may have also been a form of currency. Whatever their ultimate purpose, torcs are widely considered to be the finest examples of art created by the ancient Celts.

RENAISSANCE

Throughout most of the Middle Ages, necklaces all but disappeared. The clothes of the period—largely shapeless tunics secured by brooches—did not lend themselves to impressive neck ornaments, or even simple ones. The beginning of the Renaissance also led to a renaissance of the necklace. The development

Olga Kurylenko
wearing de Grisogono.

of tailoring engendered more form-fitting garments, as well as the much-beloved invention of décolletage, a boon for necklaces. The necklaces of this time were often referred to by the French name carcan, which denoted a prisoner's iron collar. The terminology suggests the form of these jewels, which were usually broad collars worn at the base of the neck.

These necklaces were favorite gifts of Philip the Good, Duke of Burgundy, and one exemplary purchase demonstrates the popularity of lavish collars: a necklace he bought for his wife Marguerite in 1396 was set with a sapphire, ten red spinels, 44 pearls and a large spinel pendant. The splendor of these ornaments was their only purpose; these necklaces served no

Bérénice Béjo
wearing Chopard jewelry.

practical function, but their popularity continued in tandem with that of plunging necklines until the end of the fifteenth century. The Renaissance also signaled a new way of regarding the necklace. Despite the rediscovery of and newfound appreciation for ancient culture, contemporary jewelers had no way of knowing what classical necklaces looked like, but the humanistic values of the Renaissance influenced jewelry design. Instead of jewels that distracted from natural beauty, artisans created pieces to enhance it.

SEVENTEENTH & EIGHTEENTH CENTURIES

Pearl necklaces, invariably fastened with a ribbon tie, enjoyed a long-lasting vogue towards the tail end of the Renaissance, popping up in society portraits and written records over the seventeenth century. This simple style, of one gem after another, also guides the rivière (stream) type of necklace, in which identically sized and faceted gemstones are mounted in collets and joined together.

LEFT
de Grisogono pendant.

RIGHT
Chopard pendant.

CENTER
Piaget necklace.

Bayco jewelry.

THIS PAGE
Messika jewelry.

Andreoli necklace.

French names for necklace styles such as carcan and collier du chien often sound a bit barbaric, and the esclavage style was no exception, named as it was for the institution of slavery. The women who wore esclavage necklaces, however, were weighed down only by the massive amounts of diamonds in the jewels (and by the burdens of being female in early modern Europe, but that is a topic for a different book). King Louis XV of France commissioned an esclavage necklace for his necklace Madame du Barry, and it nearly toppled the ancien régime singlehandedly. A con artist engineered an elaborate scheme of forgery and deception to get her hands on the necklace, convincing an out-of-favor courtier that Marie Antoinette herself longed for the jewel. When the bill came due, the details of the plot emerged, and the public remained convinced that the flighty queen had had something to do with the matter. Her public image was forever tarnished, as she was painted as a vain, vengeful spendthrift.

Jeanne de la Motte, the woman behind the Affair of the Necklace, most likely brought the "queen's necklace" to London and broke it up to sell

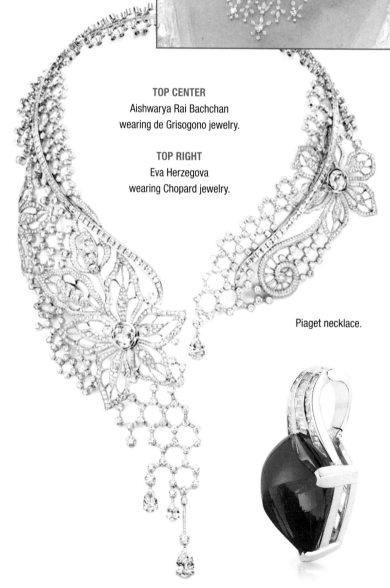

TOP CENTER
Aishwarya Rai Bachchan
wearing de Grisogono jewelry.

TOP RIGHT
Eva Herzegova
wearing Chopard jewelry.

Piaget necklace.

Takat pendant.

THIS PAGE
Piaget necklaces.

Assael necklace.

NINETEENTH CENTURY

New elements and new themes emerged for necklaces in the nineteenth century. Europe's continuing quest to colonize the rest of the world and a new interest in science led to an influx of novel ideas and materials for necklaces. For example, France's military adventures in Mexico led to the introduction of Central American themes in jewelry, just as, fifty years earlier, Napoleon's desire to link himself with the emperors of yesteryear had engendered a revival of antiquity among the fashionable set.

the stones separately. After the French Revolution, many necklaces found the same fate as their "queen," as jewels flooded the market, liquidated by down-on-their-luck aristocrats. This lowered the price of gemstones across Europe and led to the dissolution of countless historical pieces.

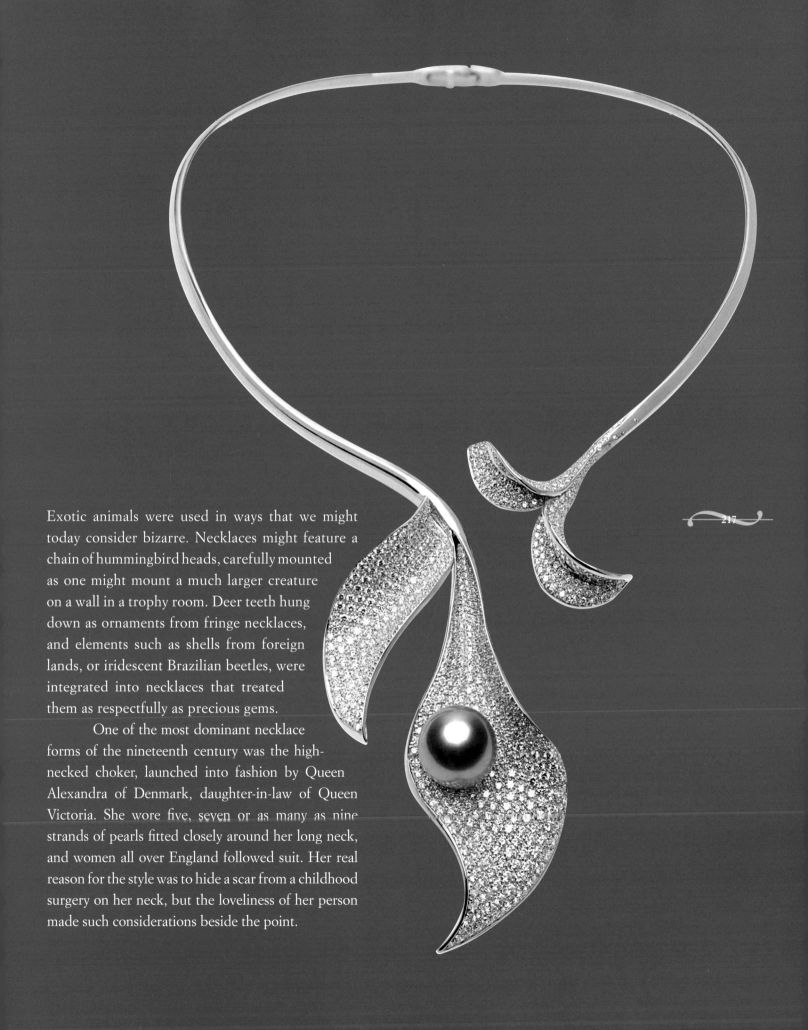

Exotic animals were used in ways that we might today consider bizarre. Necklaces might feature a chain of hummingbird heads, carefully mounted as one might mount a much larger creature on a wall in a trophy room. Deer teeth hung down as ornaments from fringe necklaces, and elements such as shells from foreign lands, or iridescent Brazilian beetles, were integrated into necklaces that treated them as respectfully as precious gems.

One of the most dominant necklace forms of the nineteenth century was the high-necked choker, launched into fashion by Queen Alexandra of Denmark, daughter-in-law of Queen Victoria. She wore five, seven or as many as nine strands of pearls fitted closely around her long neck, and women all over England followed suit. Her real reason for the style was to hide a scar from a childhood surgery on her neck, but the loveliness of her person made such considerations beside the point.

Boucheron necklace.

Despite the radical break from tradition Art Nouveau jewelers effected with respect to materials and themes, when it came to style, the designers stuck with the two types that were most popular at the turn of the twentieth century: the choker and a slightly longer style that closely girded the base of the neck. Within these confines, Art Nouveau jewelers showed off a daring design aesthetic that prized lightness and fluidity. Their influence can be felt in necklaces that curve around the neck in natural-seeming forms. "Question mark" necklaces from the late nineteenth century show a strong Art

Nouveau influence on their form, as they use diamonds and other precious stones to mimic wreaths of leaves or ivy, or flowering branches coiling around the neck. Many haute jewelry houses still include this kind of necklace among their finest creations.

TWENTIETH CENTURY & BEYOND

The strong, clean lines of Art Deco dominated the sautoirs and lariats of the 1930s, before necklaces shrank due to the material shortages of World War II—because they require so much more metal than

Andreoli necklace.

other jewels, they were proportionately more affected by rationing. The demure pieces of the '50s gave way to the explosion of colors, materials and trends engendered by the various social revolutions of the '60s, a time when independent designers dominated the conversation. Since then, necklaces have continued along the path of endless multiplicity, striking dramatic poses or discreetly bringing a bit of sparkle to the throat. Today's haute jewelry designers fully explore the nearly endless possibilities provided by a simple form, whether through a strand of pearls, a bewitching trompe l'oeil, a repeated gem-studded motif or an imposing framework for important jewels.

DIFFERENT KINDS OF NECKLACES

CHOKER

All fashionable women know that style can mean suffering, an idea reflected in the name of the choker. Haute jewelry chokers in the late nineteenth and early twentieth century usually consisted of a jeweled plaque that was either sewn to a cloth band

Naomi Campbell
wearing de Grisogono jewelry.

Bayco jewelry.

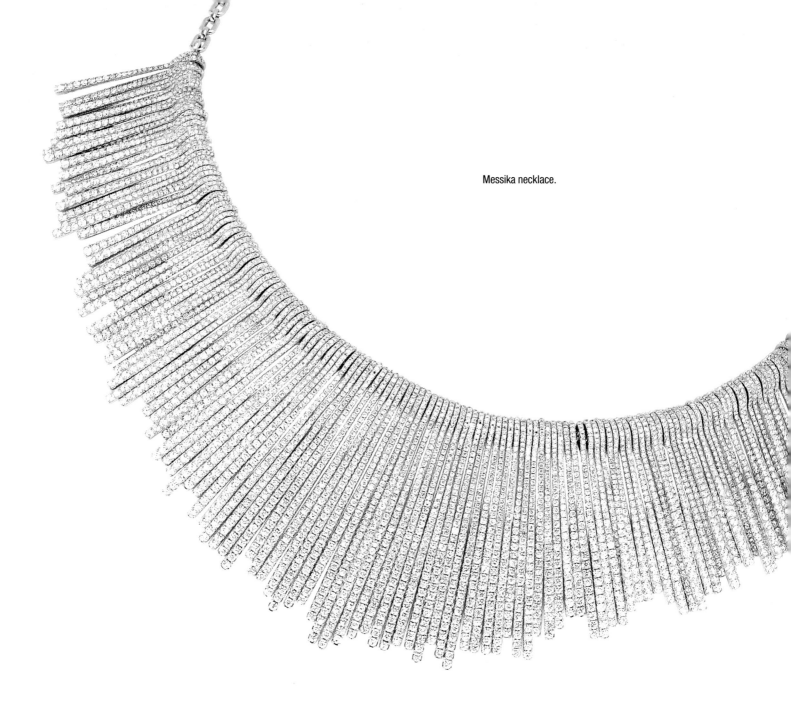

Messika necklace.

or arranged amidst row upon row of small pearls. Chokers had to be custom-made for each woman: a choker that was too loose would sag and ruin the effect, and a too-tight choker would ruin the evening for entirely different reasons. Chokers were often worn in addition to other necklaces.

FRINGE

The name of the fringe necklace is fairly self-explanatory, describing as it does a piece with a fringe of elements, graduated in size toward the center. A fringe necklace could generally also be worn as a tiara, by inverting it and affixing it to a metal hair ornament frame. Variations on the fringe design were worn in antiquity, and examples have been found from the ancient cultures of Egypt, Greece, Minos, Mycenae, Etruria and others. The style then disappeared almost completely, returning only with the archaeological revival movement of the nineteenth century. It has never completely faded since, though its popularity has waxed and waned. Haute jewelers appreciate the fringe's form, which is ideal for displaying an impressive selection of hard-to-find large precious gemstones.

RIVIÈRE & CLUSTER

The rivière, whose name means "stream" in French, possesses a simple design of identical or very slightly graduated stones set one after the other in collet or claw mounts. Any additional ornamentation is restricted to a drop at the front of the necklace. The cluster is a variation on the same design, except instead of individual stones, it is set with a group of stones set in a mass.

SAUTOIR

The sautoir as we know it came into being in 1910. As a long necklace that supports a tassel or pendant at the bottom, the sautoir is most suited to outfits with simple vertical lines.

PENDANT

The pendant necklace is one of the simplest and most endlessly adaptable styles of the form.

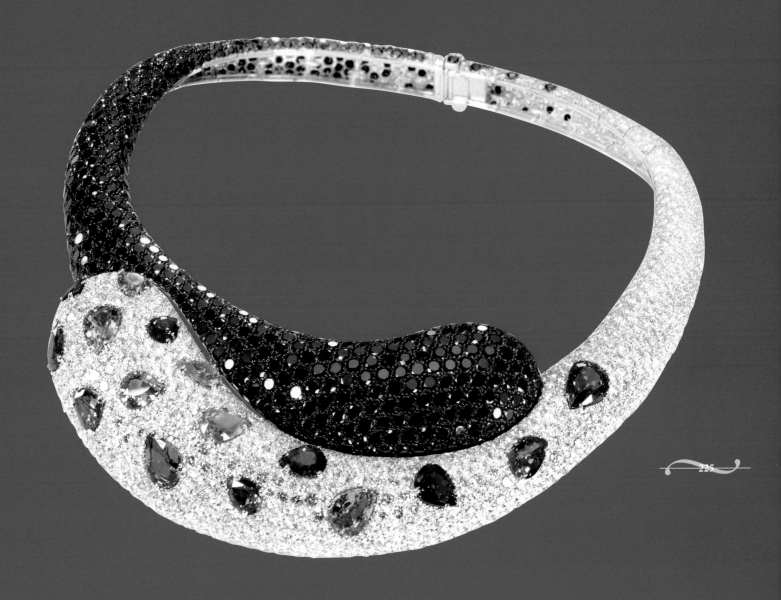

de Grisogono necklace.

People of prehistoric cultures would create pendants by boring holes in shells or rocks and threading grass, vine or sinew through the newly invented ornament. One type of pendant is a locket, which contains the photograph of a loved one. Another is a lavaliere, a longer, jeweled variety, which is named for Louise de La Vallière, the unhappy mistress of King Louis XIV.

TORC

The torc is a rigid collar, crafted in metal, most associated with the Celts of Northern Europe.

Modern torcs are much easier to take on and off than the ancient kind, which were not meant to be removed!

PEARL NECKLACES

The princess, matinee, opera or rope styles refer to lengths of pearl necklaces: 17-19 inches, 20-26 inches, 26-36 inches and 36-48 inches, respectively. Given the relative simplicity of most pearl necklaces, the length is the most crucial design element, lending an air of modest luxury or extravagant flair.

Jewelmer Joaillerie jewelry.

227

LARIAT

The lariat necklace is unusual in that it has no clasp; instead, one end of the necklace is threaded through a loop at the other end. Lariats must be quite long, naturally, in order for this system to work.

FESTOON

Festoon necklaces take advantage of a vast expanse of décolletage to weave their magic, dangling swags of chain—often set with gems or strung with pendants—from a main support. One type of festoon necklace is the esclavage necklace, which was the style of the jewel at the heart of the Affair of the Necklace that roiled pre-revolutionary France. The esclavage necklace was a common bridal gift in Normandy and other regions of France through the nineteenth century, though we do not know if its name referred to the less-than-emancipated condition of women, or the idea that bride and groom were now eternally chained together. (Either interpretation suggests a less than rosy take on the institution of marriage.)

LEFT
Ujjwala Raut
wearing de Grisogono jewelry.

RIGHT
Naomi Campbell
wearing de Grisogono jewelry.

de Grisogono necklace.

TOP
Gumuchian necklace.

LEFT
Kylie Minogue wearing Chopard jewelry.

BOTTOM
Andreoli necklace and earrings set.

BIB

An haute jewelry bib necklace is almost always
an astonishing statement piece, with a thick carpetlike
cover of jewels across the entire bust. A bib necklace
may be—but is not necessarily—a fringe necklace as
well, depending on how the gemstones are connected
to each other. The necklace has just a small clasp at
the back, completing its resemblance to a baby's bib.

TOP
Messika necklace.

LEFT
Bianca Balti
wearing de Grisogono jewelry.

BOTTOM
Assael necklace.

Bayco jewelry.

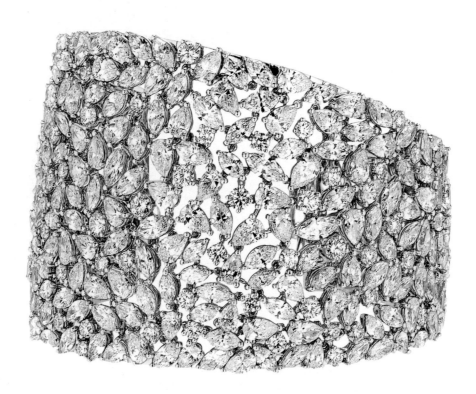

BRACELETS

Bracelets may just be the most playful form of jewelry we have yet devised. The largest, most important gemstones are usually reserved for the necklace, the ring is loaded down with millennia of layered meanings, the brooch began as a utilitarian sartorial element, but bracelets read as pure fun. The bracelet lends even more drama to impassioned gesticulations, often with an accompanying tinkle as charms or bangles find a way to brush up against each other. Often marking spot where a sleeve ends, or punctuating the length of a bare arm, bracelets contain an undeniable sensuality and beauty all their own. The linked bracelet also possesses a secret versatility that derives from the ratios of human anatomy: as the circumference of the neck is double that of the wrist, two flexible bracelets joined end to end become a chic choker necklace.

The use of bracelets has been a constant throughout human history, though the jewel's aesthetic and symbolic significance has always been in flux,

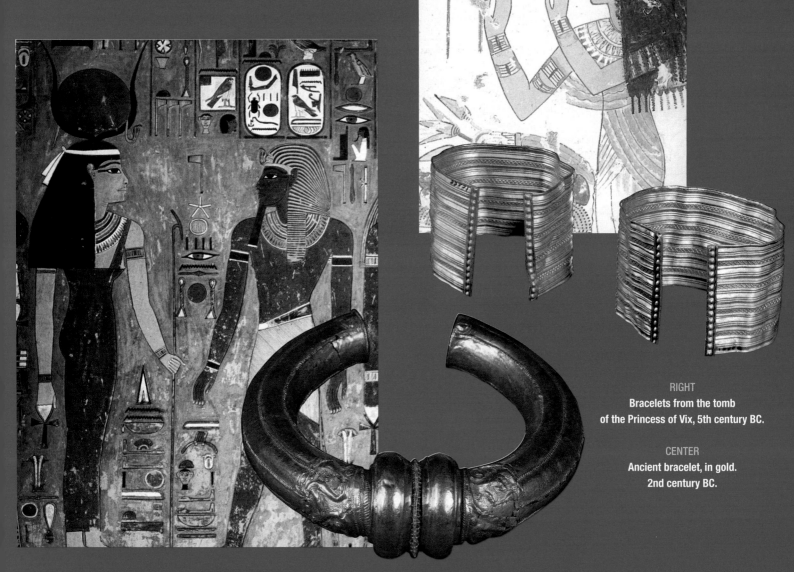

Woman presenting offerings,
copy of wall painting from Thebes,
tomb of Menna.

varying through the ages and across continents. In the contemporary Western world, the bracelet has no inherent significance, but in the nineteenth century, they carried coded love messages, and in Southern Asia, they are highly meaningful. Once we leave the realm of haute jewelry, moreover, bracelets take on countless interpretations, from the friendship bracelets made by young girls of colored string, to colored rubber bracelets that signal one's devotion to a cause, to coral bracelets that are said to protect babies against the evil eye.

One of the perks of being a bracelet devotee is the nearly endless range of ways to indulge oneself. Though wearing many necklaces or pairs of earrings would be highly unusual—and there is even a limit on the number of finger-rings it is acceptable to wear at a time—bracelets, particularly bangles, lend themselves to being worn multiply. First of all, we must take into consideration the presence of two wrists, each one as deserving of adornment as the other. As the gaze meanders upward, one might notice quite a bit of unused real estate. Why not, indeed, take advantage of

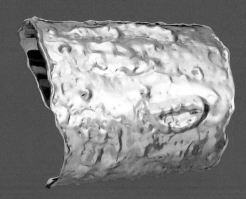

Etruscan bracelet.

LEFT
Italian revival bracelet, 1882.

RIGHT
Portrait of a Roman Egyptian
mummy wearing crown,
pendant earrings and two necklaces.

BOTTOM
Greek bracelet from 4th century BC.

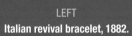

Interior of Roman Building with Figures
by Ettore Forti, late 19th century.
(J. Paul Getty Museum)

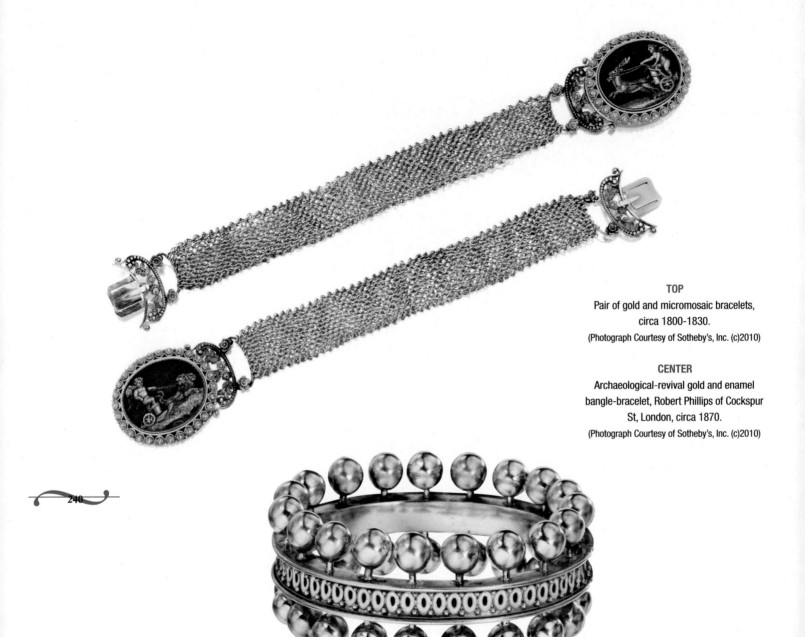

240

the entire forearm? Though very few women take things that far, it is by no means unusual to see several inches' worth of bangles on each arm, worn in odd numbers to bring good luck.

For a similarly striking statement without the jingle-jangle, a fashionable woman might don a cuff bracelet, and the exceptionally confident might go for a matching set. The most famous bracelets in popular culture take the form of matching cuffs—the indestructible, bullet-deflecting cuff bracelets worn by Wonder Woman. The basic cuff bracelet, crafted from a sheet of yellow gold, remains unchanged from the form it took thousands of years ago in material and design. However, between the earliest days of the bracelet and the present day, this flirtatious bit of beauty has taken innumerable forms.

The origins of the bracelet remain shrouded in mystery, but it is definitely no newcomer. Archaeologists working in the Siberian Denisova Cave discovered in 2008 fragments of a dark green stone bracelet that is circa 30,000-40,000 years old. In Wales, on the site of

the oldest known burial ground in Western
Europe, the so-called "Red Lady of Paviland"
(who actually turned out to be a young man) was
buried with ivory bracelets. These sparse findings
only grow more numerous, practically inescapable, as
we move from prehistory to ancient civilizations.

The Sumerian tomb of Queen Pu-abi counted
among its riches hollow bracelets of hammered
sheet gold and beaded cuffs with cylindrical beads
of lapis lazuli and gold. These bracelets shared a
certain aesthetic, due to their component materials,

with Egyptian jewelry. Crafted upon supports of gold or gilded silver, ancient Egyptian bracelets sported beads of amethyst, carnelian, lapis lazuli, green feldspar and turquoise. The malleability of gold also lent itself to elaborate bracelet designs, with broad cuff bracelets that narrated stories in picture form and pairs of bracelets that bore images of gods, serpents and lotus flowers. Thin golden strips, hammered out and soldered at the ends, served as elegant bangles. The Egyptians, lovers of finery that they were, used slightly larger beaded jewels around the ankles, and added banded golden armlets that encircled the biceps—Cleopatra was perhaps the most well-known aficionado of the style. King Tutankhamen, another famously bejeweled individual, wore gold bracelets inlaid with colored stones and glass fashioned into the form of the sacred scarab beetle.

In ancient Crete, artisans used bee and honeycomb motifs in bracelets, and all around the Mediterranean lands, people wore penannular bracelets with animal-head terminals. These motifs could be lions, bulls, rams or any animal important to the local

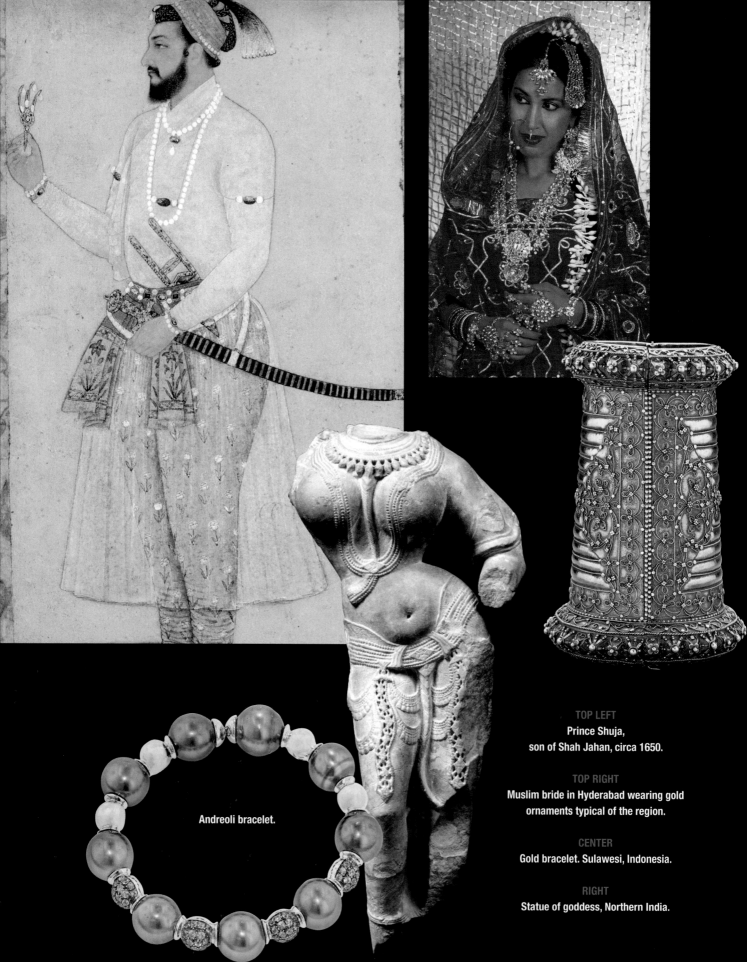

TOP LEFT
Prince Shuja,
son of Shah Jahan, circa 1650.

TOP RIGHT
Muslim bride in Hyderabad wearing gold
ornaments typical of the region.

CENTER
Gold bracelet. Sulawesi, Indonesia.

RIGHT
Statue of goddess, Northern India.

Andreoli bracelet.

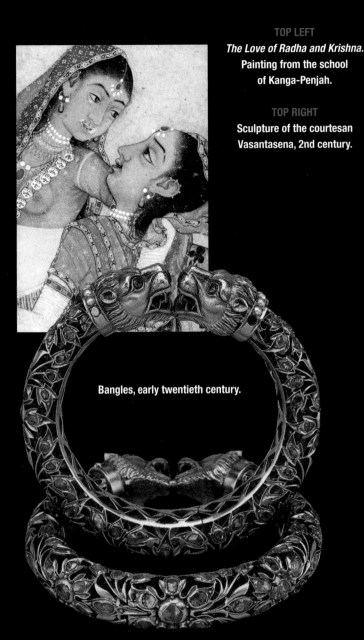

Bangles, early twentieth century.

culture. During the Hellenistic period, in the third and second centuries BC the Heracles knot was a popular motif for bracelets, which were worn by women in pairs upon the upper arms.

These bracelets worn on the upper arm, as opposed to the forearm, were called "arm rings" and were often worn by male warriors. In fact, when the contemporary literature simply refers to a "ring," it is this arm ring that is meant. (In Asia, arm rings persist as a connotation of warrior status in traditional Indonesian and Sri Lankan dress.)

The Romans loved their bracelets, men as well as women. Arm jewelry took the form of simple bangles, multiple spirals, or even more elaborate forms. In Gaius Petronius's Satyricon, the story of Trimalchio's Feast underscores the ways in which bracelets and other jewelry could be wielded as a form of social currency, or even ostentatious display, for this social climber. Trimalchio's wife, Fortunata, takes off her gold bracelets and lets her guests hold them, eventually doing the same with her anklets and gold hair net, making sure to let everyone know

Renée Puissant wearing Van Cleef & Arpels jewelry. Circa 1925.

Cartier bracelet.

LEFT
Boucheron bracelet.

RIGHT
Chopard bracelet.

exactly how pure the gold is. Trimalchio "complains" about how much all these trinkets cost, while making sure to remark upon his own expensive arm band. The two parvenus even go so far as to order a scale brought in to weigh their jewelry for the assembled guests.

Celtic armlets of the Iron Age were cast as penannular hoops with ornamentation that sprang up in relief from the jewel's surface. The terminals of these pieces sported the bright colors possible with champlevé enamel or inlaid colored glass.

Cartier bracelet.

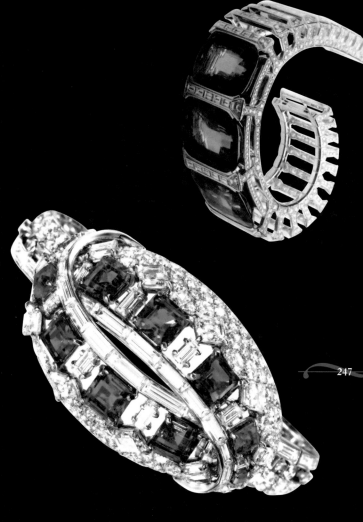

247

Cartier bracelet.

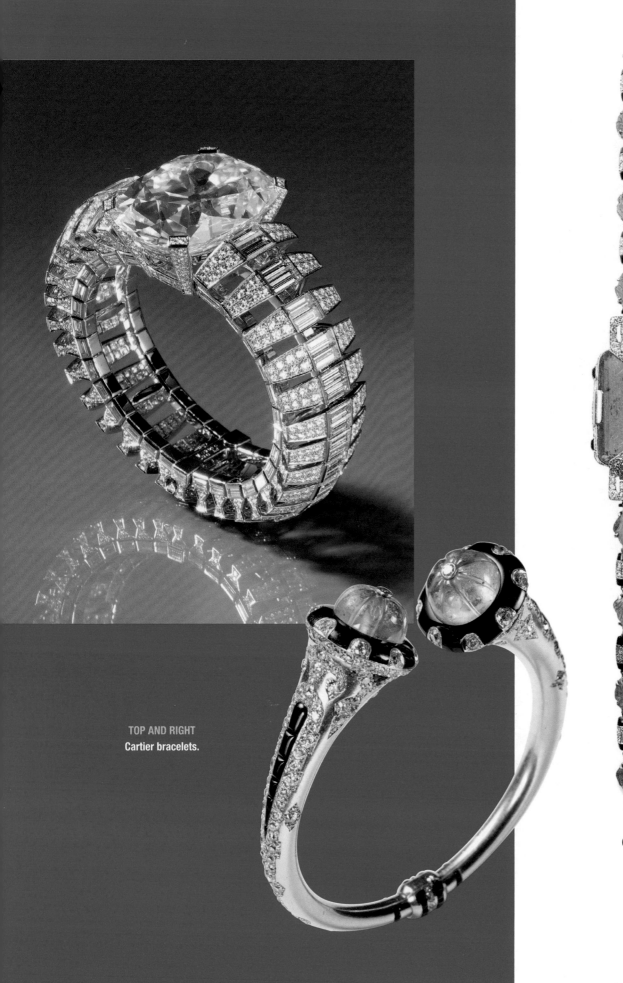

TOP AND RIGHT
Cartier bracelets.

Cartier bracelet, created
in 1930 for Aga Khan.

TOP RIGHT
Diamond and platinum bracelet
from Van Cleef & Arpels circa 1937.

TOP CENTER
Front cover of *Comoedia*
by Léon Bakst, 1909.

LEFT
Cartier bracelet, circa 1929.

Takat bracelet.

TOP LEFT
Van Cleef & Arpels bracelet, 1939.

TOP CENTER
Design in the 1939 catalog
for Van Cleef & Arpels.

LEFT
Mauboussin bracelet in yellow gold
and rubies, circa 1938.

RIGHT
Hammerman Brothers
bracelet.

CENTER
de Grisogono bracelet.

Many Celtic armlets are so massive that archaeologists originally theorized that they were made to decorate statues of gods, but as no such statues have surfaced, we are left to surmise that these armlets, weighing almost three and a half pounds each, adorned the biceps of living men and women. Uncomfortable though this may have been, it would be far from the most painful sacrifice humans have made for jewelry.

During the Byzantine era, the fashion of wearing bracelets flourished, and the golden ornaments were worn in pairs. Bangles crafted from panels of gold and inscribed with sentimental materials were quite popular, as was a style made from wide, hinged bands with motifs in repoussé gold. Precious stones and enamel added a splash of color to the gleam of yellow gold, and pearls brought their shine to bear as well.

The popularity of bracelets waxed and waned over the centuries, with a groundswell of enthusiasm and some accompanying developments in the nineteenth century. One of the most typical bracelet

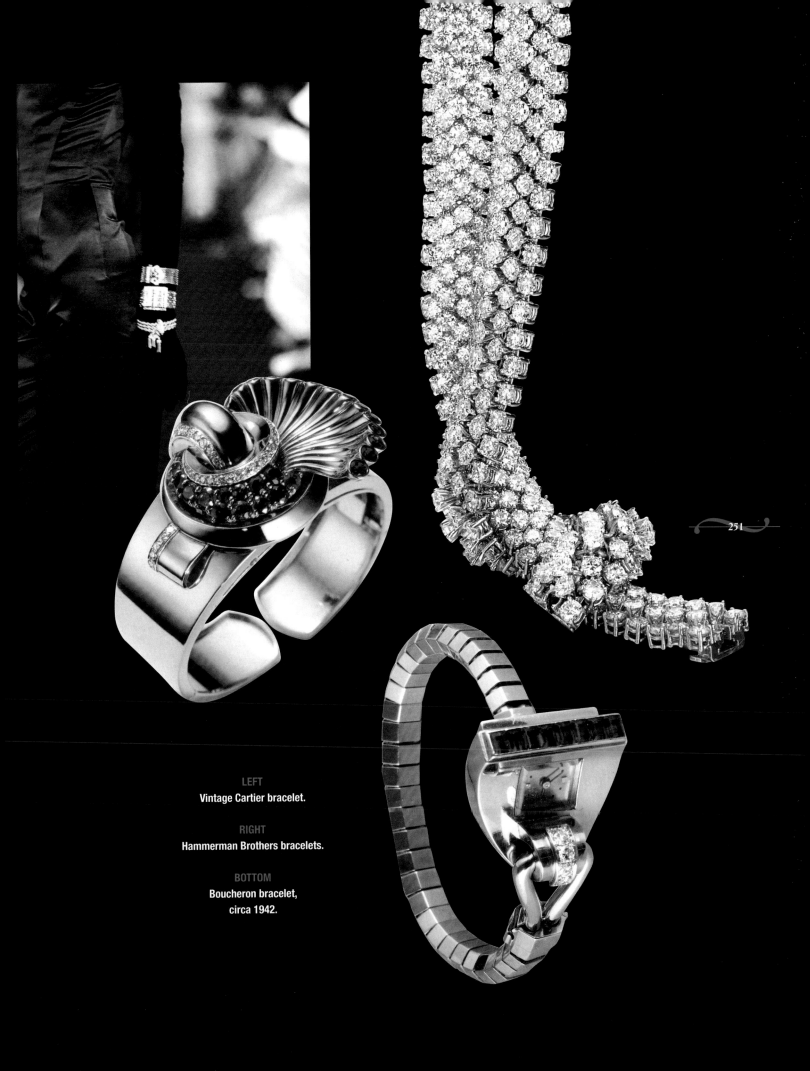

251

LEFT
Vintage Cartier bracelet.

RIGHT
Hammerman Brothers bracelets.

BOTTOM
Boucheron bracelet,
circa 1942.

de Grisogono bracelet.

TIMELE...

VA

Boucheron bracelet.

253

types of this time period was known as the "acrostic" bracelet, so called because it used the initial letters of the gems used to spell out a message. For example, an English acrostic bracelet might let a woman know she was "dearest" by including, in order, a Diamond, Emerald, Amethyst, Ruby, Emerald, Sapphire and Tourmaline. This kind of jewelry first gained favor in Napoleon's court, and his favored jeweler Marie-Etienne Nitot, founder of Chaumet, created acrostic bracelets for Marie-Louise that spelled out the names and dates of birth of the

Emperor and the Empress, as well as the dates of their first meeting and wedding.

The acrostic bracelet was soon adopted by the Victorians across the Channel, who placed a strong emphasis on the jewelry form. Heavy cable link "curb" bracelets, fastened with a heart padlock, were even used as engagement jewelry. The repressed Victorians even used jewelry to flirt with naughtiness—cuff bracelets in the shape of corsets with faux "laces" have survived to this day, leaving us to wonder just how starved our forebears were for titillation. The hollow

TOP LEFT
Andreoli bracelet.

CENTER LEFT
Claudia Schiffer wearing
Chopard jewelry.

TOP RIGHT
Laura Chiatti wearing
Chopard jewelry.

LEFT
Boucheron bracelet.

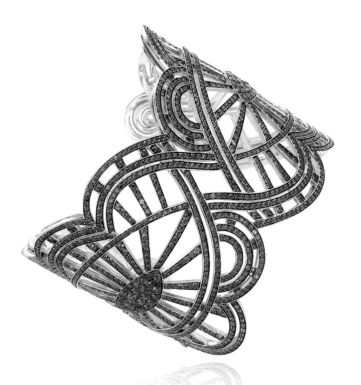

silver bangle enjoyed popularity due to the fact that it appeared impressively heavy, but was actually quite light. Bangles and linked bracelets battled for supremacy throughout the nineteenth century, and no one style triumphed for long. The historical revival styles couldn't help but sweep over bracelets as well, leaving in their wake micromosaic and cameos set in the jewels. Heavier pieces were generally worn in pairs, but as the nineteenth century approached the twentieth, the lighter styles that arrived on the scene were more apt to be worn in multiples.

The Art Nouveau movement led to more natural motifs, with sinuous vines, slithering snakes or undulating insects wrapping themselves around feminine wrists. In fact, one of the most famous bracelets in jewelry history is an arm ornament made for actress Sarah Bernhardt by Art Nouveau legends Georges Fouquet and Alphonse Mucha. It depicts a serpent with inlaid opal headed for a connected ring and is one of the emblematic pieces of Bernhardt and the entire Art Nouveau trend. Another Fouquet bracelet features turquoise cabochons that flaunt, rather than excise, the black matrix that makes

Chopard bracelet.

Jewelmer Joaillerie jewelry.

TOP LEFT
Naomi Campbell wearing
de Grisogono jewelry.

TOP RIGHT
de Grisogono bracelet.

CENTER
Jewelmer Joaillerie bracelet.

BOTTOM
de Grisogono bracelet.

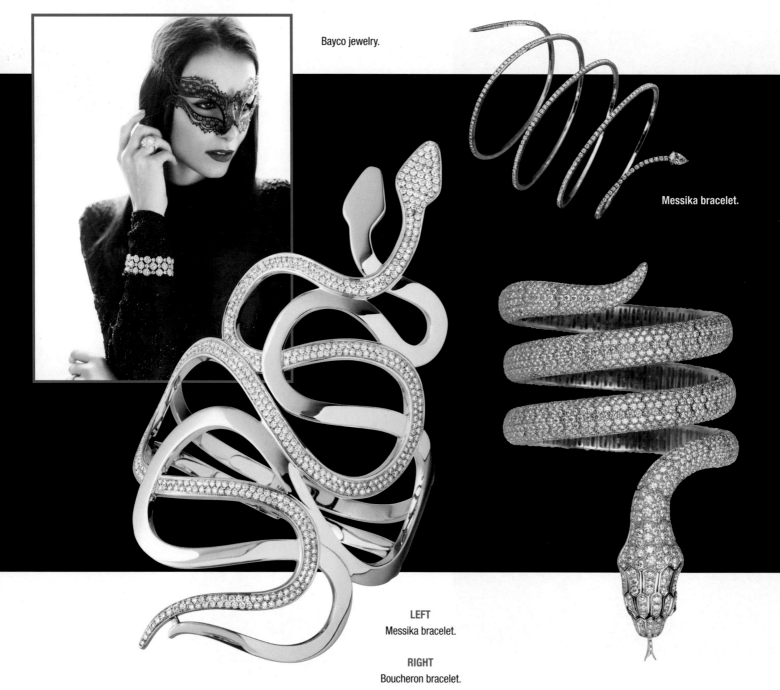

Bayco jewelry.

Messika bracelet.

LEFT
Messika bracelet.

RIGHT
Boucheron bracelet.

each one completely individual. However, a sartorial development was in the works that would change bracelets forever: the advent, in the modern Western world, of the right to bare arms.

The new freedoms of the Jazz Age were a boon for Art Deco in several ways—not the least of which was that more exposed arm, liberated by short-sleeved and sleeveless styles, meant more space for bangles and flexible bracelets. Women turned to a wide range of styles, wearing bracelets on their upper arms as well as forearms—anything from a

straight, single thin row of diamonds set in platinum to outrageous cuffs was considered fair game. Dominant fashion designer and style icon Coco Chanel wore a pair of iconic Maltese cross cuffs, inspired by Byzantine artwork she saw in her travels, and crafted by Verdura. A few decades later, another grande dame of twentieth-century fashion, Harper's Bazaar editor Diana Vreeland, wore matching cuffs as the emphatic exclamation point to her unique, terrifically self-assured sense of style.

Piaget jewelry.

Bangle bracelets bear enormous importance in South Asian cultures, particularly when it comes to marriage. Depending on the region, a bride is given bangles by her new husband, his family or her own family to denote her new status. It would be unthinkable for a married woman in many regions to go out with inauspiciously bare arms, and even children make a habit of wearing bangles. The bracelets have been excavated at archaeological sites throughout India, and the word itself comes from bungri, the Hindi word for "glass." Terminology differs throughout the subcontinent, and glass is by no means the only material from which bangles are made: gold, silver, shell, coral and even ivory are all traditional bracelet materials for young brides.

There is something almost inherently playful about the bracelet, whether it is linked, a bangle or a cuff. For one thing, the jewel is not usually used as a showcase for the most important gems. The arm moves about with too much careless, erratic force for that to be a good idea. For today's haute jewelers,

FACING PAGE
TOP
**Marion Cotillard wearing
Chopard jewelry.**

LEFT
**Mischa Barton wearing
Chopard jewelry.**

RIGHT
Messika bracelet.

CENTER
Chaumet Liens bracelet.

THIS PAGE
Cartier bracelet.

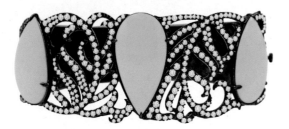

RIGHT AND BOTTOM
de Grisogono bracelet.

BELOW
Sutra bracelet.

LEFT
Milla Jovovich wearing
de Grisogono jewelry.

CENTER
Michelle Trachtenberg wearing
de Grisogono jewelry.

de Grisogono bracelet.

de Grisogono bracelet.

those who concentrate exclusively on important gemstones, a bracelet might be a way station—a place to park a handful of identical rubies while one waits for enough perfectly red stones to make a necklace. The lowered stakes of the smaller jewel are inherently more open to experimentation. Then we have the delightful aural quality that so often accompanies bracelets. The more one wears, the louder one is, as the jewels tinkle, jangle or even clatter against each other.

Today's jewelry designers appreciate the unique opportunities provided by the bracelet. The wrist is often

the first spot to welcome untraditional haute jewelry materials such as leather, horn or even wood. Cuffs might take on the disguise of stacked bangles, for a staggered look that may seem random, but is actually carefully plotted and designed. Flexible linked cuffs meld two distinct styles into a glittering showcase of visual impact that is nonetheless comfortable for the wearer. More traditional jewelers continue to take advantage of the bracelet's unique properties, setting it with a crop of precious stones in finely worked gold or platinum, and setting it loose to play peekaboo with the world

Messika bracelet.

265

LEFT AND BOTTOM
Andreoli jewelry.

Messika bracelet.

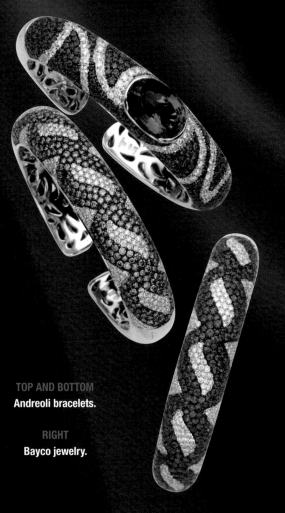

DIFFERENT KINDS OF BRACELETS°

BANGLE

The bangle is one of the simplest forms of the bracelet, and one of the most universally beloved. A thin, rigid hoop that forms a circle or oval about the wrist, the bangle might either slide on or open with a hinge to encircle the wrist with a closer fit. Of great significance in Asian cultures, the bangle is more of a playful ornament in the Western world, with a wide variety of materials and gem settings available. Though its name is derived from the Hindi word for "glass," bangles are crafted in just about any material with which we make jewelry.

Bayco jewelry.

Messika bracelet.

de Grisogono bracelet.

LEFT
Chopard bracelet.

CENTER
Gumuchian bracelet.

CUFF

Like bangles, cuffs are rigid, but they are much wider, ranging from an inch thick to striking pieces that cover several inches of skin. Cuffs may be hinged or have an opening large enough to squeeze a wrist through (but small enough so that the jewel will not fall off). Modern haute jewelers have embraced the cuff as a dramatic opportunity to display important stones in innovative designs, in combination with nontraditional materials such as leather.

LINK BRACELET

The link bracelet takes many forms: it might be a thick chain in a precious material, perhaps with gemstones set into each link. It might join clusters of gems in geometric, floral or organic arrangements, each cluster holding on to the next in a way that maximizes the collective impact. It might take the form of a series of jeweled or enameled plaques; it might, with a single chic row of diamonds, be known by that effortlessly athletic moniker of "tennis bracelet."

de Grisogono bracelet.

271

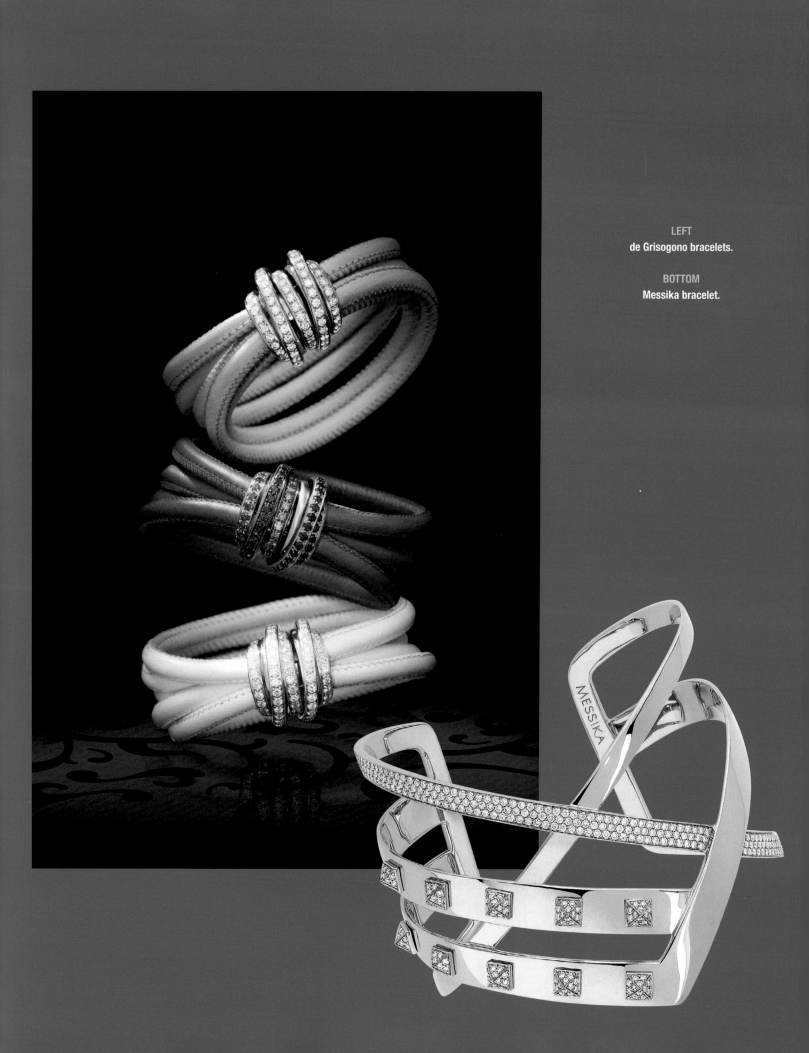

Eva Longoria wearing
Piaget jewelry.

RINGS

Of all forms of jewelry, perhaps none is as charged with significance as the ring. Not just symbols of love and fidelity, rings have also been used over the millennia to exercise power, prove identity, display belonging to a political or social group, murder enemies, attest to friendship, mourn the lost, establish legitimacy and even cure disease! Ironically for such an all-encompassing symbolic object, the ring is the simplest piece of jewelry that most people wear, with a form that has changed very little since its earliest days. The earliest, prehistoric rings were likely created as amulets to ward off disease, weakness and general bad luck, and even today, its deceptively simple form exercises a powerful hold on our imaginations. Wagner's epic opera cycle *Der Ring des Nibelungen*, which tells the story of a ring that grants the power to rule the world, still packs opera houses today. Another ring of immense power was the driving force behind the worldwide smash cinematic trilogy *The Lord of the Rings*. In popular culture, the symbolism of a ring and all it entails was evoked Beyoncé's hit single that cheekily reminded an ex-lover, "If you liked it, you should've put a ring on it!"

FACING PAGE
Guy Ellia ring.

THIS PAGE
Gong Li wearing
Piaget jewelry.

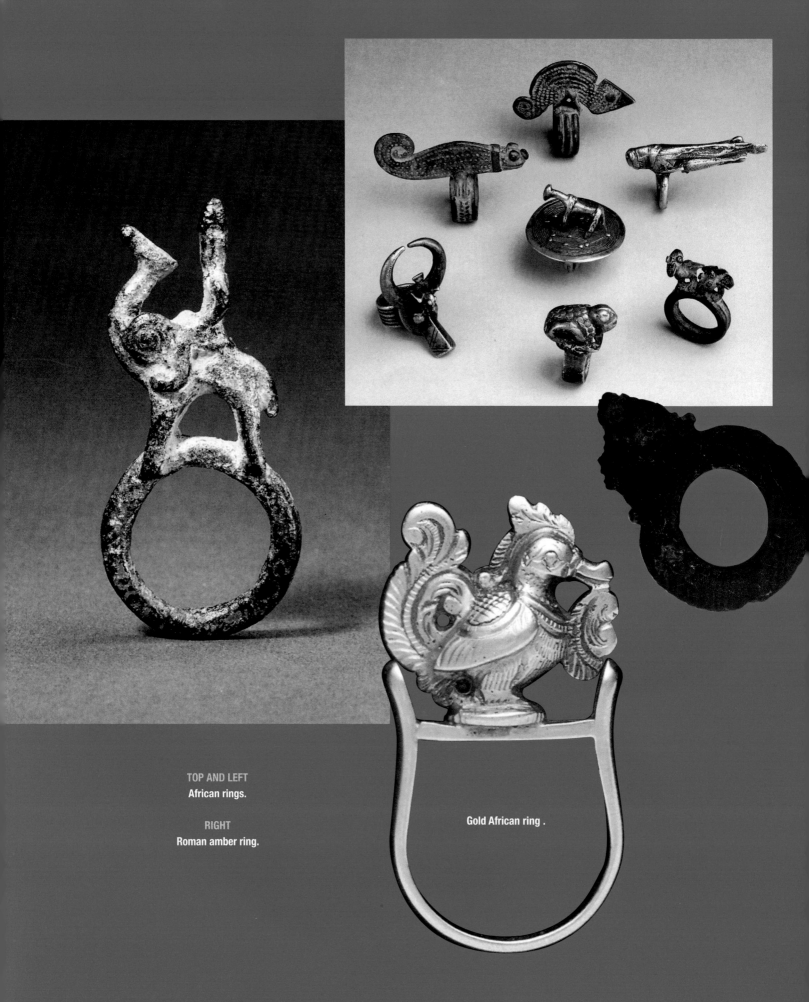

TOP AND LEFT
African rings.

RIGHT
Roman amber ring.

Gold African ring .

TOP
Bronze ring fron Nigeria.

RIGHT AND BOTTOM
African rings.

PREHISTORIC RINGS

The prehistoric rings that have been found in archaeological digs evidence early humans' impulses toward adornment, using animal bones, teeth and shells, either used as central pieces or carved into more or less identical beads to tie around the finger. The earliest Egyptian rings tapped into that culture's reverence for the scarab beetle: they were just that, a beetle tied to the finger with string. Even this crude adornment encapsulates the ring's essence, and as the Egyptians grew increasingly sophisticated, they replaced the literal scarab with representations carved

in rock crystal, amethyst or glazed soapstone, with hieroglyphs engraved on the underside. The string gave way to gold wire and eventually a hoop all but identical to one we might wear today. That simple shape—a hoop, usually coupled with a bezel—has hardly changed, but the variations that jewelers high and low, all over the world, have played upon it are nearly endless.

ANCIENT EGYPT

Rings found in Egyptian tombs show the importance of that item to the voyage of the afterlife. Hidden inscriptions under the bezel referred to names,

life events, gods and sacred animals, all with the purpose of supporting the deceased pharaoh in the afterlife. Other rings were more ornamental, but judging by the care put into them, no less important. Hollow shapes were carved out of the gold ring, with precisely engraved turquoise, lapis lazuli and carnelian slotted in to fit perfectly. In ancient Egyptian culture, the hand was symbolically important and the way in which it was depicted and adorned adhered to strict aesthetic rules. Artists and artisans crafted rings that could be worn on fingers or toes, and Tutankhamen bore rings on his left hand that covered the fingers completely.

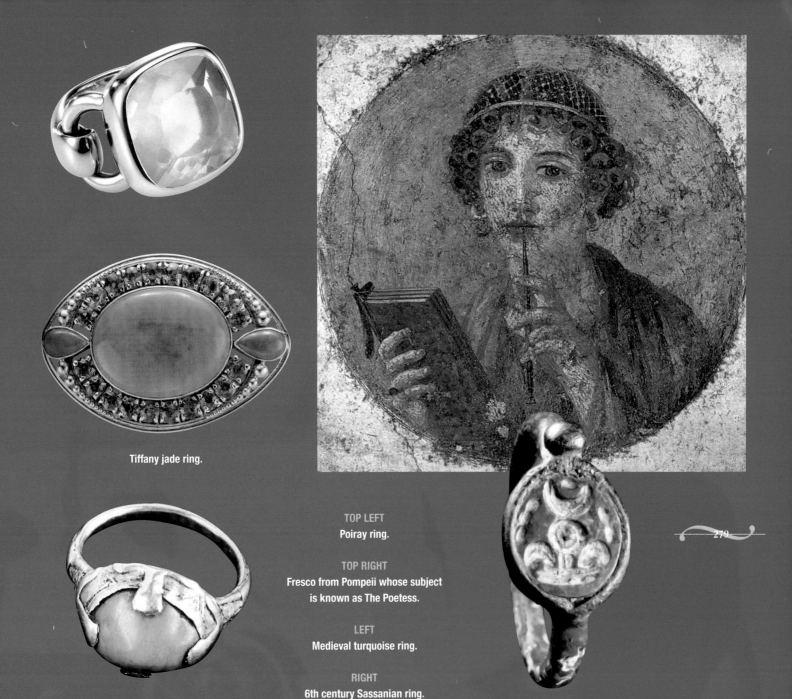

Tiffany jade ring.

TOP LEFT
Poiray ring.

TOP RIGHT
Fresco from Pompeii whose subject
is known as The Poetess.

LEFT
Medieval turquoise ring.

RIGHT
6th century Sassanian ring.

POWERFUL RINGS

While women mainly wore rings as a decoration and status symbol at this point, men were more utilitarian in their use of the jewel. One important Egyptian contribution to jewelry was the signet ring, used for millennia, in literate as well as preliterate societies, to authenticate messages, in exactly the same way we use personal signatures today.

A relief in the tomb of Huy, Viceroy of Nubia under Tutankhamen, depicts the man receiving a gold signet ring, symbol of power as well as useful administrative tool. In the Bible, when Pharaoh conferred leadership of Egypt upon Joseph, he sealed the deal by putting his own signet ring on Joseph's finger, a universally recognized symbol of the time. The idea of a ring representing this power was often conflated with the idea of the power itself residing in the ring. When a pope dies, for instance, one of the first orders of business is to destroy the Fisherman's Ring, the ring with which the pontiff sealed his bulls and briefs. The seal is destroyed to prevent forgery of documents, and a new ring, with a new, personalized seal, is made for the new pope.

Achilles among the Daughters of Lycomedes by Pietro Paolini, about 1625-1630. (J. Paul Getty Museum)

Dejanira (Autumn)
by Gustave Moreau, about 1872-1873.
(J. Paul Getty Museum)

Boucheron rings.

283

TOP LEFT
Renaissance garnet ring,
circa 1620.

TOP RIGHT
School of Fontainebleau,
detail of *Woman at her Toilette*, circa 1590.

CENTER
Vintage Marchak fire opal ring.

RIGHT
Vintage Marchak ring.

Boucheron ring.

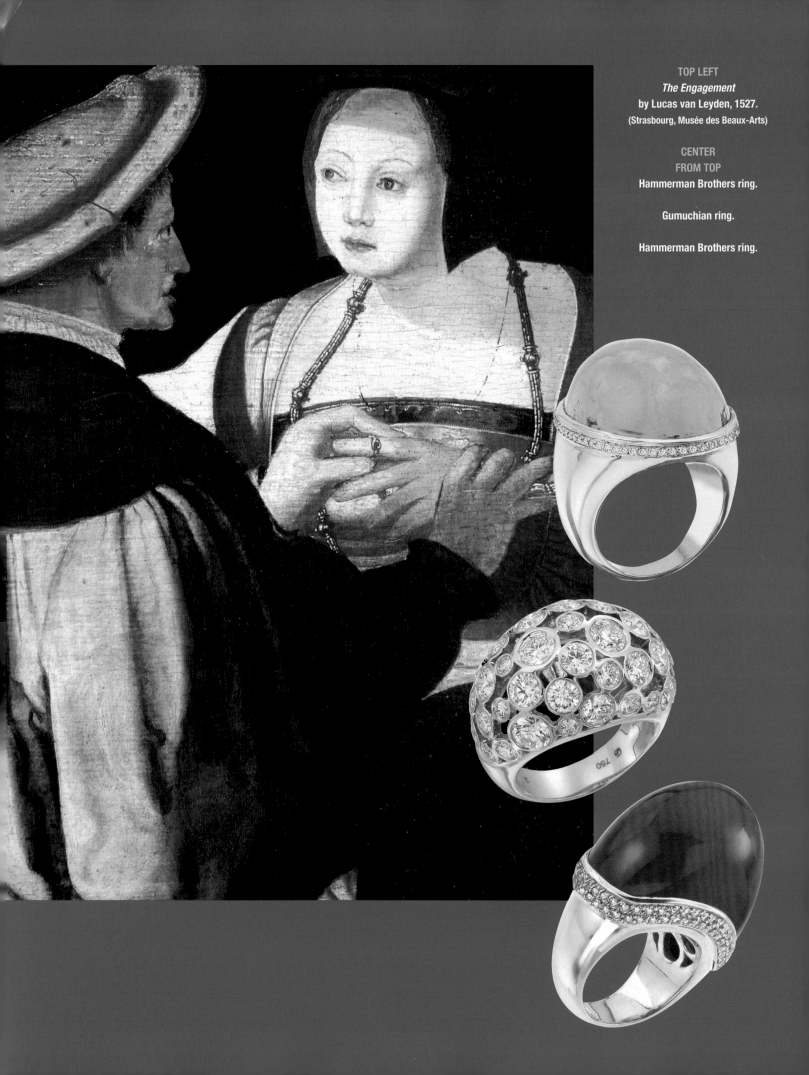

ANCIENT GREECE

In fifth-century-BC Greece, rings often featured bezels with mythological scenes or portraits carved in relief or in intaglio, similar to the coins of the day. Other motifs, such as the serpent or the Hercules knot, were more popular during the Hellenistic period. Snake rings appeared to slither several times around the finger in the form of a tiny golden reptile, which—besides having an apt body for representation in coiled jewelry—represented Asclepius, the god of healing and medicine. (Snake motifs in jewelry are nearly universal and, despite a few centuries of unpopularity in the Middle Ages, evergreen as a source of inspiration. From Queen Victoria to Cartier, jewelers continue to draw inspiration from the Greeks.) The Hercules knot—two gold loops entwined—combined new techniques with motifs from other contemporary cultures. The knot was believed to aid healing, and its association with the mythical hero doubled its presumed power. When used on a wedding ring, the Hercules ring represented the groom undoing his bride's garments after the ceremony.

ANCIENT ROME

During the Roman Empire, men used rings to display their social status, wealth and professional success. As Rome's resources grew, so did its rings, which went from plain iron bands to increasingly large rings in gold and silver, with gemstones carved by the best artists in Rome to depict portraits or events in mythology and history. Wearing gold rings was not a right that everyone enjoyed. For instance, senators and knights were among the classes entitled to wear gold rings, making the jewel a useful signifier. Even the wealthiest of men, if they had not been born free, were not allowed to wear gold rings, instead contenting themselves with gilding iron ones. These sumptuary laws did not last forever in such strict form, and by the third century AD all soldiers were allowed to wear gold rings.

Vintage Marchak ring.

Portrait of Eleonora Gonzaga
by Titian, 1538.
(Galleria degli Uffizi)

Julius Caesar wore a ring engraved with a portrait of Venus to celebrate his self-declared lineage, and his partisans did likewise. Rings set with intaglios of Nike, the goddess of victory, celebrated military triumphs, and less high-minded rings portrayed love and lust in its various forms. Describing the ostentation of the time, Seneca noted, "We adorn our fingers with rings, and a jewel is displayed on every joint." As Christianity spread in the early centuries AD, Saint Clement of Alexandria argued that signet rings—the only permissible form of jewelry, he believed, for Christians—should not bear pagan or immoral scenes, preferring instead the Christian symbolism of the fish, fisherman, ship and anchor.

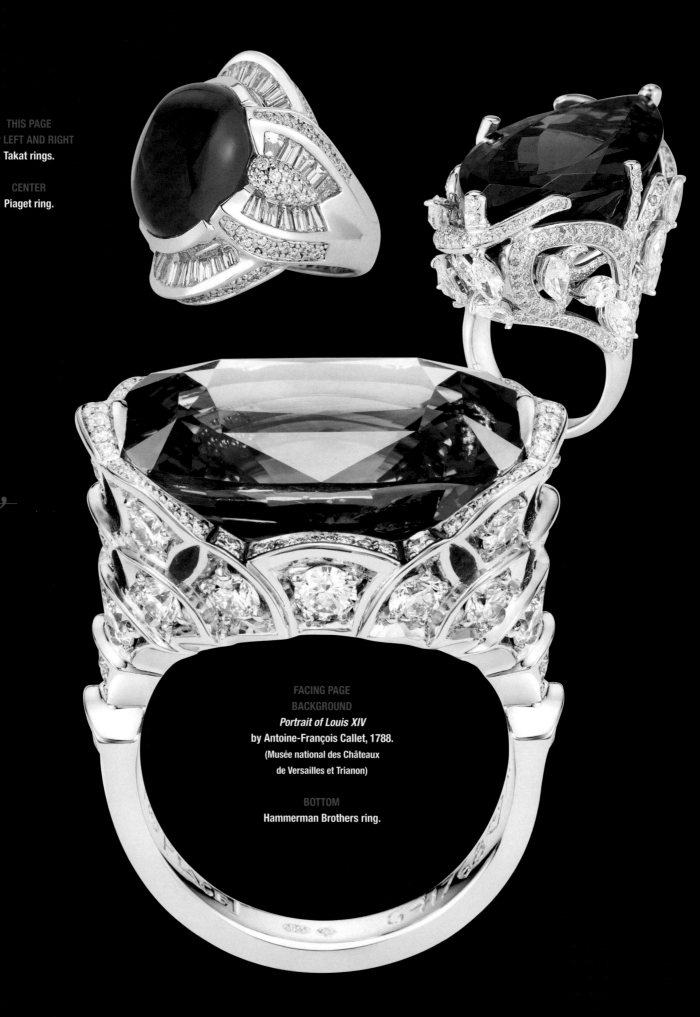

THIS PAGE
TOP LEFT AND RIGHT
Takat rings.

CENTER
Piaget ring.

290

FACING PAGE
BACKGROUND
Portrait of Louis XIV
**by Antoine-François Callet, 1788.
(Musée national des Châteaux
de Versailles et Trianon)**

BOTTOM
Hammerman Brothers ring.

MEDICINAL RINGS

For thousands of years before the advent of modern medicine, people ascribed healing powers to rings. Precious stones were, of course, ascribed fantastical qualities—sapphires were supposed to preserve chastity and rubies to protect against storms—but even lowlier materials turned rings into folk medicine. A donkey's hoof presumably cured epilepsy and fossilized fish teeth acted as treatment for dropsy. These beliefs had ancient origins: Marcellus, an ancient Roman physician, prescribed a pure gold ring, engraved with Greek letters, to be worn on Thursday during the waning moon, all to cure a pain in the side. One fourth-century physician treated abdominal pain and gall bladder complaints using an eight-sided iron ring, with an engraving that commanded the bile to plague a lark in lieu of the patient. As late as the turn of the nineteenth century, as European culture tiptoed into modernity, there are reports of illness cured by rings under highly specific circumstances. *The Gentleman's Magazine* instructs readers that a silver ring will do the trick, as long as it is made from the melted metal of five sixpences collected from five bachelors, none of whom

MAGICAL RINGS

The mystical power contained in rings crops up in fictional tales about real-life heroes. For example, Charlemagne, the "Father of Europe," was said to have fallen desperately in love with a beautiful young woman, so much so that he spent every moment basking in her company and more or less ignoring affairs of state. When she died, he fell into a grief equal to his passion, which was not any more conducive to the tasks of governing. The Archbishop of Cologne, having finally separated the distraught young ruler from the corpse of his beloved, found a ring set

know the intended use of their donations. The smith must be a bachelor, as must the man who gives him the coins. No less an authority than the 1815 *London Medical and Physical Journal* tells of an epileptic patient cured by wearing a silver ring donated by twelve young women.

296

TOP LEFT
Assael ring.

RIGHT
The Bar at Maxim's
by Pierre-Victor Galland, 1906.

CENTER
Chopard ring.

BOTTOM
Cartier ring.

Boucheron ring.

with a precious stone in her mouth. When the Archbishop removed it, Charlemagne's grief was immediately forgotten. To protect the monarch against any other unscrupulous people who might come across the ring, the Archbishop threw it into a lake near Aix-la-Chapelle. This did not exactly nullify the power of the ring, as Charlemagne developed an intense affection for the lake, eventually building a palace on its shore and governing from the spot. For a very different kind of tale of enchanted jewelry, consider that Joan of Arc, another European icon, was accused of charming rings to ensure victory in battle.

MIDDLE AGES

In the Middle Ages, rings took on new connotations, and it became fashionable to wear them on every finger, sometimes even on more than one knuckle at a time! They might be attached to attached clothing or hats, or worn on chains around the neck or wrist as well; why should having only ten fingers be an impediment to wearing as many rings as one wishes? Sapphires, rubies, garnets and spinels showed up more and more as central stones, often cut as cabochons. Point-cut, pyramid-shaped diamonds, which echo the natural shape of the crystal, came into

de Grisogono ring.

fashion around 1400. A ring might bear the image of
a saint to capture the protection of that saint against
various misfortunes, or a Biblical inscription
that added to the piece's protective power.
Extremely common was the fede motif,
featuring two clasped hands, and
the gimmel ring, in which two
linked bands combine to form
a single jewel. The custom of
romantic engravings known as
posies was extremely popular
at this time and for centuries
afterwards, with set phrases
or individualized engravings.
Even centuries after the Middle
Ages, in 1660, Samuel Pepys
wrote in his famous diary about
his family composing phrases to be
engraved on Roger Pepys's wedding
ring, as a way to pass the time while
the lamb they were to have for dinner was
roasting. Sometimes the engravings were in the

de Grisogono ring.

Rings from Chaumet's
Liens collection.

form of rebuses, such as "LMME," which when pronounced phonetically became "elle aime aimer," meaning "she loves to love." In the mid-eighteenth century, a noblewoman who had outlived three husbands inscribed this flippant posy on her fourth wedding ring: "If I survive / I will have five."

WEDDING RINGS

For many people, the only piece of jewelry they wear is a wedding band. The juxtaposition of the endless shape of the hoop and the scratchproof durability of the diamond provides a doubled symbol of eternal devotion for the happy couple. In addition, the ring's use as a tool of authentication made it the perfect symbol – Among fifteenth-century European peasants, wedding ceremonies sometimes concluded with a bizarre wrestling match: as the groom attempted to place the ring on his bride's finger, she would obstinately try to knock it out of his hands. In many cases, the presence of a ring was the deciding factor in judging the legitimacy of a union, and in England

301

de Grisogono ring.

Sutra ring.

Andreoli ring.

Chaumet Hortensia ring.

Jewelmer Joaillerie jewelry.

RIGHT
Jewelmer Joaillerie
jewelry.

CENTER
de Grisogono ring.

it was only slowly, in the eighteenth century, that the presence of witnesses and church registers supplanted the ring itself as proof. This did not, however, diminish the symbolic importance of the wedding band. After the Battle of Waterloo, Lord Raglan had to have his arm amputated, but kept the severed limb long enough to remove his wedding ring and put in on the hand that remained, at which point he shouted, "Look, I've still got it!"

The fourth finger on the left hand has long been the preferred spot for wedding bands since ancient times, with varying reasons proposed. The British Apollo, an

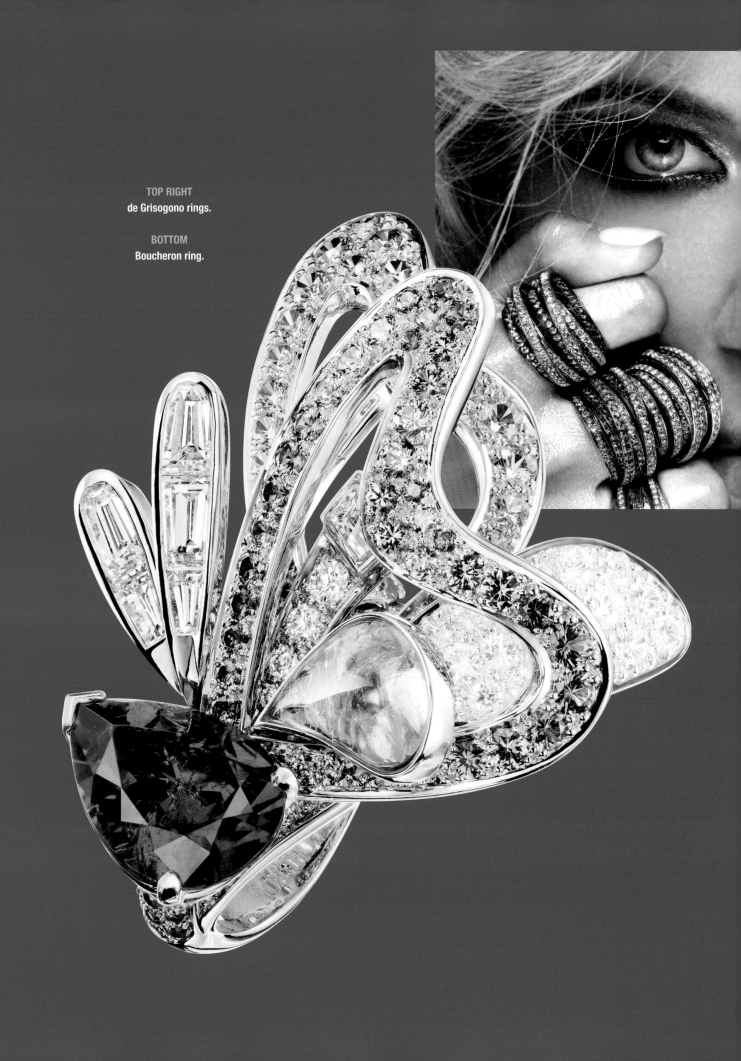

TOP RIGHT
de Grisogono rings.

BOTTOM
Boucheron ring.

de Grisogono ring.

eighteenth-century newspaper that sought to provide answers for an eclectic variety of questions (a proto-Wikipedia, if you will), gave the rationale for the choice as follows: "There is nothing more in this than that the custom was handed down to the present age, from the practice of our ancestors, who found the left hand more convenient for such ornaments than the right, in that 'tis ever less employed; for the same reason they chose the fourth finger, which is not only less used than either of the rest, but is more capable of preserving a ring from bruises, having this one quality peculiar to itself, that it cannot be extended but in company with some other finger, whereas the rest may be singly stretched to their full length and straightened."

Other theories held that a vein ran straight from this finger to the heart, making it uniquely suited to bear a ring with such an emotional connection.

FRIENDSHIP RINGS

Weddings are not the only occasion on which to exchange rings, however. Two friends might exchange rings as a sign of Platonic affection. The nineteenth-century French writers Maxime Du Camp and Gustave Flaubert exchanged rings in this way, with Du Camp

THIS PAGE
Bayco rings.

Chopard rings.

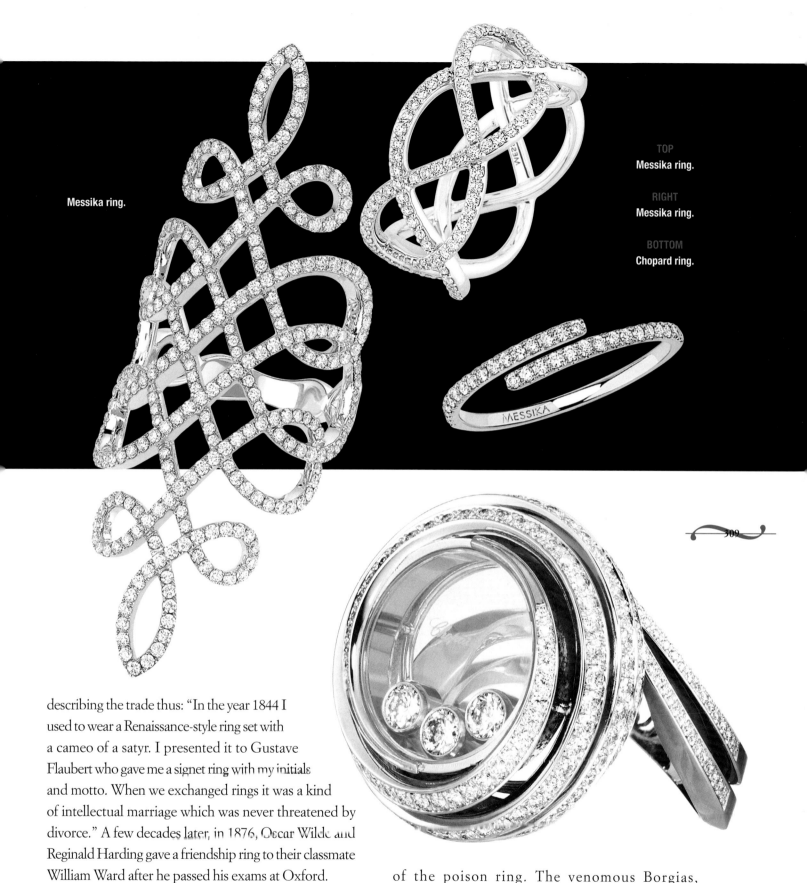

Messika ring.

TOP
Messika ring.

RIGHT
Messika ring.

BOTTOM
Chopard ring.

describing the trade thus: "In the year 1844 I used to wear a Renaissance-style ring set with a cameo of a satyr. I presented it to Gustave Flaubert who gave me a signet ring with my initials and motto. When we exchanged rings it was a kind of intellectual marriage which was never threatened by divorce." A few decades later, in 1876, Oscar Wilde and Reginald Harding gave a friendship ring to their classmate William Ward after he passed his exams at Oxford.

POISON RINGS

Far from the joyous symbolism of the wedding or friendship ring is the sinister implication of the poison ring. The venomous Borgias, particularly Lucrezia, were notorious for poisoning their political enemies, and the poison ring was just one tool in the arsenal. Even after the rings fell into disuse, they could still cause problems for the

LEFT
Sharon Stone wearing
Jacob & Co. jewelry.

RIGHT
Boucheron ring.

CENTER
Jacob & Co. ring.

BOTTOM
Piaget ring.

Bayco ring.

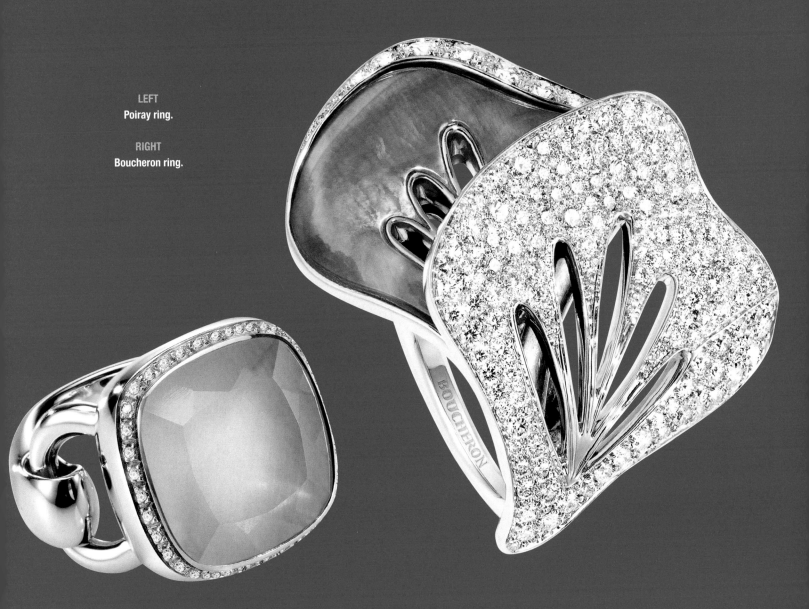

unwary: there were nineteenth-century French reports of a man who scratched himself with an antique ring and almost immediately fell seriously ill. The doctor who cured him identified the ring as a Venetian "death" ring: the seemingly decorative steel lion's claws that formed part of the ring's design were surprisingly sharp, and filled with poison. One not-so-friendly handshake, and the victim was done for, prey to a poison that still retained much of its fatal power hundreds of years later.

A 2013 archaeological dig in Bulgaria unearthed a likely ring of this type, probably designed to be worn on the pinky finger of a man's right hand and dating from the 14th century. A hollowed out central ornament would have been the perfect vehicle for a lethal dose to be surreptitiously poured into a noble's wine goblet. Experts in Kavarna, the region in which the ring was found, hypothesized that it had belonged to Dobrotitsa, a noble of Kavarna at that time, whose retinue experienced an unseemly number of untimely deaths.

THIS PAGE

TOP LEFT
Hammerman Brothers ring.

TOP RIGHT
de Grisogono ring.

FACING PAGE
Gumuchian jewelry.

ELIZABETHAN RINGS

Legendary for all sorts of reasons, Queen Elizabeth I counted a passion for jewelry among her extravagant qualities, and rings were no exception. Hentzner's Travels in England, a 1598 book, describes the reception of a Bohemian baron by the queen: she "gave him her right hand to kiss, sparkling with rings and jewels—a mark of particular favor." Her love for rings backfired when her coronation ring became too small for her finger (or rather, when her hand grew too fat for her ring)

CENTER
Chaumet Liens ring.

BOTTOM
Bayco ring.

Andreoli jewelry.

LEFT
de Grisogono ring.

BOTTOM
Vintage Piaget ring.

317

and had to be filed off; the superstitious queen, as well as many others, viewed this as a bad omen.

Queen Elizabeth exchanged many rings with her cousin, Mary, Queen of Scots, as tokens of affection, but when things soured between the two monarchs, all the eternal devotion and fidelity the rings promised must have felt like a cruel joke to Mary. A letter from Mary describes Elizabeth's empty promises: "I believed the jewel I received as a pledge of your friendship would remind you that when you gave it me I was not only flattered that with great promise of assistance from you, but you bound yourself on your royal word to advance over the border to my succor, and to come in person to meet me, and that if I made the journey into your realm that I might confide in your honor." She was, of course, sorely disappointed.

LEFT
Bayco ring.

BOTTOM
Boucheron ring.

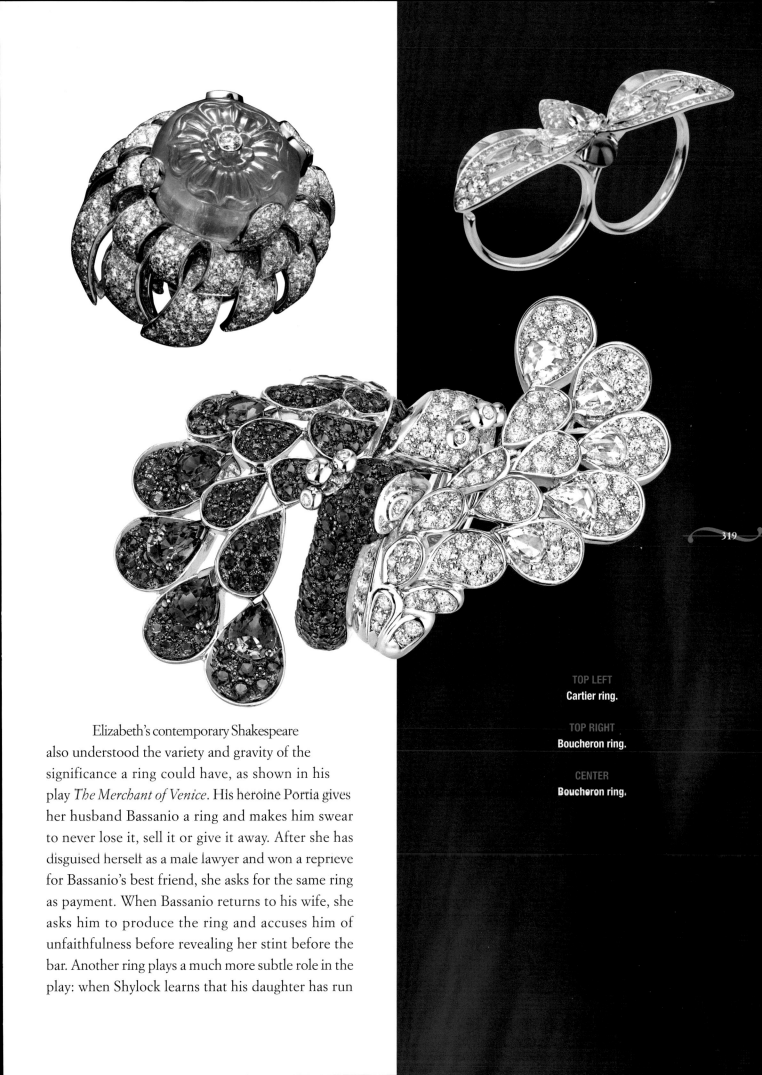

Elizabeth's contemporary Shakespeare also understood the variety and gravity of the significance a ring could have, as shown in his play *The Merchant of Venice*. His heroine Portia gives her husband Bassanio a ring and makes him swear to never lose it, sell it or give it away. After she has disguised herself as a male lawyer and won a reprieve for Bassanio's best friend, she asks for the same ring as payment. When Bassanio returns to his wife, she asks him to produce the ring and accuses him of unfaithfulness before revealing her stint before the bar. Another ring plays a much more subtle role in the play: when Shylock learns that his daughter has run

TOP LEFT
Cartier ring.

TOP RIGHT
Boucheron ring.

CENTER
Boucheron ring.

away with a Christian, and traded a ring she had stolen from him for a monkey, he laments, "I had it of Leah when I was a bachelor. I would not have given it for a wilderness of monkeys." Even before his momentous "Hath not a Jew eyes?" speech, Shakespeare shows us the humanity of his villain by his reaction to the loss of a ring.

The importance of the ring in this Shakespeare play, is not surprising, for the sixteenth century was awash in rings. Anyone who issued orders, sent correspondence or even bills—from the highest of the nobility to clergymen, merchants and lawyers—had

his own signet ring, with an intaglio carving that was unique to him.

TWENTIETH CENTURY AND BEYOND

Throughout the 1920s and '30s, waves of fashion brought about innovations in ring style that remain with us to this day. Cocktail rings introduced the idea of a huge stone, real or fake, as a perfect accessory to an illicit alcoholic indulgence. Art Deco rings used more inexpensive materials such as rock crystal to make an oversized visual impact. These trends meant that large rings colonized hands, with

LEFT
Chopard rings.

RIGHT
Jewelmer Joaillerie rings.

de Grisogono rings.

Messika rings.

LEFT
Andreoli jewelry.

BOTTOM
Piaget ring.

central gems that reached all the way to the knuckle. In partnership with Jean Cocteau, Louis Cartier created the house's iconic Trinity ring, upon which three sleek hoops of yellow, white and red gold intertwine, symbolizing fidelity, friendship and love respectively, and hearkening back to medieval gimmel rings. Van Cleef & Arpels introduced the invisible setting, which allowed rings to boast an unbroken wave of color and light across the finger using a mesh of gold or platinum wire to secure gems instead of prongs. Eternity rings, which consist of a plain metal hoop set entirely with diamonds or other precious stones, were another trend that cropped up in the 1930s and displayed remarkable staying power—in 1938, one *Vogue* article asked,

"What better emblem of unending devotion than eternity rings?"

324

In the 1950s, the punchy cocktail ring had become de rigueur for partygoers; the hint of danger that it exuded during Prohibition had been completely subsumed by its power as pure fashion statement.

Over the last 50 years, women have increasingly broken with tradition in the arena of rings as well as in… everything else imaginable. Because of their small size and relatively small stakes, rings lend themselves to being treated as wearable art, a low-risk form of experimentation for even the most traditionally minded among us. Even as we seem to treat the ring as simple jewelry—we no longer expect it to cure disease, or act as a legal signature—it still contains an undeniable symbolic force, as evidenced by a plotline on the television show *Sex and the City* in which the heroine wears an engagement ring (from a man she doesn't want to marry) around her neck rather than on her finger. Unusual shapes, materials, themes and designs are par for the course, and whether simple or elaborate, large or small, valuable or practically disposable, rings are as popular now as they have ever been.

WATCHES

Similar to the bracelet, yet entirely distinct, the wristwatch is the youngest major type of jewelry. Though the wristwatch didn't take off as an essential modern accessory for men until after the first World War, jewelers and horologers created individual pieces here and there, starting in the early nineteenth century, and the jeweled wristwatch was the province of the feminine elite. The modern jeweled wristwatch takes a myriad of forms, from a discreet bezel setting of diamonds to an all-out gem-set extravaganza coupled with sophisticated mechanical complications.

While the origins of the first necklace, ring and earrings are long lost in the mists of time, rotting away millennia ago in preliterate societies, the earliest wristwatches are much better documented. Given the technical sophistication required to fabricate any timekeeping device, let alone in miniature—*let alone* set with gemstones—the first wristwatches were, unsurprisingly, royal commissions.

Once the basic mechanism of the clock was invented—after sundials, water clocks and other less-than-satisfactory timekeeping devices—would-be

Portrait of Caroline Murat, Queen of Naples, by Louise Elisabeth Vigée Le Brun, 1807.

TOP LEFT
**Breguet Reine
de Naples watch.**

TOP RIGHT
**Detail, *David Meeting Abigail*
by the workshop
of Peter Paul Rubens,
circa 1620s.
(J. Paul Getty Museum)**

CENTER LEFT
**Patek Philippe,
1868 wristwatch.**

CENTER BOTTOM
**Van Cleef & Arpels
watch bracelet, 1938.**

329

**A pineapple watch
bracelet from Verdura.**

horologers set themselves to the endless task of making improvements. Springing up nearly simultaneously in Italy, Germany and France near the end of the fifteenth century, the mechanical watch revolutionized the notion of timekeeping, making it a personal concern as opposed to a monumental public one. Though the pocket-watch dominated for centuries, there were other options for the horologically inclined. François I of France ordered a pair of watches set in the hilts of two daggers in 1518, and Elizabeth I of England wore a ring watch that would slightly scratch her finger as an alarm. Although the seventeenth-century philosopher and mathematician Blaise Pascal was the first person known to actually wear a watch around his wrist, his brainchild consisted of simply tying his pocket-watch around his wrist with a piece of string, and it did not start a trend. It was not until the beginning of the nineteenth century that the first well-known wristwatches came about, and it would take another century for them to achieve something like ubiquity.

DUNAND
RUE HALLE 72
PARIS

RIGHT
Vintage Boucheron watch.

TOP
Astrolabe, Italy circa 1640.

CENTER
Pocket-watch in steel inlaid
with gold, 1918.

No less a personage than Abraham-Louis Breguet shone as an early player in the wristwatch game. Inventor of uncountable devices and ameliorations to the personal watch, including the ever-popular tourbillon, Breguet designed a "repeater in oblong form for bracelet," commissioned For Caroline Murat, the Queen of Naples, in 1810. Not only was the oval shape a highly unusual one for a watch, but the "repeater" part of the request was also significant: Breguet created, not only a wristwatch, but one that could chime the hours and minutes. To this day, minute repeaters are considered one of the most

challenging complications, and Breguet's addition of the complication to the brand-new wristwatch form, with its unprecedented acoustical qualities, speaks to the watchmaker's daring, yet meticulous, expertise. Today, the company that bears Breguet's name offers a "Reine de Naples" collection, combining exquisite workmanship and elegant femininity.

Another of the first wristwatches was actually two watches, in a delightful set that gave the time and date indications each its own stage on which to shine. In 1811, François-Regnault Nitot, the then

LEFT
Vacheron Constantin watches, circa 1955.

RIGHT
Vintage Cartier watch.

BOTTOM
Guy Ellia Queen watch.

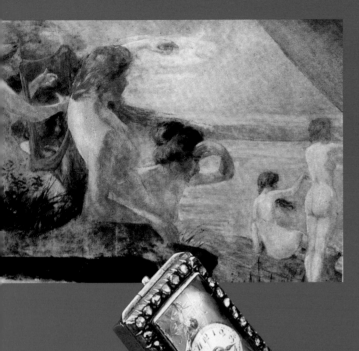

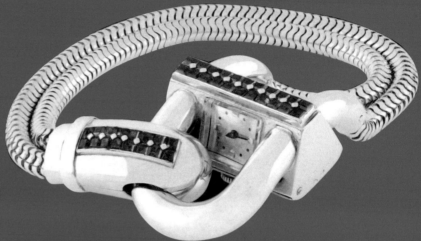

leader of Chaumet, created a pair of wristwatches, a jeweled matched set destined for the wrists of Princess Augusta of Bavaria. At this point, paired bracelets were all the rage, and these watches evinced the jewelry excellence inherent to Chaumet's creations. A delicate yellow-gold motif traced a floral design around the wrist, set with pearls and emeralds. An exquisite piece of jewelry as well as a leap forward in wristwatch history, Chaumet's first pair of wristwatches engendered a tradition of haute jewelry applied to watchmaking that continues to this day.

Throughout the nineteenth century, wristwatches were considered to be fanciful decorations, not utilitarian tools, and were worn almost exclusively by women. One famous example, and the first evidence of wristwatches tiptoeing their way into the mainstream, was the 1868 creation of such a piece by Patek Philippe for Countess Koscowicz of Hungary. Just twelve years later, the wristwatch broke two important barriers, when Girard-Perregaux produced an order for the German Imperial Navy. For the first time, wristwatches were being mass-produced—and for a male audience.

Cartier watch.

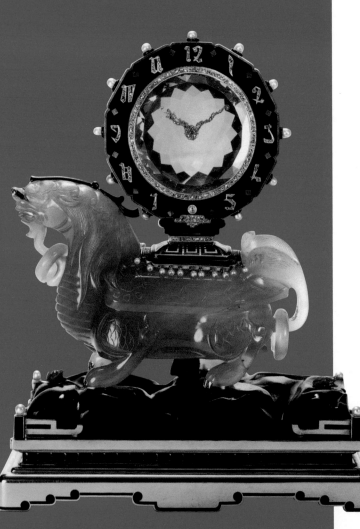

Cartier clock.

Piaget watch, 1976.

The nascent field of aviation demanded an easily accessible timekeeping device, and many of today's most prestigious watchmakers created close partnerships, with instruments that belonged in the cockpit. Louis Cartier created a wristwatch for his friend, the aviation pioneer Alberto Santos-Dumont, in 1904. However, it took the advent of World War I to produce one of the most iconic wristwatches of the twentieth century: Cartier's Tank watch, inspired by Louis Cartier's time on the front and the Renault tanks he saw there. Originally created in 1917, it has been interpreted dozens of times in the

Chopard Red Carpet watch.

TOP LEFT
Cartier secret watch.

TOP CENTER
Piaget watch, 1965.

TOP RIGHT
Cartier secret watch.

BOTTOM
Chopard L'Heure
du Diamant watch.

TOP
Piaget watch, 1976.

CENTER
Piaget Limelight Couture
Précieuse watch.

BOTTOM
de Grisogono Nº Uno watch.

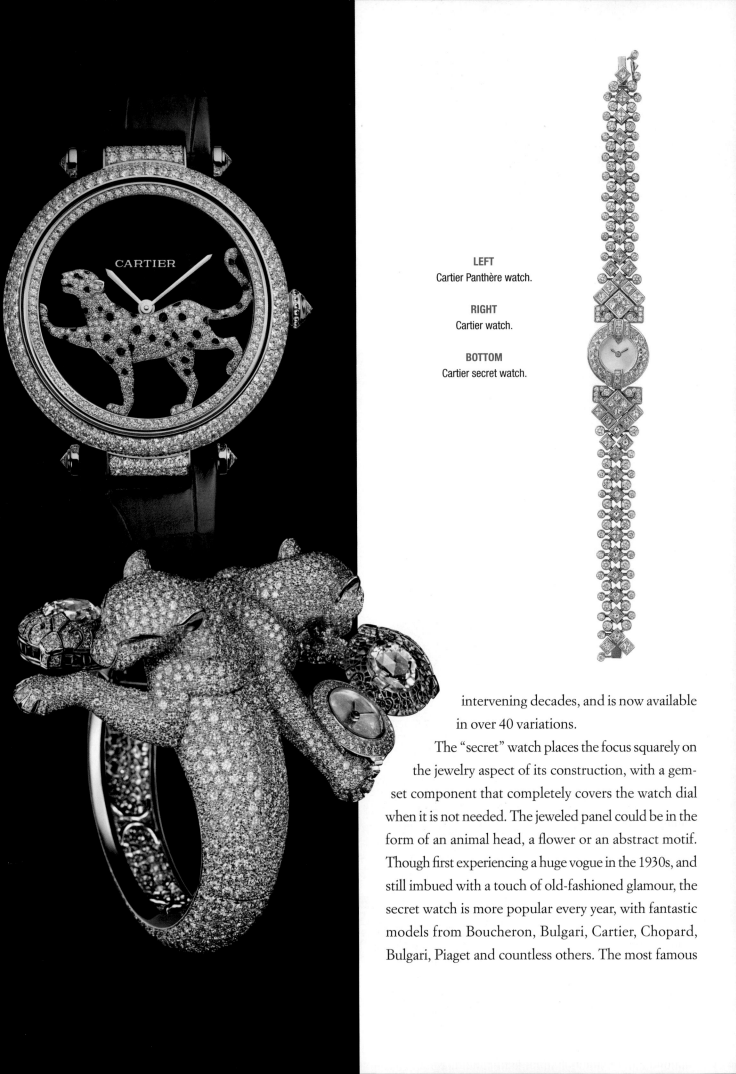

intervening decades, and is now available in over 40 variations.

The "secret" watch places the focus squarely on the jewelry aspect of its construction, with a gem-set component that completely covers the watch dial when it is not needed. The jeweled panel could be in the form of an animal head, a flower or an abstract motif. Though first experiencing a huge vogue in the 1930s, and still imbued with a touch of old-fashioned glamour, the secret watch is more popular every year, with fantastic models from Boucheron, Bulgari, Cartier, Chopard, Bulgari, Piaget and countless others. The most famous

Cartier secret watch.

LEFT
de Grisogono Boule necklace watch.

RIGHT
de Grisogono Instrumentino watch.

BOTTOM
Guy Ellia Circle watch.

TOP LEFT
Chaumet watchmaking
workshops.

TOP RIGHT
Chaumet Attrape-Moi...
Si Tu M'aimes watch.

CENTER
Chaumet Attrape-Moi...
Si Tu M'aimes watch.

BOTTOM LEFT
Breguet Reine de Naples watch.

Piaget Limelight Couture
Précieuse watch.

de Grisogono jewelry.

LEFT
Cartier secret watch.

RIGHT
Guy Ellia Circle "La Petite"
watch in white gold and in red gold.

BOTTOM
Chopard Red Carpet
watch design.

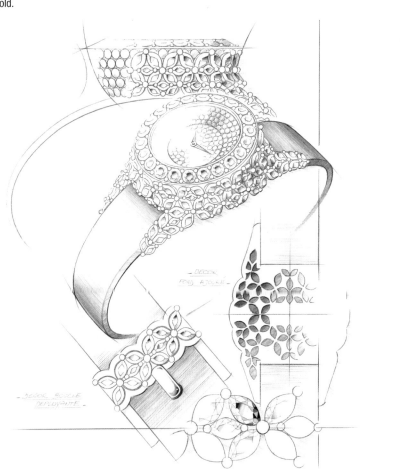

secret watch is a Chopard model that gained fame for being the most expensive watch in the world—the 201-Carat Watch. With a blinding setting of 163 carats of white and yellow diamonds on the dial, case and bracelet, this superlative timepiece also bears three heart-shaped diamonds—a 15-carat pink, a 12-carat blue and an 11-carat white—that move aside at the touch of a button to reveal the time. This extraordinary piece was sold in 2000 for $25 million.

Complicated watches serve up another opportunity for constant one-upmanship among the most prestigious haute horology houses. With

TOP LEFT
Guy Ellia Time Space watch.

TOP RIGHT
David and Victoria Beckham
wearing Jacob & Co. jewelry.

LEFT
Guy Ellia Dazzling Lady
secret watch.

RIGHT
Boucheron Epure Blé d'Or watch.

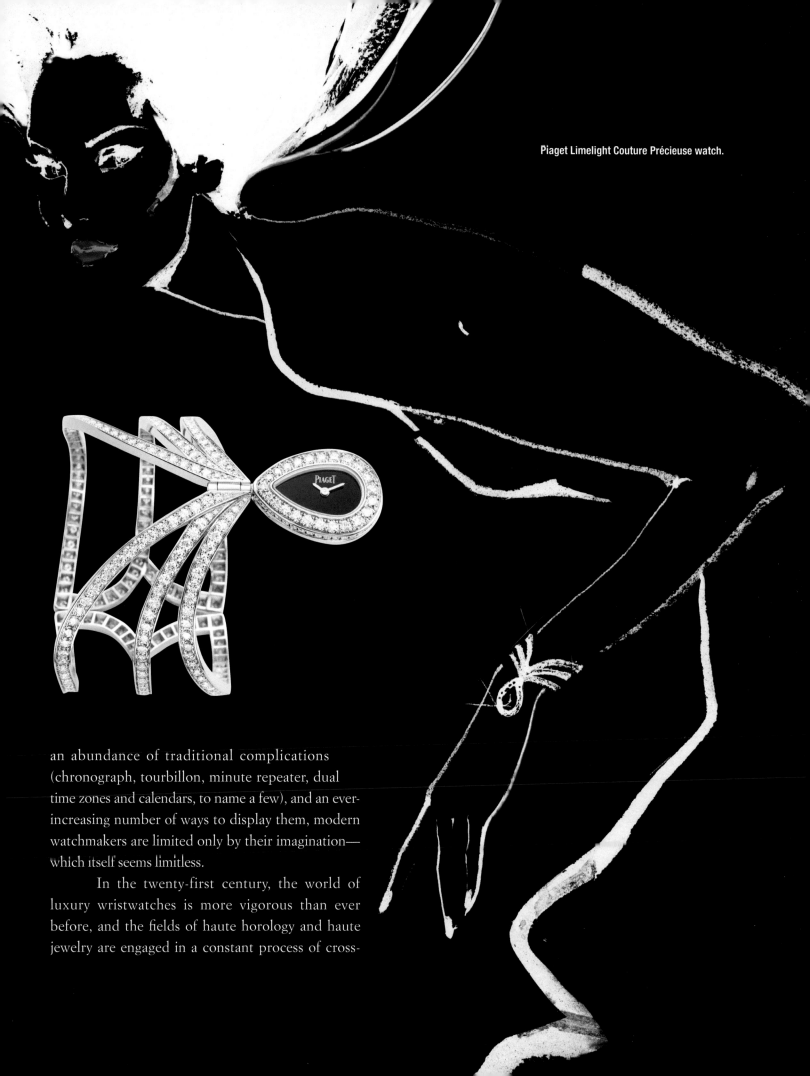

Piaget Limelight Couture Précieuse watch.

an abundance of traditional complications (chronograph, tourbillon, minute repeater, dual time zones and calendars, to name a few), and an ever-increasing number of ways to display them, modern watchmakers are limited only by their imagination—which itself seems limitless.

In the twenty-first century, the world of luxury wristwatches is more vigorous than ever before, and the fields of haute horology and haute jewelry are engaged in a constant process of cross-

de Grisogono Tondo
by Night watches.

TOP
Cartier Temps Modernes watch.

LEFT
Piaget watch.

RIGHT
Gong Li wearing Piaget jewelry.

pollination. Wristwatches are one of the few jewels that allow men to indulge themselves as thoroughly as women, though instead of gemstone-studded cases and dials, men often opt for complicated timepieces, upon which the main attraction is not a sultry sparkle but a miniature mechanical marvel, whether it is a chronograph, moonphase, innovative time display or a minute repeater.

Cartier Rotonde watch.

BROOCHES

Of all jewelry worn, a brooch is undoubtedly the most practical. It may sound odd to apply that adjective to a piece of jewelry, whose sole purpose, it seems at times, is to be decidedly *un*practical—to serve as a token of everlasting love, a symbol of rank or simply a sign of freewheeling delight in the beauty proffered by the generous earth. But the brooch follows a trajectory slightly different from other kinds of jewelry. Rather than becoming useful through its symbolic significance, like the signet ring,

the brooch started out as a plain, utilitarian tool: a safety pin *avant la lettre*, before most people had any letters at all. Because humans have a natural propensity to beautify our surroundings, it was not long before we looked at the brooches holding our clothes together and thought of the marvelous possibilities it offered. Another important way in which the brooch differs from other jewels is what it adorns: rather than touching the skin directly, a brooch pierces the clothing, providing more aesthetic freedom for the wearer.

The brooch has a touch of split personality: although it was born to serve a particular function, it can be just as useless or as gloriously symbolic as any other jewel, perhaps even more so, given the fact that the same rules don't quite apply to this unique gem. Unconstrained by the need to fit between fingers or hang from an earlobe, the brooch can be much larger and heavier than these ornaments. Freed from the tyranny of the O-, U- or Y-shapes that dominate bracelets and necklaces, the brooch can take any form it wishes, seeming to float unsupported on the garment, with no chain to remind the admirer of the claims of gravity.

Another hint of a dual personality comes through when pondering the distinction between daring and demure. During the Victorian Era—a time so prudish that people referred to the "limbs" of chairs to avoid uttering the indecent word "legs"—plunging necklines were hugely in fashion, and the most typical spot for a brooch was at the very center of the neckline, drawing the attention to the décolletage. In the 1948 film The Three Musketeers, the revealing dresses

*Portrait of Leonilla, Princess
of Sayn-Wittgenstein-Sayn
by Franz Xaver Winterhalter, 1843.*

TOP
Portrait of Adelaide of Saxe-Meiningen
by Sir William Beechey, circa 1831.

LEFT
Portrait of Elisabeth of Bavaria,
nineteenth century.

CENTER
Cartier lace bow brooch, 1906.

RIGHT
Vintage Cartier brooch.

LEFT
Brooch from the Netherlands, 1630.

RIGHT
Portrait of William III of England,
seventeenth century.

by Angela Lansbury and Lana Turner were deemed much too risqué by Hollywood censors. To satisfy the morals police, the costume department affixed large brooches to conceal the offending cleavage. In general, however, we affix jewels where we want to draw the eye. One of the people in present-day popular culture who exhibits the most affection for the brooch is the character of Joan Harris, née Holloway, on the television series *Mad Men*. Interestingly, she is an extremely intelligent woman whose smarts often go unnoticed

because of her body. A penchant for bracelets or rings would not tell quite the same story.

Another modern brooch aficionado—this one a real person—is renowned for her intellect. Former Secretary of State Madeleine Albright owns a collection of over 200 brooches and even wrote a book (*Read My Pins*) about them and their relation to her career—an auto-broochography, if you will. She often used her jewelry as a way of making a subtle, or occasionally not so subtle, statement on her diplomatic work. For instance, during a meeting with then-

TOP
Van Cleef & Arpels stork brooch.

LEFT
Boucheron brooch.

President of Russia Vladimir Putin, Albright donned a pin with the famous "see no evil, hear no evil, speak no evil" monkeys, a pointed reference to Russia's policy on Chechnya. Putin and President Clinton both understood the dig; neither one was happy about it.

Even the etymology of the word "brooch" distinguishes it from other ornaments, in whose names lurks the body part for which they are destined. The Middle English word "broche" came from the Latin word for "spike," and meant a sharp instrument, like a dagger or a meat spit. (Even today, food cooked on skewers is said to be en brochette.) Thus a brooch was always noted for its more utilitarian side; the jewels and other ornamentation came later, and its form stayed simpler longer than other kinds of jewelry. Women used brooches in pairs, one for each shoulder, to keep simple tubular dresses in place. The truly fashion forward strung a strand of beads between the two pins. However, the brooch would come into its own, taking on ornamentation and motifs that complemented other jewelry or stood apart to shine in its difference.

Animals of all families have found a welcoming habitat upon the brooch, which offers nearly unlimited freedom of shape and size. When the animal is posed

horizontally, you may notice that the brooch will always have the sharp end of the pin pointing toward the head. This is because when a right-handed woman affixes a brooch to her garment, the tendency will be for her to fasten it with an upward tilt as it goes to the left. Were the animal's hindquarters on the same side as the pin, they would be higher than its head after fastening.

In Ancient Egpyt, brooches were not as prevalent as some other forms of jewelry, but they did exist. The term "pectoral" usually refers to a large necklace, but it could also mean a brooch ornament, which was decorated with the same iconography and with the same materials as other ornaments.

The ubiquity of the brooch in ancient Greece, and its usefulness, take a sinister turn in an account told by Herodotus of the ongoing rivalry between Athens and nearby island Aegina. When the Athenians attacked and tried to carry off a couple of sacred statues, their plan failed disastrously, perhaps with help from the gods themselves, and only one man returned to Attica to carry the news of the rout. The city of new

Cartier brooch.

widows advanced upon the luckless survivor, each one removing the brooch that fastened her dress. One by one, the women stabbed the soldier with their brooches, each one demanding to know where the body of her husband had been left. As punishment for this murder, the Athenian women were forced to change their dress to the Ionian style, which did not require pins. (One explanation for this strangely light discipline is that the story might be apocryphal, concocted to explain certain shifts in the culture—including a move away from brooches—after the fact.)

The use of the brooch was so widespread in Rome that the Latin word for it—fibula—persists in modern Romance languages. Due to a visual similarity, it is the same word as the word for on of the bones found in the shin. Fibulae replaced the straight pins that had fastened clothing in the Bronze

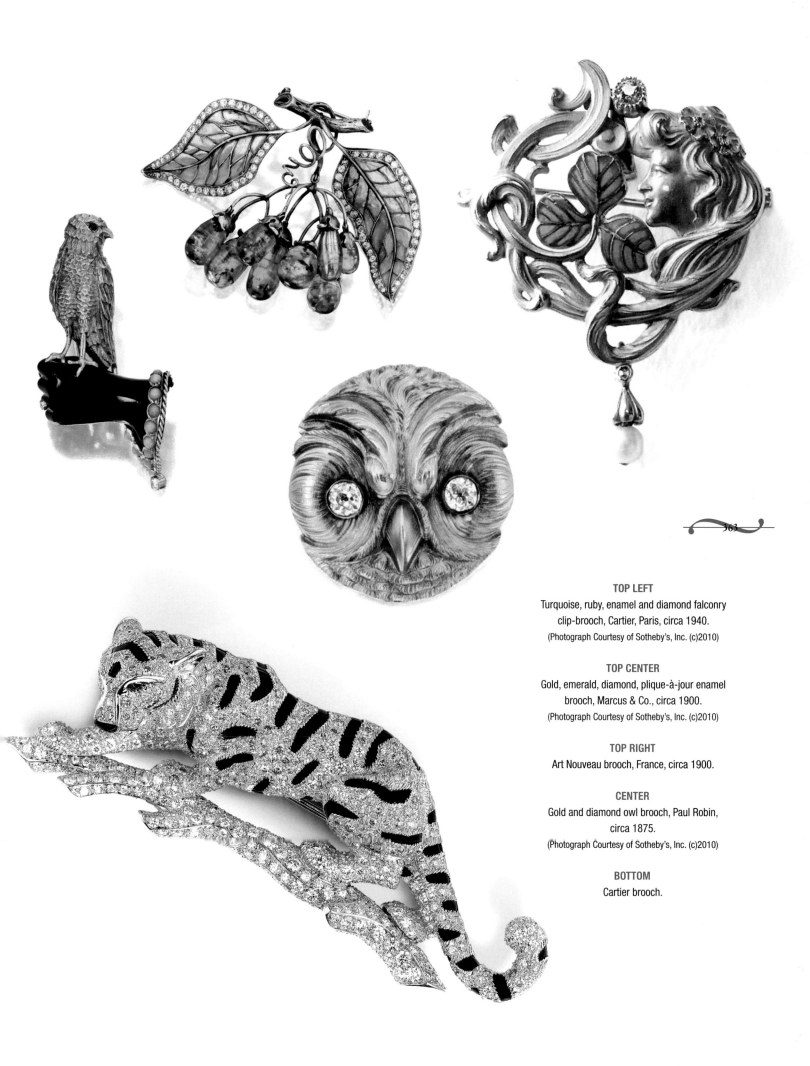

TOP LEFT
Turquoise, ruby, enamel and diamond falconry
clip-brooch, Cartier, Paris, circa 1940.
(Photograph Courtesy of Sotheby's, Inc. (c)2010)

TOP CENTER
Gold, emerald, diamond, plique-à-jour enamel
brooch, Marcus & Co., circa 1900.
(Photograph Courtesy of Sotheby's, Inc. (c)2010)

TOP RIGHT
Art Nouveau brooch, France, circa 1900.

CENTER
Gold and diamond owl brooch, Paul Robin,
circa 1875.
(Photograph Courtesy of Sotheby's, Inc. (c)2010)

BOTTOM
Cartier brooch.

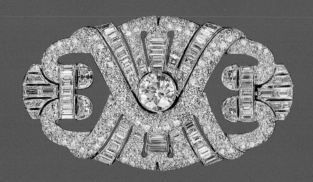

TOP RIGHT
Van Cleef & Arpels diamond
and platinum clip, 1928.

RIGHT
Vintage Van Cleef & Arpels
diamond clip, 1931.

LEFT
Onyx brooch set with diamonds,
a sapphire and cabochon rubies.
American, circa 1930.

CENTER
Vintage Boucheron brooch, 1925.

Age, acting as the ancestor of today's safety pin. The fibula had several advantages over the straight pin: it did not fall out as often, and the bow or plate of the fibula offered much more room for decoration than the head of the straight pin. The designs crafted on fibulae often signified marital status, profession or rank. There were several different types of basic design: the violin bow fibula, resembles the modern safety pin, as well as (unsurprisingly) a violin bow. The common quality among the different kinds of violin bow fibulae was that the bow always ran flat and parallel to the pin. Other forms featured an arched bow, spirals or a triangular shape. The spread of the Roman Empire in the first century AD led to a corresponding explosion of the fibula's popularity throughout the territory. Craftsmen experimented with new shapes and enameled designs, eventually developing designs that were unique to each area of what is now Europe.

Celts and other Europeans favored brooches throughout the Iron Age, Roman Empire and early

Van Cleef & Arpels brooch, 1928.

365

Andreoli brooch.

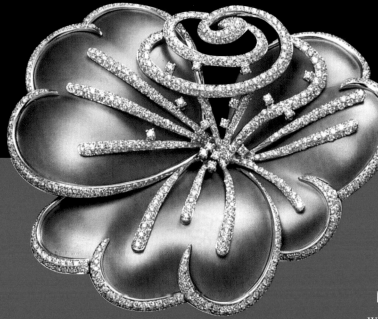

took on more intricate, elaborate detail. The brooches from the Roman period in Britain are plain and generally crafted in iron or bronze, but around 700, brooches undergo a metamorphosis, with goldwork and jewels transforming the humble object into a sign of rank. The penannular shape, which forms an almost complete ring with two larger terminals, holds a pin that moves freely about the ring. Women and men alike wore these pins, and they were so universal that Ireland actually had laws to sort out who was at fault if one person was injured by

medieval period. Characterized, jewelry-wise, by the penannular torcs, Celts turned to a similar shape for their brooches. Although they began as clothes fasteners, in the eighth and ninth centuries, these brooches began to be worked in precious metal and

another's brooch. (Answer: it depended on how far the pin stuck out.) Another law addressed the kinds of brooches suitable for different members of the aristocracy: sons of minor kings were to have silver brooches, while those of major kings would wear gold brooches set with crystal.

The fashion of Medieval Europe, favoring as it did a covered-up look, was highly conducive to the wearing of brooches. Women usually wore a long tunic with a mantle on top, which would be fastened at the neck with a brooch. Among the aristocracy, jeweled pins, along with rings, were by far the most common form of ornament to be found.

Brooches were extremely popular during the prosperous Renaissance, not least as a way to flaunt wealth once one ran out of room on the body. Bodice ornaments were crafted in gold, diamonds and colored precious gemstones, and ingeniously mounted on springs, so that the entire piece would quiver as the wearer moved. Another much-loved jewel of the seventeenth century was the stomacher brooch, which

TOP LEFT
**Queen Elizabeth II
and Princess Anne.**

TOP CENTER
**Cartier's Edelweiss brooch,
set with the Williamson
diamond, 1953.**

FAR RIGHT
Van Cleef & Arpels brooches.

LEFT
**Mauboussin sapphire brooch
from the 1970s.**

Andreoli brooch.

might cover the entire bodice of the constricting dress of the time, and was often constructed in two or three pieces to allow the wearer to move. The stomacher brooch also went by the more appealing name devant de corsage.

Victorians adored brooches, and used them for all sorts of symbolic gestures. Love brooches drew upon a tremendously varied symbolic language of flowers to convey messages of friendship (ivy leaves), constancy (bluebells), remembrance (forget-me-nots) and a wide array of subtly graded emotions. Mourning brooches might be crafted in jet or

Chaumet Hortensia brooch.

Boucheron brooch.

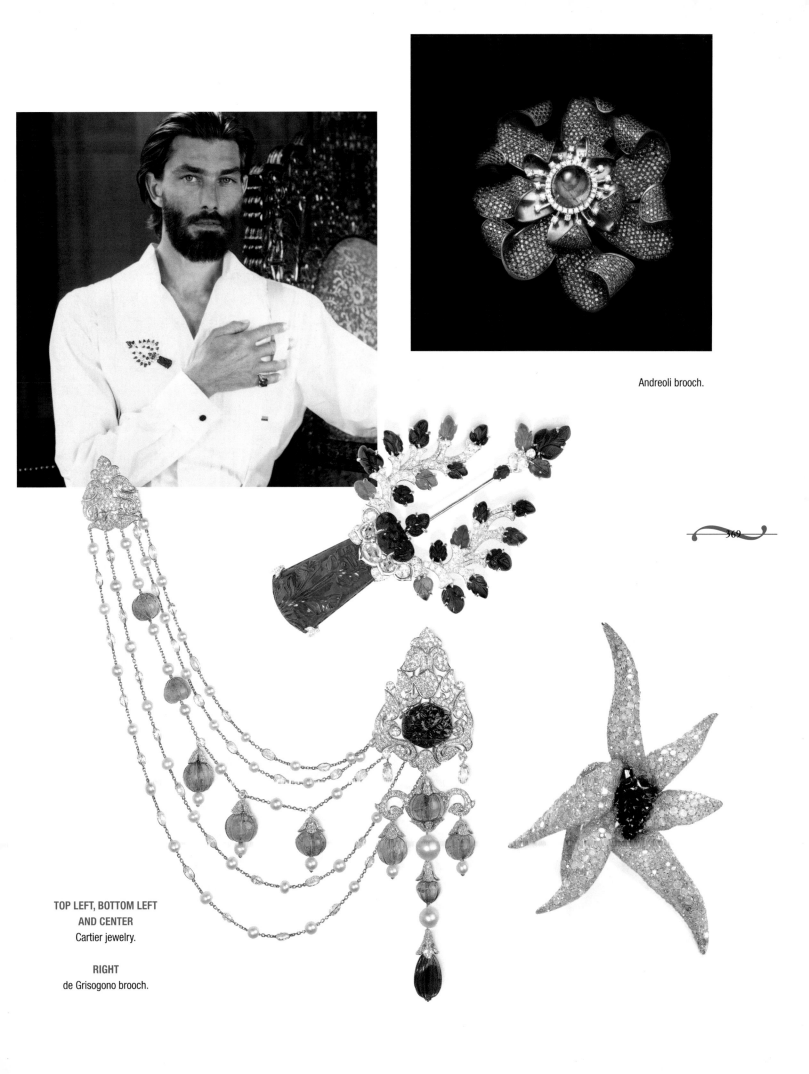

Andreoli brooch.

**TOP LEFT, BOTTOM LEFT
AND CENTER**
Cartier jewelry.

RIGHT
de Grisogono brooch.

Chanel brooch.

other black materials and incorporate
hair or a photograph of the deceased.
(Keep in mind that these photographs were
usually taken posthumously.) They could also
commemorate nationwide events, such as Queen
Victoria's Golden and Diamond Jubilees, which
marked the fiftieth and sixtieth years of her reign,
respectively. Rather than one or two large pieces, by
the end of the nineteenth century, small brooches were
popular, and worn in profusion all over the bodice.

 In the early years of the twentieth century,
oversize, painting-style brooches were popular. Art

Nouveau fit this trend perfectly, using
natural materials to create a compelling
scene that was freed from the constraints of
other types of jewelry. With the advent of Art Deco,
however, the brooch took on an entirely different
character. Straight lines and geometric motifs ruled
the day, untouched by the need for rounded forms to
accommodate the living body. Brooches became an
abstract interpretation of form and color, exuding a
chic, modern feel that persists to this day.

 The concept of a jeweled pin is not restricted
to dresses or blazers. In the Middle Ages and the

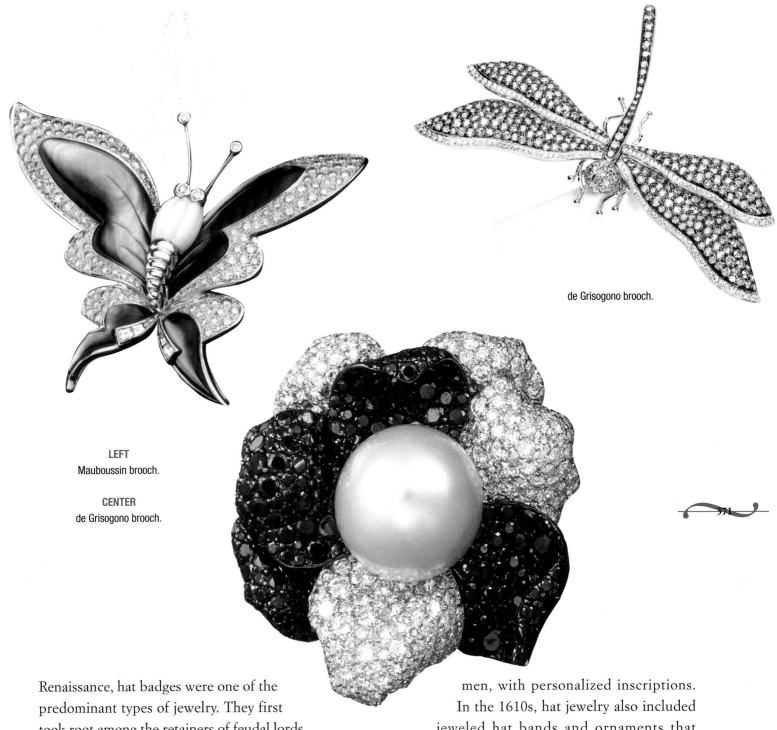

de Grisogono brooch.

LEFT
Mauboussin brooch.

CENTER
de Grisogono brooch.

Renaissance, hat badges were one of the predominant types of jewelry. They first took root among the retainers of feudal lords and princes, who demonstrated their affiliation by pinning the heraldic badges of their masters to their headgear. Medieval pilgrims picked up on the practice, using pins that represented patron saints or particular shrines they had visited. As the custom migrated to the upper classes, and the pins became more elaborate, they lost the original overtones of fealty and faith. Now in gold, with embossed motifs or those cast in relief, the hat badge became a fashion accessory for wealthy men, with personalized inscriptions.

In the 1610s, hat jewelry also included jeweled hat bands and ornaments that recreated elaborate feathers in diamonds and pearls. Moving away from the idiosyncratic nature of inscriptions and individual motifs, this new form of hat jewelry focused on large stones and functioned as a simple display of wealth and taste.

This form of jewelry reached its apotheosis in the courts of India, with the turban ornaments, known as sarpesh, that incorporated a profusion of extremely large gemstones. The turban ornament

Cartier brooch.

TOP
Naomi Harris wearing
Chopard jewelry.

RIGHT
Boucheron brooch.

LEFT
Chopard brooch.

also played a huge role in royal jewelry in Persia, where it was known as the jiga. Named for the egret bird whose feathers often adorned such jewels, the aigrette was a hugely popular motif for these turban ornaments, limning the vanes in diamonds and often featuring a huge colored stone near the end, resembling plumes from that other dazzling avian: the peacock. As many sovereigns exchanged valuable gifts of jewelry to cement alliances and relationships between nations, Shah Abbas I of Persia sent a jiga featuring an engraved

ruby, a pearl and black heron feathers to Jahangir, the Mughal Emperor of India. The Shah's gift, worth 50,000 rupees, started an Indian fashion of wearing both the sarpesh and the jiga upon aristocratic turbans.

In a way that hearkens back to its roots as a simple sartorial tool, the brooch proffers a versatility that is unmatched in the world of jewelry. The central jeweled plaque of Queen Alexandra's famous "dog collar" necklaces could be removed and worn on its own, and many haute jewelry pendants have to option

to wear the central element as a pin. A brooch might also have other jewels or chains that are suspended from the main jewel. Its generous size relative to other forms of jewelry means that the brooch can easily support jeweled decorations.

One of the most famous brooches bears two diamonds that have migrated from crown, to tiara, to necklace, to pin. The stones, Cullinan III and Cullinan IV, are the third and fourth largest diamonds to be carved from the Cullinan Diamond, still—by an enormous margin—the most massive diamond ever found, originally weighing in at an unbelievable 3,106 carats. The two largest diamonds, Cullinan I and II, adorn the English Sovereign's Scepter and Imperial State Crown, respectively. Cullinan III and IV were given to Queen Mary by the South African government, and after trying them out in various forms, she set them in a magnificent brooch that bears no other adornment: just a pear-shaped 94.4-carat diamond, suspended from a square-cut 63.6-carat diamond. Queen Elizabeth II, Queen Mary's granddaughter, who is never seen in public without a carefully chosen brooch, often wears the Cullinan III and IV, referring to the brooch as "Granny's chips." Other diamonds carved from the Cullinan find have

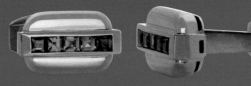

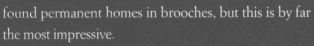

upon the bust. The most imposing gemstones, as ever, need no further interpretation, sitting in splendor with the natural-born aplomb of true royalty. Having outgrown the demands of practicality, the brooch is free to join other precious jewels in a topsy-turvy world in which beauty and elegance dictate every turn.

CUFFLINKS

Discreet yet elegant, gem-studded yet utilitarian, cufflinks are one of the last remaining jewels left to the less fair sex. Introduced during the reign of Louis XIV—the heyday of male personal adornment—cufflinks began as set of glass buttons connected by a short chain, with which men could fasten their shirt sleeves. These "boutons de manchette" figured in the Sun King's jewelry wardrobe as well, making an appearance in diamond form when he set the world record (as far as anyone can tell) for most diamond carats worn at once. The design has not changed altogether much in the intervening centuries, apart from the innovation of using a short post in place of a linked chain to connect the two studs.

Whether set with gemstones, decorated with enamel or left to shine unadorned, cufflinks generally

found permanent homes in brooches, but this is by far the most impressive.

The twenty-first-century brooch is under fewer constraints than ever: the use of lightweight titanium has made even more elaborate designs possible, and materials such as mother-of-pearl, dyed or naturally hued, bring a beautiful splash of color from end to end. The piece's versatility and transformability continues unabated, as haute jewelers create elements that can metamorphose from brooch to pendant, to bracelet, and back again. Animals continue to be a favorite motif, stalking, floating, swimming, flying, lolling or frolicking

TOP LEFT
de Grisogono cufflinks.

TOP RIGHT
Jewelmer Joaillerie jewelry.

Vintage Cartier
clip brooches.

fall into the "double-panel" category: two decorated discs connected by a chain or post. In order to use them properly, the wearer needs a shirt whose cuffs sport two buttonholes (level with each other) but no buttons. The wearer pushes one end through both holes, swiveling the post if necessary to keep the accessory in place. Some cufflinks mimic stud earrings, piercing the hole in the sleeve and fastened by a removable back.

The enduring popularity of the cufflink, in this age of miracle fabrics and invisible, flexible fasteners, speaks to a few eternal truths about human habits. Men in the Western world may have been systematically stripped of jewels, relinquishing personal adornment as "frivolity," which they saw as a strictly feminine quality. However, the taste for cufflinks has lingered. Subtle as they are, tucked away among folds of fabric at the wrist, cufflinks nonetheless provide a bit of sparkle, a bit of showmanship and a bit of flair to formal occasions. Men can stick with classic studs in precious materials, or get whimsical with animal motifs or other playful themes.

Andreoli
376

THIS PAGE
A breathtaking white-gold tutti frutti set glows with emerald drops, sapphire beads and carved emeralds, rubies and sapphires, with glinting diamond accents.

FACING PAGE
Crafted in rose gold, this flexible cuff bracelet is set with emeralds, rubies and sapphires, with 3 ruby cabochons as the highlight of the piece.

Andreoli

From the simplest jewelry to the most elaborate pieces, from an inventive use of enamel and semiprecious materials to classic motifs with immense precious gemstones, Andreoli expresses a jeweler's sensibility on both an epic and an intimate scale. Whatever the material, whatever the medium, Andreoli brings Italian style and craftsmanship to every jewel in its wide-ranging collections.

LEFT
White diamonds and multi-colored sapphire dance delightfully on this playful white-gold set.

BOTTOM
Rose-gold earrings describe foliate filigrees set with white diamonds, ending in black onyx blossoms.

Andreoli speaks the language of rings fluently, knowing that sometimes, the smallest pieces of jewelry can be among the most significant. These pieces adorn the fingers with wit, flair and grace, utilizing a variety of materials and motifs to convey a serious taste for unserious attitudes. Size matters: a large colored stone might take center stage, offset by a carefully considered shade of flawless enamel or a swirling filigree of white and colored diamonds. Or the jeweler might paint a picture using smaller stones, pavé-set in floral or abstract motifs for a shimmering Pointillist effect. The woman wearing Andreoli's rings on her fingers talks with her hands, letting the world know she is a force to be reckoned with. Like their wearers, rings must be strong as well as beautiful, able to withstand the rigors of the daily hands-on world.

Of all jewelry, it is possible that earrings have the most varied forms of expression. They can go from tiny studs to long, draping chandeliers, and Andreoli

Brown diamonds and multi-colored sapphires paint the petals of this yellow-gold ring.

A smoky topaz cabochon takes center stage, surrounded by swirls of brown diamonds, on this yellow-gold ring.

White diamonds combine with yellow sapphires to brighten a dramatic set in white gold.

BOTTOM
White gold and white diamonds bring an elegant sparkle to a set composed of a necklace, a ring and earrings.

explores this territory with verve and confidence, often using titanium to facilitate intricate designs that dangle from delicate earlobes. Andreoli's earrings range from classic and traditional to starkly modern, with much in between, such as one playful pair that highlights flower-carved emeralds nestled inside diamond-set hoops.

The jeweler's bracelets hold a special sensual allure all their own, marking the spot where a long sleeve gives way to soft skin. Not as intimate as the neck, nor as public as the fingers, the wrist is a nexus of flirtation, where a would-be lover might touch woman and Andreoli has created a myriad of ways to make the spot even more irresistible. Pearls of richly exotic hues encircle the wrist, or a garden of precious colored

CENTER
Yellow gold provides a rich backdrop for brown diamonds on this warmly luxurious ring.

RIGHT
A cabochon of yellow jade gleams like the sun on this yellow-gold ring, which is also set with smoky topaz.

A classic design envelops these platinum and diamond earrings with a vintage aura.

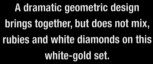

A dramatic geometric design brings together, but does not mix, rubies and white diamonds on this white-gold set.

stones springs to life, loosely draped around a forearm. Andreoli's thick, striking bangles use inventive design and playful colors—in gems, metals and enamel—to express the wearer's individuality.

With exuberant craftsmanship and impeccable showmanship, Andreoli's necklaces always stand out. Not content with simple strands, the jeweler explores myriad ways to make a statement—some pieces drip with oversized coral beads in dramatic colors, accented with precious gemstones. Other necklaces take the form of pendants, interspersing brightly colored stones with strips of Andreoli's signature dyed mother-of-pearl.

This ring uses an undulating shape for its diamond- and sapphire-set white gold, evoking the sea.

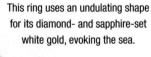

Diamonds flank a Burmese sapphire on this simple, elegant platinum ring.

TOP RIGHT
Angel-skin coral makes a dramatic contrast with black diamonds in this rose-gold set.

TOP LEFT
A bold use of color defines this set, strung with beads in angel-skin coral and emeralds. White diamonds set in white gold sparkle where one element meets the next.

BOTTOM
Crafted in white, yellow and rose gold, these three pearl rings frame their central beauties with diamonds and beads in ruby, sapphire and emerald, respectively.

Of course, the necklace provides the broadest canvas for a jewelry designer to work with, and with an immense collection of sapphires, rubies and emeralds at its disposal, Andreoli can work wonders, as in one bib necklace in the time-honored tutti frutti style, whose enormous dangling emerald drops provide a gorgeous counterbalance to the smaller carved gems that decorate the upper area. With pieces that are elegant, imposing, approachable and playful all at once, Andreoli stakes a claim to one of the most vulnerable parts of the human body, creating necklaces that serve as both armor and invitation.

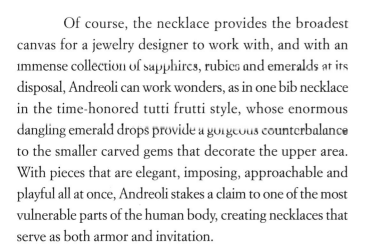

Black diamonds set a chic stage for turquoise drops on these earrings.

CENTER AND BOTTOM
Turquoise drops spill from this white-gold set of necklace and earrings, with diamonds and blue sapphires set in between.

LEFT
Faceted amethysts adorn the terminals of these enamel bracelets, with gems that seem to drip down the hoop.

BOTTOM
This intricate white-gold ring is set with an array of multi-colored sapphires for a shimmering rainbow of light.

Fearlessly blending precious and semiprecious materials or placing contrasting colors side by side, Andreoli knows that variety is the spice of life. The jeweler's parures—sets that combine a necklace with other complementary

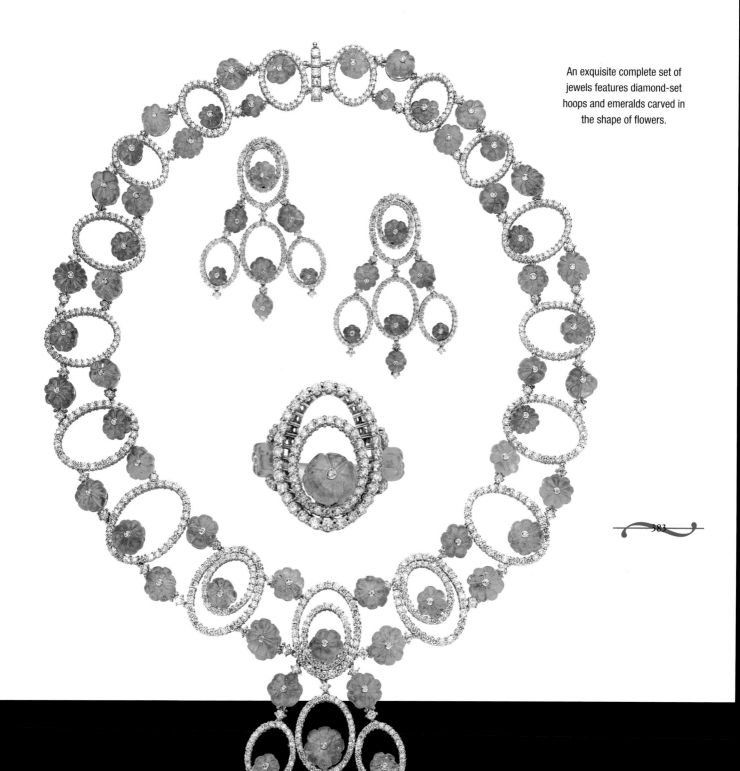

pieces—showcase the imagination that goes into the creation of each jewel. The coral drops of a vivid necklace repeat at the ears, emphatically echoing the more elaborate piece. Emerald flowers within diamond hoops explore the different variations on the motif and how it might play out within the confines of a ring, two earrings, a bracelet or a stunning necklace. Ultimately, Andreoli's art resides within this coherent vision of a varied world of jewelry.

THIS PAGE

These earrings feature lustrous white pearls suspended from platinum surmounts set with 6 pear-shape diamonds (3.34 carats) and 10 marquise-cut diamonds (4.94 carats). The accompanying necklace of South Sea pearls is strung with 23 16-20mm pearls, and its platinum ball clasp sparkles with 60 pavé-set diamonds (8.36 carats).

FACING PAGE

Smoldering with the dark glow of 25 15-18.3mm Tahitian natural color pearls, this necklace fixes with a platinum ball clasp set with 72 round-cut diamonds (6.11 carats).

Assael

Though the classic, white, lustrous pearl — known as the South Sea pearl — is the best known of its kind, the oceans provide a vast array of possibilities. The Tahitian Natural Color Black pearl made a dramatic entrance into New York in 1976, when Salvador Assael returned from his pearl farms in Tahiti with a set of exquisite black pearls. He created the perfect black necklace, as he had done so many times before with white pearls, and then went to his old friend, the legendary Fifth Avenue jeweler Harry Winston, and challenged him to sell the necklace. The deal was made, the necklace was sold, and Salvador J. Assael had introduced a new gem to the world market.

Two exquisite pieces from the Angela Cummings for Assael Collection: a pair of earrings hung with baroque South Sea pearls of 16.1-16.1-19.5mm in dimensions and set with round-cut diamonds (2.42 carats), with a necklace strung with 18 baroque South Sea pearls of 16.7-18.7mm and suspending a baroque South Sea pearl drop of 18.5-19.3-24.7mm in dimensions, set with 171 diamonds (5.03 carats). Both pieces display a cunning diamond-set coral branch motif in platinum and white gold.

That is a great, great story," said his wife, Christina Lang Assael, who today is continuing the business after her husband passed away in 2011. "Assael is one of the world's leading pearl houses, specializing in haute joaillerie and precious stones. We are a wholesale business that supplies the greatest jewelers and also creates our own, found at top retailers throughout the United States."

"The family business originated in Europe in the early twentieth century, as Assael-Ventura, with my father-in-law, James Assael, a diamond dealer and co-founder of the Diamond Bourse in Milano. He moved his family to Cuba and then to the United States during the Second World War. His son Salvador served with distinction in the U.S. Army in Europe, and then started working for his father, dealing in diamonds and later, his preference, the colored precious stones. In 1972 Salvador took over the business and changed the name to Assael International. Today the firm is simply known as Assael."

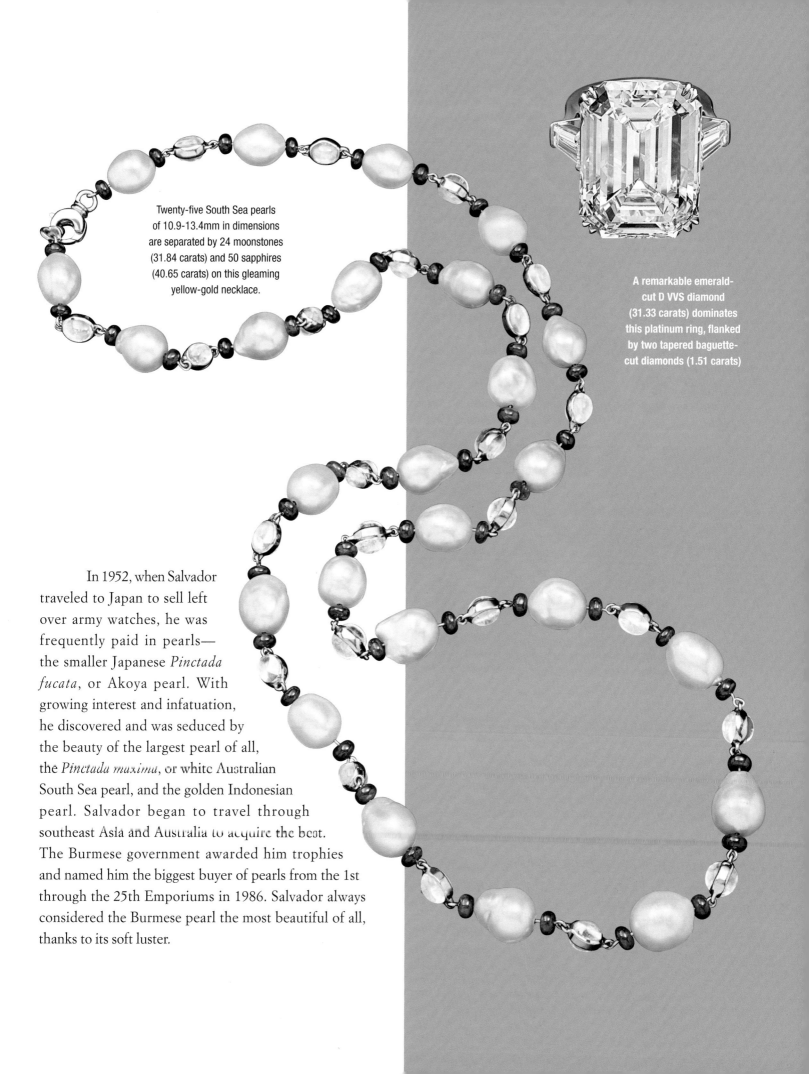

Twenty-five South Sea pearls of 10.9-13.4mm in dimensions are separated by 24 moonstones (31.84 carats) and 50 sapphires (40.65 carats) on this gleaming yellow-gold necklace.

A remarkable emerald-cut D VVS diamond (31.33 carats) dominates this platinum ring, flanked by two tapered baguette-cut diamonds (1.51 carats)

In 1952, when Salvador traveled to Japan to sell left over army watches, he was frequently paid in pearls—the smaller Japanese *Pinctada fucata*, or Akoya pearl. With growing interest and infatuation, he discovered and was seduced by the beauty of the largest pearl of all, the *Pinctada maxima*, or white Australian South Sea pearl, and the golden Indonesian pearl. Salvador began to travel through southeast Asia and Australia to acquire the best. The Burmese government awarded him trophies and named him the biggest buyer of pearls from the 1st through the 25th Emporiums in 1986. Salvador always considered the Burmese pearl the most beautiful of all, thanks to its soft luster.

White diamonds (4.91 carats) enhance the natural glow of a South Sea button pearl of 14.5-15.2mm on this platinum ring.

BOTTOM
Crafted in platinum and white gold, this Angela Cummings for Assael Swirl necklace mimics the sea's movement with 10 round South Sea pearls of 12-12.7mm in diameter and 280 round-cut diamonds (55.87 carats).

CENTER
Sixteen diamonds (5.24 carats) radiate out from 2 South Sea button pearls of 15-15.2mm on an elegant pair of platinum earrings.

At the suggestion of a friend, Salvador traveled to Tahiti and was introduced to the *Pinctada margaritifera* or black Tahitian pearl, which became his special baby. He had reached the source, soon realizing that with ownership came full market and quality control. Salvador became a producer, investing in pearl farms in Southern Polynesia that yielded more than half the world's supply. His idea of discarding pearls that did not meet his standard, making certain that only the finest pearls would be available on the world market, was a costly practice, but ensured that the gem would keep its value.

In order to produce a great pearl, the oyster must remain in the water for two to three years, vulnerable to typhoons that could mean disaster to a whole crop. The perfectly round pearl is a rarity, accounting for just 5–10% of a crop. The rarest necklaces take several years to create.

A splendid necklace of 40 baroque South Sea pearls of 16.1-22.5mm in dimensions exemplifies the jeweler's reputation for excellence.

An emerald-cut Burma sapphire (50.55 carats) brings a deep azure to this platinum ring, whose mounting is set with 6 baguette-cut diamonds (2.39 carats).

Needing to persuade jewelers of the value of the gem, Salvador lobbied the Gemological Institute of America (GIA) for certification of color authenticity, which helped set Tahitian cultured pearls apart from Japanese black pearls, which are dyed. The GIA also created a grading system according to their luster, clarity of surface, shape, tone and size, which ranges from 8–16 mm. "My husband's love affair with the pearl made him known as the Pearl King in the press, as his pearl necklaces were seen in all the best places. The most expensive necklace ever was a South Sea necklace my husband sold in 1993 at a Sotheby's auction in New York for $2,300,000—a world record. I was privileged to share his life, travel with him and learn from him. Salvador was a giant in the pearl world. He lived and breathed pearls—he loved them."

Twenty diamonds (9.46 carats) rise up like white flames from 2 golden South Sea button pearls of 13.1-14.0mm on these platinum earrings.

Luscious 14-16mm golden South Sea Pearls set the scene on this splendid necklace, with a yellow-gold clasp set with white diamonds (4.19 carats).

The Angela Cummings Collection

Last year I had the wonderful opportunity of signing a contract with famed US jewelry designer Angela Cummings. After many years as Tiffany's top designer, and then close to two decades under her own name, Ms. Cummings retired a few years ago. Then, quite by chance, when a mutual friend brought us together, we decided that the time was right for us to join forces.

Three iconic strands of pearls
in three hues—golden, white
and Tahitian—incarnate Assael's
commitment to classic pieces with
extraordinary materials.

This winning yellow-gold seahorse
brooch from the Angela Cummings for
Assael collection is set with 68 round-cut
diamonds (1.41 carats) and supports
a single baroque South Sea pearl of
16.1-18.4-20.5mm in dimensions.

Seeing master craftsmen turn Angela's drawings into beautiful pieces of jewelry is a very exciting process. Her creative approach is fresh and playful, chic and sophisticated all at once. The Collection is available in select stores across the country.

My husband worked with designers in the past. Today I am proud to present Angela Cummings for Assael.

Christina Lang Assael, New York, 2014

Bayco's extensive collection of ruby jewelry includes these ruby and diamond earrings set with a pair of oval rubies (13 carats total), this ruby and diamond ring centered upon a 13-carat oval-cut ruby and this ruby and diamond bangle bracelet (also pictured on facing page) set with 5 oval rubies (42 carats total).

Bayco

Long renowned as the home of the world's most impeccable, most extravagant, and most exceptional colored gems, Bayco continues to write new chapters in the story of couture jewelry. To cite just one example, the house's Imperial Emerald is a new standard bearer for a company—and a family—that has always sought out emeralds, sapphires and rubies of unparalleled quality and color, and always at impressive sizes. The Hadjibay family travels to the ends of the earth to find enchanting materials, which then become, in Bayco's hands, truly awe-inspiring jewelry—the envy of royalty.

These cool blue sapphire and diamond earrings bear a pair of oval sapphires (15 carats total).

Bayco

The rhymed couplet of the jewelry world, rings are generally considered to be the simplest way of displaying a one-of-a-kind gemstone: against the delicate backdrop of the human hand, stones appear larger, and the central gem of a ring can stand alone, requiring no mate or chain of matching stones that must be sourced and painstakingly analyzed to assure a perfect color match. However, Bayco flips this paradigm on its head, often using two or even three identical precious gems on the ring's relatively petite frame. Even singleton gems often find themselves flanked by generously proportioned diamonds or colored stones that match each other. Let us not forget, either, Bayco's colored eternity rings, which take the idea of a white diamond-set band and paint it with bold strokes of lush green, heavenly blue, passionate red or even a shocking shade of pink. These unconventional rings require many smaller stones that must match each other exactly to live up to Bayco's demanding standards.

LEFT
The Majestic: this regal sapphire and diamond necklace features a 55-carat "Royal Blue" Burmese sapphire.

BOTTOM
Scintillating with monochrome sophistication, this rose-cut diamond ring surrounds a 2 carat oval rose-cut diamond with diamond micropavé.

This intricate ring uses a pavé diamond setting to highlight the central 14-carat square cushion-cut sapphire.

Strictly speaking, earrings traditionally require just two identical stones, but here again, Bayco brings its own brand of extravagant excellence, dangling two or three show-stopping gems from each earlobe. When a single ruby graces the ear, the jeweler frames it with a bushel of white diamonds, their sparkle setting off the fiery elegance of the central gem. Bayco's drop earrings draw appreciative attention to a graceful neck, and tassels of sapphire beads sway and swing with their wearer's movements, catching the light in a myriad of ways. Cleverly constructed eternity hoops also use a dense row of colored stones to bring a splash of color to the open space below the earlobe.

A sonnet contains just 14 lines, no more, no less, and the bracelet's size is similarly circumscribed. With a set of several matched gems, the bracelet becomes possible. Only at Bayco, however, would a simple bangle sport five large rubies, neatly arranged one snug against the next for maximum visual impact. Only at Bayco would a shimmering blue strap wrapped around the wrist turn out, on closer inspection, to be composed entirely of sapphires. Only at Bayco would a wide, flexible diamond bracelet have dozens of emeralds nestled within as many diamond-set links. The gems become their own vocabulary, arranging the jewels in sparkling sestets and quatrains. The simplicity of the styles brings a self-assured confidence to the entire piece: a timeless setting for an eternal fascination.

This set of ruby and diamond jewelry includes earrings with a pair of cushion-cut rubies (20 carats total), a ring that bears an exceptional 43-carat oval-cut ruby and a bracelet comprised entirely of rubies.

LEFT

Crafted in dramatic black gold, this pair of ruby and diamond earrings consists of 6 rubies, each set within a diamond micropavé surround.

TOP RIGHT

Diamond micropavé brings a unique sparkle to this ring, mounted with a 6-carat pear-shaped rose-cut diamond.

TOP CENTER

A fiery 10-carat cushion Burmese ruby is flanked by white diamonds and surrounded by diamond micropavé on this elegant ring.

BOTTOM

Cushion-cut rubies (20 carats total) dangles from these spectacular earrings with a border and pendant element in white diamonds.

Of course, the jeweler's most impressive work sparkles around the wearer's neck: an epic in the most traditional sense of the word. Necklaces are the perfect showcase for the Hadjibays' talents for many reasons, chief among them being that as a precious gem increases in size, it also increases not only in weight (a disadvantage for earrings) but also in fragility (a disadvantage for rings and bracelets). The necklace, therefore, is the ideal piece with which to feature Bayco's most magnificent gemstones, with feminine décolletage as a warm backdrop for the mineral beauties. The other notable quality of the necklace is the demands its size places on the jeweler. Bayco's necklaces usually entail several sizable gemstones, as focal points that catch the eye in several different places. What the average person does not know, however, is the extreme difficulty of finding seven or eight—or nine or ten—emeralds of comparable size and quality, with identical takes on the perfect shade of green. It can take ten years, or even more, for the Hadjibays to gather enough perfect gems for a Bayco necklace. But what is a decade when Bayco crafts heirlooms that can be passed down from generation to generation?

TOP

A pair of pear-shaped emeralds
(10 carats total) stars in these show-
stopping emerald and diamond earrings.

BOTTOM

Three oval rose-cut diamonds (4 carats
total) gain even more impact from a
diamond micropavé surround on this
eye-catching ring.

TOP

Eight rose-cut diamonds,
each surrounded by diamond
micropavé, catch the light on
these earrings.

TOP

This intricate emerald and
diamond ring bears as its central
stone a 10-carat antique French
cushion-cut Colombian emerald.

THIS PAGE
Actress Diane Kruger wears
Cypris earrings in white and
blackened gold, set with
diamonds and rubies.

FACING PAGE
This ring from the **Cypris**
collection flaunts a dual
personality, featuring swans
in white and blackened gold
set with diamonds, black
sapphires and rubies.

Boucheron

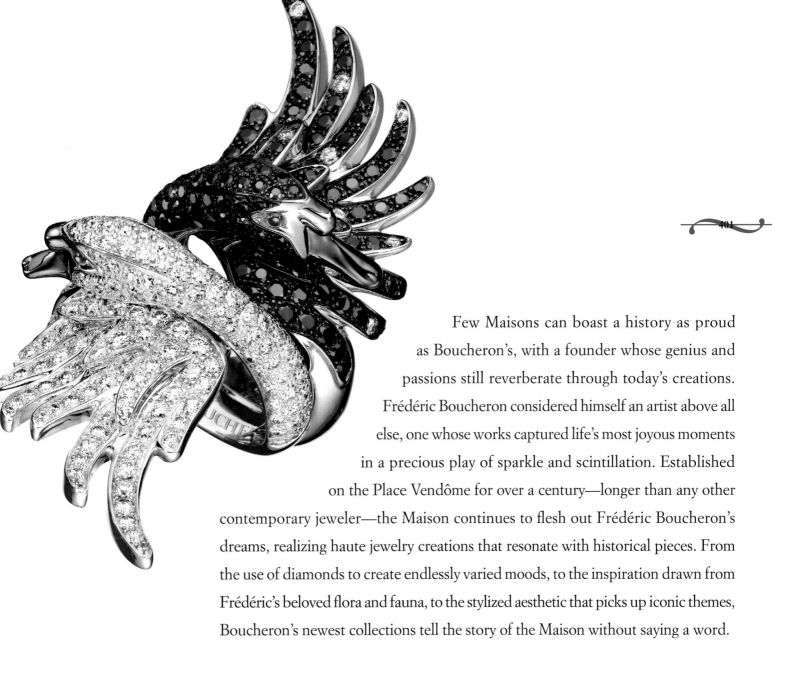

Few Maisons can boast a history as proud as Boucheron's, with a founder whose genius and passions still reverberate through today's creations. Frédéric Boucheron considered himself an artist above all else, one whose works captured life's most joyous moments in a precious play of sparkle and scintillation. Established on the Place Vendôme for over a century—longer than any other contemporary jeweler—the Maison continues to flesh out Frédéric Boucheron's dreams, realizing haute jewelry creations that resonate with historical pieces. From the use of diamonds to create endlessly varied moods, to the inspiration drawn from Frédéric's beloved flora and fauna, to the stylized aesthetic that picks up iconic themes, Boucheron's newest collections tell the story of the Maison without saying a word.

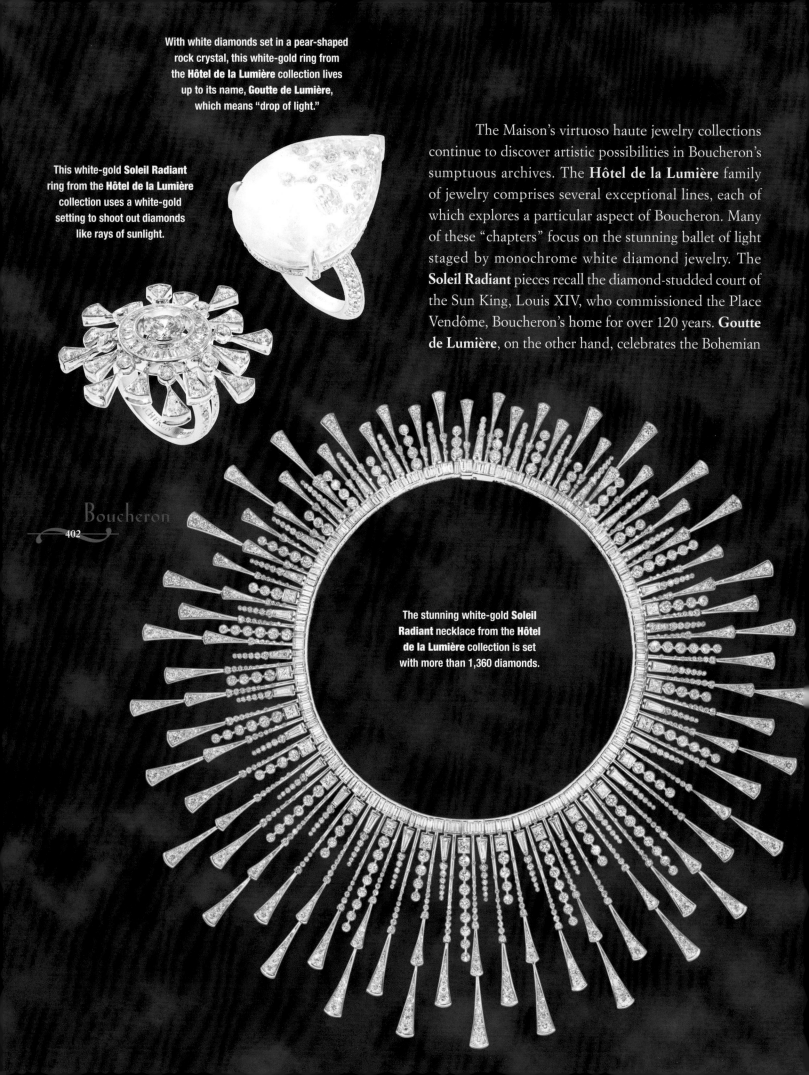

With white diamonds set in a pear-shaped rock crystal, this white-gold ring from the **Hôtel de la Lumière** collection lives up to its name, **Goutte de Lumière**, which means "drop of light."

This white-gold **Soleil Radiant** ring from the **Hôtel de la Lumière** collection uses a white-gold setting to shoot out diamonds like rays of sunlight.

The Maison's virtuoso haute jewelry collections continue to discover artistic possibilities in Boucheron's sumptuous archives. The **Hôtel de la Lumière** family of jewelry comprises several exceptional lines, each of which explores a particular aspect of Boucheron. Many of these "chapters" focus on the stunning ballet of light staged by monochrome white diamond jewelry. The **Soleil Radiant** pieces recall the diamond-studded court of the Sun King, Louis XIV, who commissioned the Place Vendôme, Boucheron's home for over 120 years. **Goutte de Lumière**, on the other hand, celebrates the Bohemian

Boucheron

402

The stunning white-gold **Soleil Radiant** necklace from the **Hôtel de la Lumière** collection is set with more than 1,360 diamonds.

The **Lierre de Paris** ring and necklace from the **Artisan du Rêve** collection craft Paris's indigenous ivy and famous cobblestones using only white gold, faceted and rough diamonds. The ring is set with a central round diamond, and the primary ivy leaf on the necklace bears a pear-shaped diamond.

BOTTOM
Boucheron's charming chameleon from the **Artisan du Rêve** collection clings to a leaf on this **Caméléon** brooch, crafted in white gold and pavé-set with white and gray diamonds.

Queen Rania of Jordan wears Boucheron's **Princess Tiara** in blackened gold set with emeralds.

spirit of Gabrielle Boucheron, Frédéric's wife, with an astonishing mélange of rock crystal and white diamonds that seem to float weightlessly inside.

With Boucheron's varied collections for the Biennale des Antiquaires 2012, the Maison again looked to its founder and his fascinations. For instance, when the nineteenth-century enthusiasm for meticulously manicured gardens was at its height, Frédéric recognized the beauty of the wild ivy that enhanced the architecture of his beloved city. The **Lierre de Paris** set makes the city come to life before our eyes, using only a combination of rough and faceted diamonds.

This scaly, evocative brooch and ring from the **Serpent Bohème** collection are crafted in yellow gold and set with diamonds.

The Place Vendôme jeweler has always had a soft spot for the vast and varied menagerie of animals that might pad, slither, climb or prowl, their natural camouflage compromised by their incarnations in diamonds, gold, opal and precious colored gemstones. These spirit guides influence a range of Boucheron's collections, including **Serpent Bohème**, which uses a pavé diamond setting to simulate the cool, muscular tension of snakeskin. The snake—the epitome of mysterious reptilian elegance—is also the star of a collection that Boucheron created for the Biennale des Antiquaires, called **Serpent Opalescent**. These reptiles have all hatched from the same egg: a serpentine necklace given by Frédéric Boucheron to his wife, with the promise of a joyful life together. The pieces acquire a second layer of meaning when one considers the ease with which a snake sheds her skin. Symbolizing a constant process of renewal and the courage to reinvent

Stud earrings from the **Serpent Bohème** collection use white diamonds set in white gold to represent smooth scales.

oneself, Boucheron's snake jewelry speaks to women who enjoy the freedom of expressing different facets of their personality with a well-chosen jewel.

Other collections cast a wider net within the animal kingdom, catching up insects, birds, lizards and even mammals. The **Hera** collection presents that goddess's favorite pet, the peacock, in a spray of diamonds or sapphires. **La Plume de Paon**, another collection created by Boucheron for the Biennale des Antiquaires, presents a stylized take on the same iconic bird, with a single feather as a point of departure for a series of emerald-set jewels.

TOP

This **Hera** ring represents the iconic peacock in white gold, diamonds and sapphires.

RIGHT

Actress Salma Hayek wears Boucheron's **Grace** necklace and **Ava** earrings in diamond-pavé white gold.

405

Opal captures the essence of shimmering snakeskin on these **Serpent Opalescent** pendant earrings from the Artisan du Rêve collection, crafted in white gold and set with opals and diamonds.

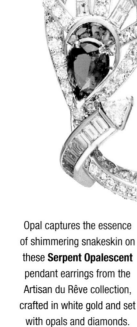

A loyal reptile grips a feather on this **Caméléon Plume de Paon** brooch from the **Artisan du Rêve** collection, set with a pear-shaped emerald, in white gold, pavé-set white diamonds and emeralds.

This charming **Caméléon Perle au Trésor** brooch from the **Artisan du Rêve** collection comes to life in white gold pavé-set with diamonds, pearls, opals and mother-of-pearl.

This **Quatre** pendant in pink, yellow and white gold, set with diamonds, plays with color and iconic Boucheron motifs for an understated yet evocative look.

TOP
Quatre Lumière hoops in yellow and white gold, set with diamonds, bring the collection's self-assured mix of materials to the ears.

CENTER
The **Quatre White Edition** ring in white, pink and yellow gold evokes femininity and strength.

TOP
Actress Kristin Scott Thomas wears the Boucheron **Quatre** ring in yellow, pink and white gold, set with diamonds.

CENTER
Gleaming in white gold and diamonds, this **Quatre Radiant Edition** ring deftly uses texture to create visual intrigue.

RIGHT
Adding a chic row of black, this **Quatre Black Edition** ring in white gold speaks of urban style.

The **Quatre** collection, which celebrates its tenth anniversary in 2014, combines highly symbolic motifs for jewels that are laden with layered significance. In its most fundamental iteration, the **Quatre** ring is comprised of four distinct bands in four different precious metals: yellow gold, white gold, Boucheron "chocolate" gold and pink gold. Each band features its own aesthetic, complementary to the others, which represents an aspect of Boucheron's artistic history. A line of diamonds nods to the Maison's reputation for impeccable jewelry, grosgrain and gadroon motifs quote emblematic Boucheron design elements, and the clous de Paris level echoes the cobblestones of the Maison's historic Place Vendôme address.

The Maison Boucheron also draws inspiration from the world of haute couture and the suppleness of the finest draped fabrics. Its **Delilah** collection

deftly works gold as an organic thread, knitting together finely wrought chains to form a delicate-feeling mesh that is nonetheless strong enough to be worn as a luxurious scarf. Other collections in the same vein nudge the couture inspiration along a more stylized vein, such as the **Halo Delilah** line, based on a Jean Cocteau-designed necklace from 1953 that was itself inspired by a knotted handkerchief. For the Biennale des Antiquaires, Boucheron created equally flexible pieces completely set with diamonds, morganite and colored sapphires, breathing vivacious life into a versatile classic.

TOP
Actresses Carole Bouquet and Muriel Mayette wear Boucheron creations.

LEFT
This **Halo Delilah** ring from the **Hôtel de la Lumière** collection, in white and pink gold, features a luscious pink morganite (14.73 carats) as a central stone.

Elizabeth, Queen of Belgians, wore a garland style diamond and platinum diadem created for her by Cartier in 1910.

Cartier

It is hard to imagine a universe without Cartier, a House with a narrative that has absorbed the world's seismic changes and remains haute jewelry's most immediately recognizable name. Having created the iconic Tutti Frutti style, jeweled panther, Trinity rings and early wristwatches, Cartier is by no means content to rest on its laurels. The jeweler continues to produce breathtaking, important pieces, turning to its time-honored sources of inspiration, as well as the magic and mystery within the stones themselves. The jeweler's collection for the Biennale des Antiquaires joins its Odyssée collection as a testament to the unparalleled artistic mastery of this haute jewelry legend.

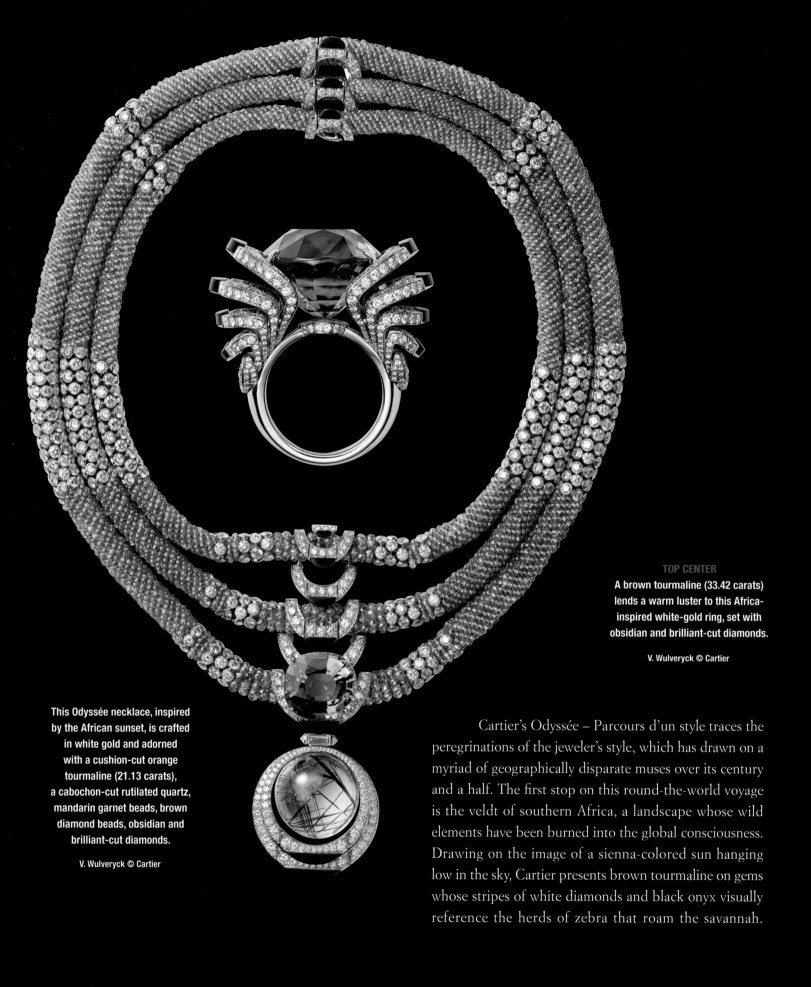

Cartier's Odyssée – Parcours d'un style traces the peregrinations of the jeweler's style, which has drawn on a myriad of geographically disparate muses over its century and a half. The first stop on this round-the-world voyage is the veldt of southern Africa, a landscape whose wild elements have been burned into the global consciousness. Drawing on the image of a sienna-colored sun hanging low in the sky, Cartier presents brown tourmaline on gems whose stripes of white diamonds and black onyx visually reference the herds of zebra that roam the savannah.

Hearkening back to Cartier's long relationship with Indian royalty, this platinum necklace suspends a carved sapphire (67.94 carats) from a magnificent support set with carved sapphire leaves, melon-cut sapphire and emerald beads and brilliant-cut diamonds.

H. Herrmann © Cartier

Representing the Art Deco skyline of the Platonic "city," this platinum bracelet sparkles with cushion- and brilliant-cut diamonds.

V. Wulveryck © Cartier

411

Representing the elegance and style of China, this platinum bracelet features two dragons, set with onyx and brilliant-cut diamonds, guarding a carved rubellite (66.43 carats) that is also set with diamonds.

V. Wulveryck © Cartier

A spectacular necklace showcases an orange tourmaline and a cabochon-cut rutilated quartz as central elements, with three thick cable-like strands. The strands are crafted with brilliant-cut diamonds, brown diamond beads and mandarin garnet beads, skillfully worked to resemble the sophisticated beaded jewelry of the people indigenous to the area. The rutilated quartz—whose wayward golden strands recall a lion's mane—seems to float unsupported in the center of the piece, framed by a diamond-set border that betrays the singular aesthetic of the Parisian jeweler.

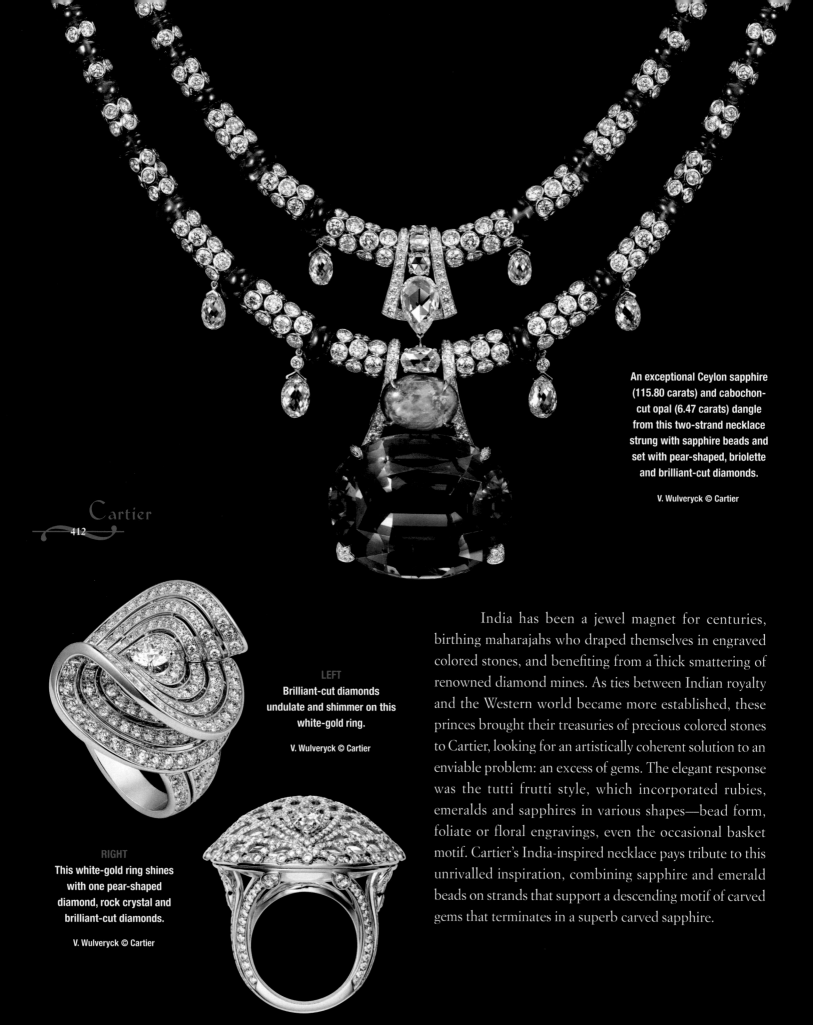

An exceptional Ceylon sapphire (115.80 carats) and cabochon-cut opal (6.47 carats) dangle from this two-strand necklace strung with sapphire beads and set with pear-shaped, briolette and brilliant-cut diamonds.

V. Wulveryck © Cartier

Cartier

412

LEFT
Brilliant-cut diamonds undulate and shimmer on this white-gold ring.

V. Wulveryck © Cartier

RIGHT
This white-gold ring shines with one pear-shaped diamond, rock crystal and brilliant-cut diamonds.

V. Wulveryck © Cartier

India has been a jewel magnet for centuries, birthing maharajahs who draped themselves in engraved colored stones, and benefiting from a thick smattering of renowned diamond mines. As ties between Indian royalty and the Western world became more established, these princes brought their treasuries of precious colored stones to Cartier, looking for an artistically coherent solution to an enviable problem: an excess of gems. The elegant response was the tutti frutti style, which incorporated rubies, emeralds and sapphires in various shapes—bead form, foliate or floral engravings, even the occasional basket motif. Cartier's India-inspired necklace pays tribute to this unrivalled inspiration, combining sapphire and emerald beads on strands that support a descending motif of carved gems that terminates in a superb carved sapphire.

The effect of China on Cartier's design process also receives its due in this collection, in the form of a diamond-set bracelet with dragons defending an impeccably carved pink tourmaline that ripples outward like a miniature reflecting pool. At the end of this journey, the exotic hues fall away and Cartier enters the "city." Alluding to a cosmopolitan concept more than a specific reference, these pieces bring back the influential years of Art Deco (a movement that started in Paris and ended up… everywhere), using its pleasing geometric shapes and monochrome splendor to showcase the jeweler's art.

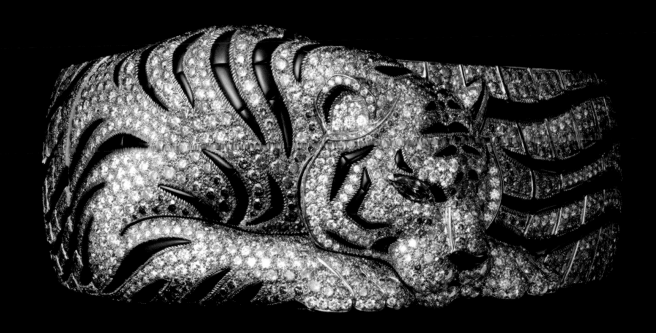

Cartier
414

At the Biennale des Antiquaires, the
most prestigious jewelers of the Place Vendôme
gather to exhibit haute jewelry that expresses
a singular aesthetic with singular precious
stones—even though the visions on display, as
well as the materials that incarnate them, are
endlessly varied. Cartier entered the arena with
an astonishing collection of pieces that hearkened to
the House's past as "jeweler of kings, king of jewelers,"
its penchant for big cats, its unerring sense of chic and its
collection of extraordinary gemstones. Enormous gems,
including aquamarine, green tourmaline, sapphire, opal
and ruby, receive the trappings they deserve, with precious
beads, accents and diamond-set delineations of Cartier's
timeless aesthetic. With unique pieces of unmatched—
unmatchable—caliber, Cartier lives up to its reputation
with the fierce elegance of a jeweled panther.

This extraordinary platinum ring
is set with a 35.73-carat green
tourmaline, highlighted with
brilliant-cut diamonds.

Julien Claessens
& Thomas Deschamps © Cartier

Chaumet

Among the most prestigious Houses of haute jewelry, few have the profound history or impeccable pedigree of Chaumet. Founded in 1780, Chaumet prevailed through the French Revolution, adorning Napoleon and figuring prominently in his mission to use Parisian finery as a luxurious diplomatic tool. Soaring through the Restoration, the Belle Epoque and our own modern times, Chaumet has demonstrated at every turn what it means to craft impeccable showcases for the world's finest gemstones. True to its rich background, Chaumet continues to develop and evolve as a creator of jewels, producing collections that interpret the world around us and the world within us. Three new lines from the Place Vendôme jeweler reinterpret eternal themes.

Featuring an oval-cut pink tourmaline (11.25 carats) and two cushion-cut diamonds of 2.02 carats each, this long Chaumet Hortensia necklace is crafted in pink gold and set with pink and angel-skin opal, brilliant-cut diamonds, marquise-cut pink tourmalines and brilliant-cut pink sapphires. It can be transformed into two short necklaces and a bracelet.

Delicate blossoms in pink and angel-skin opal, marquise-cut pink tourmalines and brilliant-cut diamonds cascade down these pink-gold Chaumet Hortensia earrings, which each bear a brilliant-cut diamond of 0.81 carat.

This pink-gold Chaumet Hortensia ring features a bright floral spray of pink opal, brilliant-cut and baguette-cut diamonds, brilliant-cut pink sapphires and a cushion-cut pink tourmaline (1.42 carats).

Chaumet

418

Laetitia Casta wears earrings and a necklace in white gold, diamonds and blue sapphire, with a ring in white gold, fully paved with diamonds at the Cannes International Film Festival, May 2013.

For the Chaumet Hortensia collection, Chaumet draws inspiration from the bloom known as the hydrangea, whose petals can be quite startling in their profusion, perfect geometry and vivid color. Each aspect of this once-familiar plant is transformed into a highly significant artistic element. The pale pink of budding emotion inhabits six pieces, which are carefully crafted in pink gold. Artfully evoking the confused jumble of emotions that accompanies first love, these pieces burst with flowers of different shapes, sizes and materials, created from a profusion of pink and angel-skin opal, pink sapphires, pink tourmaline and white

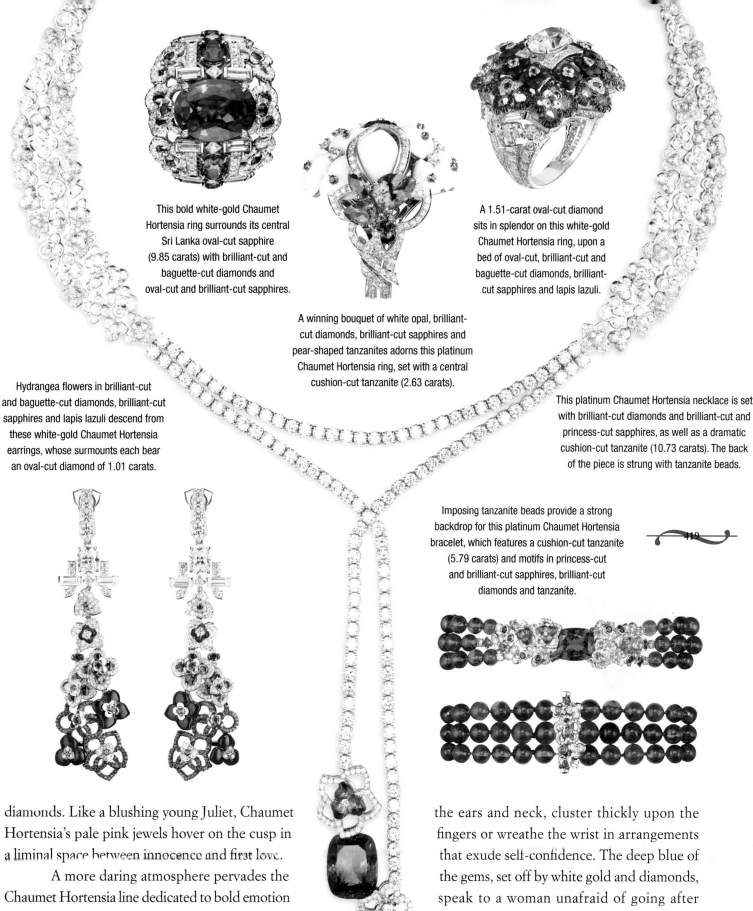

This bold white-gold Chaumet Hortensia ring surrounds its central Sri Lanka oval-cut sapphire (9.85 carats) with brilliant-cut and baguette-cut diamonds and oval-cut and brilliant-cut sapphires.

A winning bouquet of white opal, brilliant-cut diamonds, brilliant-cut sapphires and pear-shaped tanzanites adorns this platinum Chaumet Hortensia ring, set with a central cushion-cut tanzanite (2.63 carats).

A 1.51-carat oval-cut diamond sits in splendor on this white-gold Chaumet Hortensia ring, upon a bed of oval-cut, brilliant-cut and baguette-cut diamonds, brilliant-cut sapphires and lapis lazuli.

Hydrangea flowers in brilliant-cut and baguette-cut diamonds, brilliant-cut sapphires and lapis lazuli descend from these white-gold Chaumet Hortensia earrings, whose surmounts each bear an oval-cut diamond of 1.01 carats.

This platinum Chaumet Hortensia necklace is set with brilliant-cut diamonds and brilliant-cut and princess-cut sapphires, as well as a dramatic cushion-cut tanzanite (10.73 carats). The back of the piece is strung with tanzanite beads.

Imposing tanzanite beads provide a strong backdrop for this platinum Chaumet Hortensia bracelet, which features a cushion-cut tanzanite (5.79 carats) and motifs in princess-cut and brilliant-cut sapphires, brilliant-cut diamonds and tanzanite.

diamonds. Like a blushing young Juliet, Chaumet Hortensia's pale pink jewels hover on the cusp in a liminal space between innocence and first love.

A more daring atmosphere pervades the Chaumet Hortensia line dedicated to bold emotion and painted with blue sapphire, tanzanite and sculpted lapis lazuli. Lacy blossoms dangle from the ears and neck, cluster thickly upon the fingers or wreathe the wrist in arrangements that exude self-confidence. The deep blue of the gems, set off by white gold and diamonds, speak to a woman unafraid of going after what she wants—it is Juliet, remember, who proposes marriage to Romeo.

This splendid pink-gold Chaumet Hortensia necklace celebrates the thrill of passion with brilliant-cut rubies and pink sapphires, cushion-cut and troidia-cut rhodolite garnets, motifs of rhodolite garnets, cabochon-cut red tourmalines, 3 cushion-cut pink tourmalines (13.64 carats, 6.83 carats and 7.31 carats respectively), a cushion-cut red tourmaline (8.05 carats) and a cabochon-cut pear-shaped red tourmaline (25.68 carats).

Pink-gold earrings from the Chaumet Hortensia collection sparkle with brilliant-cut rubies, troidia-cut garnets, cabochon-cut red tourmalines and 2 drops of red tourmaline (8.57 carats).

After the initial intrigue and the thrill of the chase, comes the true flood of passion, celebrated in Chaumet Hortensia's pieces of deep emotion. True red is of course the color that dominates here—rubies, red garnets and tourmalines to signify the fiery essence of life, the salt and spice that flavors our every perception. The red hydrangea blooms upon these pieces with extravagant power, holding nothing

With a pink-gold dial pavé-set with rubies, and a pink-gold case set with petal-shaped and drop-shaped rubellites, diamonds, rubies and pink sapphires, this 34mm Chaumet Hortensia watch resembles a flower upon a bracelet of 3 rows of pearl-cut rubies with a rubellite-set clasp (119.56 carats total).

421

A bead of red tourmaline (23.83 carats) is the fiery star of this pink-gold Chaumet Hortensia ring, set with brilliant-cut rubies and pink sapphires.

back. Whether envisaged as one precious bloom of red tourmaline, as on the rings, or a wilderness of crimson flowers that covers the décolletage and provides a stunning setting for the aesthetic impact of large red and pink tourmalines, these jewels embody the all-encompassing pull of passion, which we are powerless to resist.

A flower blooms around a round faceted checkerboard pink tourmaline (8.61 carats), with brilliant-cut rubies, pink sapphires and diamonds set in pink gold, as well as petals in drops of red tourmaline, on this Chaumet Hortensia ring.

The rings of Chaumet's Liens collection take its theme—the French word liens means "ties" in English—very seriously. This family of twelve one-of-a-kind rings establishes ties both metaphorical and literal, incorporating Chaumet's distinctive blue into the jewels as an emblematic design element. The hoop of each ring is set with diamonds or blue sapphires in discrete, tight rows that call to mind a strong rope or cord. This gem-studded thread loops around the finger, creating intriguing, knotty designs of its own or plaiting with other gemstone motifs to convey a strong statement in white gold. Whether the central element consists of a woven white-gold lattice or an extraordinary gemstone—a role played in turn by blue sapphire, white diamond, violet tanzanite and blue tourmaline—the rings of the Liens collection stand in strong solidarity.

Chaumet

422

This white-gold Liens ring lassoes its central cushion-cut sapphire (7.33 carats) with loops of 34 sapphires and 27 baguette-cut diamonds.

A cushion-cut sapphire (10.69 carats) dominates this white-gold Liens ring, accented by 224 brilliant-cut diamonds and 4 triangular sapphires (2.84 carats each).

A geometric design guides this white-gold Liens ring, set with 14 baguette-cut diamonds, 100 brilliant-cut diamonds, 232 sapphires and featuring an emerald-cut sapphire (10.81 carats).

A pink-gold spider indicates the hours and a pink-gold fly the minutes on this unconventional complicated watch from the Attrape-Moi... Si Tu M'Aimes collection, which is crafted in white gold and set with 64 brilliant-cut diamonds (1.64 carats) on the case and 83 brilliant-cut diamonds on the mother-of-pearl dial.

The enchanting scene on the dial of this Attrape-Moi... Si Tu M'Aimes watch is comprised of a lapis lazuli sky (with pierrite dust representing the stars), inlaid with a white moon worked in seawater mother-of-pearl with pearl-effect. The flower appliqués are polished cabochon-cut dumortierit, the dragonfly, snails and caterpillar are engraved rounded mother-of-pearl, and the grass and ladybugs are painted in miniature by hand.

Butterflies in hand-cut blue polished agate and mother-of-pearl flutter among clouds set with 164 brilliant-cut diamonds on the dial of this Attrape-Moi... Si Tu M'Aimes watch.

Chaumet turned its attention to precious wristwatches in 1811, a full century before the notion of wearing a clock on the wrist had become widespread. The House continues an exquisite tradition with its extraordinary collection Attrape-Moi... Si Tu M'Aimes. The line uses the miniature dial of ladies' timepieces to depict a miniature world, a microcosmos of mayflies, dragonflies, butterflies and spiders that drift in the moonlight, flutter in concert or sidle up to their next meal. We are invited to think small, to recognize the perfect moments that pass by unnoticed in the hustle and bustle of everyday life. The minutely observed minutes—and hours—impress upon the imagination the wonder all around us, just as the finest haute jewelry reveals the astonishing treasures that the Earth holds just out of sight.

Chopard

The silver screen has long beckoned to those who work in gold and diamonds. Talented, magnetic, compelling women adorn themselves with jewels onscreen and—more often—off, sashaying down the red carpet in one-of-a-kind statement pieces from prestigious jewelry houses. Chopard understands this symbiotic relationship more profoundly than any other House, partnering with the Cannes International Film Festival in ways both large and small that underscore the jeweler's intimate relationship with cinema. World-class actresses from all over the globe embrace Chopard, wearing carefully crafted jewels that transform a special night into an unforgettable one.

Chopard

The partnership between Chopard and the Cannes Film Festival dates back to 1997, when the president of the Festival asked Caroline Scheufele, Co-President and Artistic Director of Chopard, to reinterpret the Festival's top prize—the iconic, highly coveted Palme d'Or. Caroline's fluid design, upon which the palm seems to be in gentle motion, soon become legendary in its own right. A closer look reveals two touches that betray Chopard's reverence for its subject: the palm's stem terminates in a heart shape, symbolizing a love of cinema, and the emerald-cut rock crystal upon which it sits is as inherently individual as a work of art.

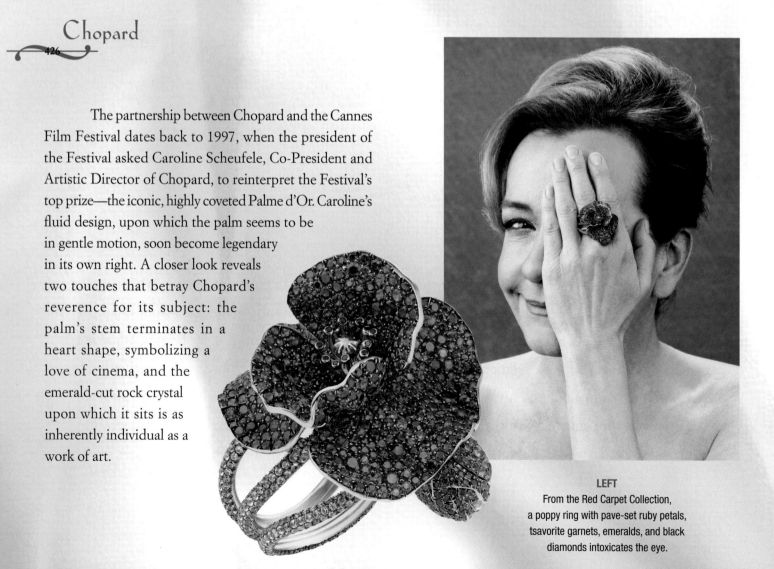

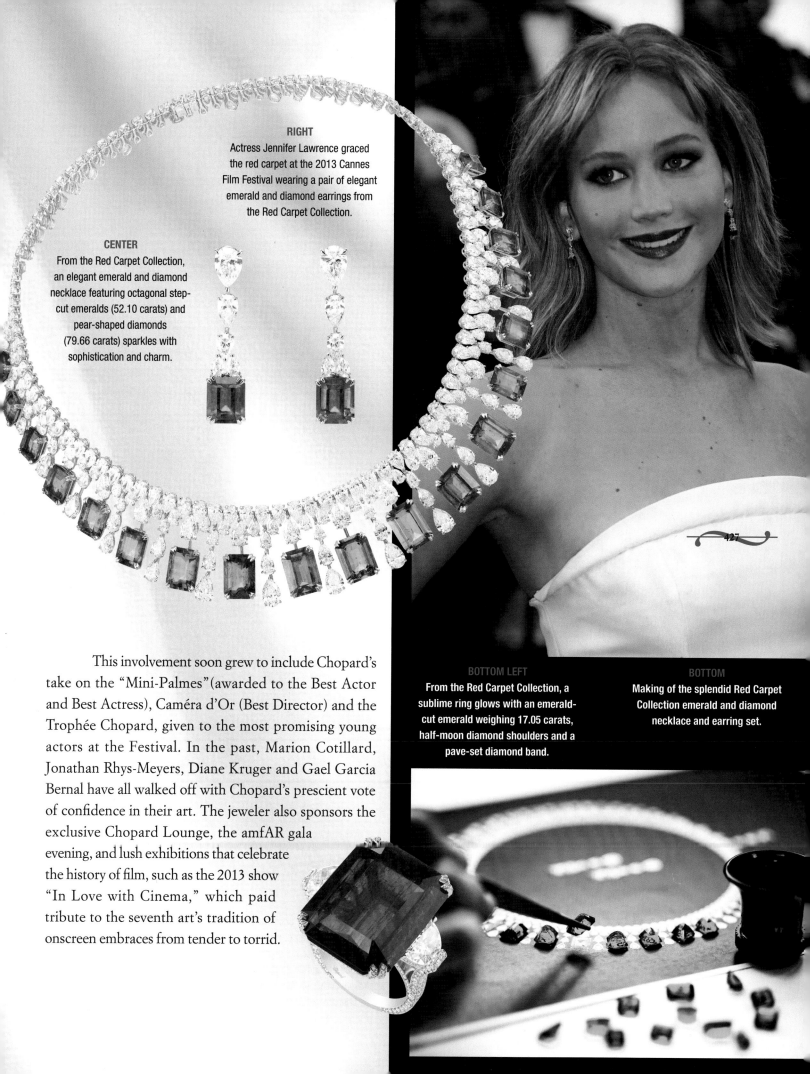

RIGHT
Actress Jennifer Lawrence graced the red carpet at the 2013 Cannes Film Festival wearing a pair of elegant emerald and diamond earrings from the Red Carpet Collection.

CENTER
From the Red Carpet Collection, an elegant emerald and diamond necklace featuring octagonal step-cut emeralds (52.10 carats) and pear-shaped diamonds (79.66 carats) sparkles with sophistication and charm.

BOTTOM LEFT
From the Red Carpet Collection, a sublime ring glows with an emerald-cut emerald weighing 17.05 carats, half-moon diamond shoulders and a pave-set diamond band.

BOTTOM
Making of the splendid Red Carpet Collection emerald and diamond necklace and earring set.

This involvement soon grew to include Chopard's take on the "Mini-Palmes" (awarded to the Best Actor and Best Actress), Caméra d'Or (Best Director) and the Trophée Chopard, given to the most promising young actors at the Festival. In the past, Marion Cotillard, Jonathan Rhys-Meyers, Diane Kruger and Gael Garcia Bernal have all walked off with Chopard's prescient vote of confidence in their art. The jeweler also sponsors the exclusive Chopard Lounge, the amfAR gala evening, and lush exhibitions that celebrate the history of film, such as the 2013 show "In Love with Cinema," which paid tribute to the seventh art's tradition of onscreen embraces from tender to torrid.

At its heart, however, Chopard is a jeweler, and the most fitting way in which it honors the grandeur and glamour of the Cannes Film Festival is in its preferred medium of precious materials and impeccable craftsmanship, directed by a passionate imagination. The Red Carpet collection is a unique family of haute jewelry pieces that Chopard's artisans create from scratch every year. The number of pieces in the collection always matches the number of Festival editions to date; for the Festival's 66th year in 2013, Chopard sent out 66 precious jewels to adorn the ears, fingers, wrists and throats of the Festival's most elite attendees as they participated in the famous "mounting of the steps" ritual on Cannes's Croisette.

For the 2013 Red Carpet collection, Caroline drew inspiration from cinema's great love stories. "Love is universal," she explains. "It illuminates women's beauty, like a beautiful piece of jewelry. I very much wanted to pay tribute to the finest sentiments. The Red Carpet collection is thus adorned in shimmering colors, red accents, like the fire of passion and heart-shaped precious stones, one of favorite cuts." Each piece is its own love story, acted out in miniature. A ring costumed as an intoxicating poppy

From the Red Carpet Collection, this extraordinary pair of earrings is set with two round-cut emeralds (22.66 carats and 24.86 carats respectively), surrounded by briolette-cut diamonds.

From the Red Carpet Collection, this exquisite ring features a cushion-shaped emerald (30.07 carats) upon a meadow of diamond flowers and diamond set band.

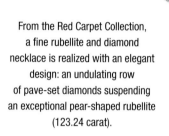

From the Red Carpet Collection,
a fine rubellite and diamond
necklace is realized with an elegant
design: an undulating row
of pave-set diamonds suspending
an exceptional pear-shaped rubellite
(123.24 carat).

flower flings its petals across
the fingers, or a heart-shaped
Paraiba tourmaline commands
the stage. Rubies, emeralds,
tanzanites, sapphires and—of
course—white diamonds follow
wildly creative scripts, appearing first
in one guise, then another. Lighthearted romps shine in the
collection, as do lush period pieces, sober, serious dramas
and artistic works that defy categorization.

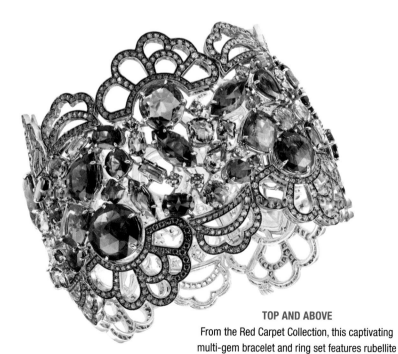

TOP AND ABOVE
From the Red Carpet Collection, this captivating
multi-gem bracelet and ring set features rubellite
tourmalines, spinels, amethysts, morganites,
blue sapphires, tanzanites, pink sapphires, rubies,
violet sapphires and diamonds.

429

**Supermodel Erin Heatherton
sparkled in an opulent ruby
and diamond necklace from
the Red Carpet Collection
at the 2013 Cannes Film Festival.**

Reese Witherspoon, Cara Delevingne and Fan Bingbing shined in Chopard at the Cannes Film Festival.

Chopard

430

From the Red Carpet Collection, this heartfelt ring, crafted in 18-karat white gold, is set with a heart-shaped Paraiba tourmaline (15.05 carats) and diamonds.

From the Red Carpet Collection, this ring, crafted in 18-karat white gold, is set with a pear-shaped Paraiba tourmaline (22.89 carats) entwined with pavé-set diamonds.

From the Red Carpet Collection, this spectacular ring featuring a pear-shaped diamond weighing 23.02 carats and a pavé-set diamond band.

The Red Carpet collection joins Chopard's other exquisite lines with its characteristic blend of exuberance and refinement. The care and meticulousness apparent in a detail like the Chopard "diamond ribbon" that cradles a ring's impressive central stone plays a role in all of Chopard's creations. Perhaps this is why the world's loveliest women choose Chopard on the biggest nights of their lives.

From the Red Carpet Collection, this sublime diamond watch features diamond flower petals.

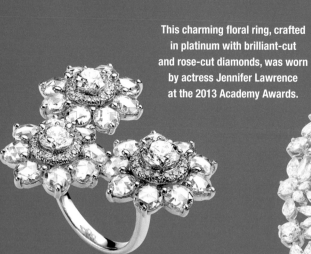

This charming floral ring, crafted in platinum with brilliant-cut and rose-cut diamonds, was worn by actress Jennifer Lawrence at the 2013 Academy Awards.

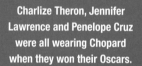

From the Red Carpet Collection, this divine necklace is set with a series of diamond-set rising sun motifs (43.95 carats).

Crafted in 18-karat white gold, these earrings set with old-cut and rose-cut diamonds were worn by actress Jennifer Lawrence at the 2013 Academy Awards.

OSCAR'S LUCKY CHARM

Some actors may have a hidden reason for choosing Chopard: the small gold statuette that Hollywood considers the ultimate accessory. Chopard has dressed winners of the Academy Awards for 10 consecutive years. Given the number of Oscar winners who have collected their trophy while wearing Chopard's elegant jewelry and watches—a list that includes Charlize Theron, Hilary Swank, Rachel Weisz, Helen Mirren, Marion Cotillard, Kate Winslet, Penelope Cruz, Mo'Nique, Colin Firth, Michel Hazanavicius and Jennifer Lawrence— one might be forgiven a touch of superstition!

Charlize Theron, Jennifer Lawrence and Penelope Cruz were all wearing Chopard when they won their Oscars.

de GRISOGONO

The Haute Jewelry collection released by de GRISOGONO to celebrate its twentieth anniversary is replete with the unique sparks that characterize all the house's pieces. A breathtaking necklace highlights emeralds and diamonds with an opulent, maximalist flair, flaunting several strands of gems in varying sizes and cuts. A row of extraordinary Colombian emerald cabochons draws the eye to the center of the piece. This necklace highlights much of what makes de GRISOGONO such an important house: the meticulously designed, yet relaxed, lines of the piece, the profusion of precious stones and the impeccable craftsmanship that graces every millimeter.

Every once in a great while, a visionary bursts onto the scene. His or her particular gift is not just bringing to life the fantastical pictures one sees in dreams; it is making the rest of us see the world through a new set of eyes. de GRISOGONO, which celebrated its twentieth anniversary in 2013, brought to light such an exceptional talent in its founder Fawaz Gruosi. Not only does the house create a host of spectacular creations year after year, but it has also introduced wholly new precious materials to a field in which less imaginative people thought there was nothing left to discover.

In 1993, Fawaz brought his dream of jewelry to life. He saw a gap between what fine jewelry currently had to offer—a lovely yet tradition-bound selection of

de GRISOGONO

This ferocious hippo bracelet, crafted in white and pink gold, sparkles with 1,705 brown diamonds (121.50 carats), 61 gray diamonds (1.98 carats), 110 white diamonds (1.88 carats), 38 rubies (2.00 carats), 22 pink sapphires (1.65 carats), 2 cabochon rubies (1.90 carats) and 2 oval

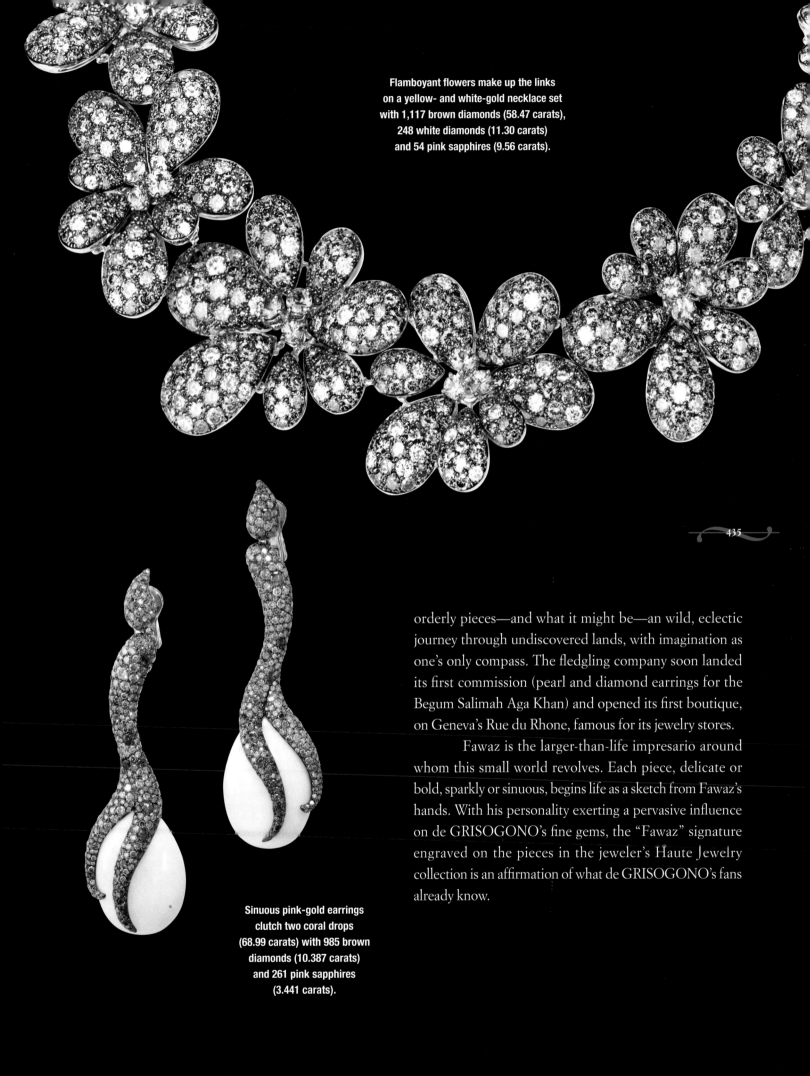

Flamboyant flowers make up the links on a yellow- and white-gold necklace set with 1,117 brown diamonds (58.47 carats), 248 white diamonds (11.30 carats) and 54 pink sapphires (9.56 carats).

Sinuous pink-gold earrings clutch two coral drops (68.99 carats) with 985 brown diamonds (10.387 carats) and 261 pink sapphires (3.441 carats).

orderly pieces—and what it might be—an wild, eclectic journey through undiscovered lands, with imagination as one's only compass. The fledgling company soon landed its first commission (pearl and diamond earrings for the Begum Salimah Aga Khan) and opened its first boutique, on Geneva's Rue du Rhone, famous for its jewelry stores.

Fawaz is the larger-than-life impresario around whom this small world revolves. Each piece, delicate or bold, sparkly or sinuous, begins life as a sketch from Fawaz's hands. With his personality exerting a pervasive influence on de GRISOGONO's fine gems, the "Fawaz" signature engraved on the pieces in the jeweler's Haute Jewelry collection is an affirmation of what de GRISOGONO's fans already know.

Dramatic and playful, these white-gold haute jewelry earrings star one round-cut white diamond K VS1 (10.25 carats) and one round-cut white diamond J VVS1 (10.07 carats), with a surrounding of 2,120 white diamonds (33.35 carats) and 795 rubies (4.44 carats).

Expertly selected gems abound throughout the Haute Jewelry collection: diamonds, emeralds, rubies, yellow and blue sapphires—and, of course, Fawaz's cherished black diamonds. These gems have long been the special sign of de GRISOGONO and Fawaz, who discovered their particular luster in the mid-1990s. Recognizing the dramatic potential inherent in this heretofore underappreciated stone, Fawaz embraced its challenges, releasing an entire collection devoted to exploring its possibilities. A mere two years later, the value of black diamonds had increased by a factor of 35! Not content to rest on his laurels, Fawaz turned his sights to other materials that had slipped under the radar, creating haute jewelry pieces with Icy Diamonds (milky-looking gems with a high degree of fluorescence) and Browny Brown Gold (a warm, chocolate-y version of the beloved metal).

LEFT AND RIGHT
Supermodel Irina Shayk wears de GRISOGONO's Haute Jewelry earrings and Tubetto ring in white gold, set with 235 white diamonds (7.27 carats).

TOP LEFT
Supermodel Bianca Balti wears de GRISOGONO at amfAR's 20th Annual Cinema Against AIDS gala.

TOP RIGHT
Displaying de GRISOGONO's affection for the black diamond, these white-gold earrings are set with 1,038 black diamonds (25.014 carats), which set off 659 white diamonds (2.175 carats) and 6 fancy-shape white diamonds (15.088 carats).

CENTER
A series of concentric circles dominates this white-gold Haute Jewelry ring, set with one round-cut diamond H VS1 (6.39 carats) surrounded by 79 white diamond discs (8.54 carats), 448 white diamonds (0.79 carat) and 513 black diamonds (12.72 carats).

This open attitude and willingness to leap headfirst into new passions defines what jewelry aficionados love about de GRISOGONO. The jeweler's pieces are immediately recognizable, and completely distinct from any other company's work. Not only do the designs spiral in all directions, using unexpected combinations of material and color to play with our notions of movement and symmetry, but they each feature impeccable craftsmanship, down to the intricately carved backing of each piece, which has become a hallmark of the house.

Fan-shaped white-gold earrings use arcs to convey motion with 2 round-cut white diamonds F VS2 (10.16 carats), 119 white diamond discs (10.01 carats), 832 white diamonds (3.14 carats) and 415 black diamonds (13.68 carats)

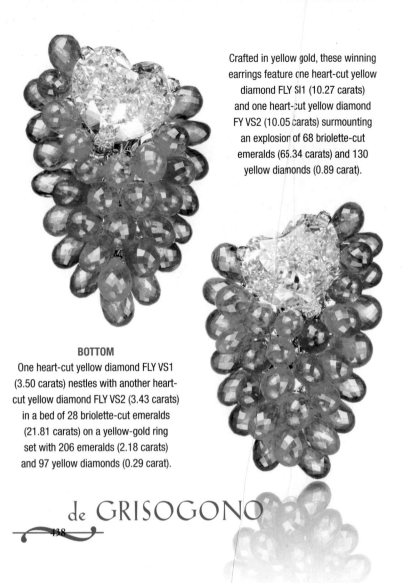

Crafted in yellow gold, these winning earrings feature one heart-cut yellow diamond FLY SI1 (10.27 carats) and one heart-cut yellow diamond FY VS2 (10.05 carats) surmounting an explosion of 68 briolette-cut emeralds (65.34 carats) and 130 yellow diamonds (0.89 carat).

BOTTOM
One heart-cut yellow diamond FLY VS1 (3.50 carats) nestles with another heart-cut yellow diamond FLY VS2 (3.43 carats) in a bed of 28 briolette-cut emeralds (21.81 carats) on a yellow-gold ring set with 206 emeralds (2.18 carats) and 97 yellow diamonds (0.29 carat).

de GRISOGONO

Among the fervent followers of Fawaz are some of the world's most beautiful women. At the opening of the jeweler's first boutique, film legend Sophia Loren graced the evening with her presence, marking the start of a tradition cherished by the jeweler and its famous fans alike. In 2001, de GRISOGONO became a presence at the Cannes Film Festival, throwing a spectacular party that left the whole festival abuzz... and Cannes hasnot stopped buzzing since! Fawaz has said of his relationship with the famed festival, "The most memorable party for me was the first one in Cannes. It's like having your first child." Sharon Stone, Naomi Campbell Isabelle Adjani and Irina Shayk are just a few of the world-class stunners who conider it a privilege to wear de GRISOGONO down the worlds most elegant red carpet.

RIGHT
Supermodel and philanthropist
Petra Nemcova wears Haute Jewelry
pieces from de GRISOGONO.

LEFT
Layered luxury swings freely with
these pink-gold earrings from the
Jane collection, set with 1,144 white
diamonds (19.82 carats) and 624 white
Icy diamonds (42.36 carats).

BOTTOM
A fantastical flower set with
2,664 white diamonds is the stunning
centerpiece of this one-of-a-kind
pink-gold bracelet.

The unique perspective of de GRISOGONO's collections is so specific that it ultimately becomes universal. Atypical of any particular time or place, the design becomes a point of view that anyone in the world can adopt, and the world has taken this project very seriously. de GRISOGONO pieces appear in fine jewelry establishments on five continents, and the jeweler's own boutiques pepper the European landscape, as well as operating in the United States, Russia and the Middle East. The inspiration that Fawaz draws from nature, abstractions in color and crystal, shines a light into all corners, irresistibly drawing lovers of haute jewelry towards de GRISOGONO like so many moths to the flame of unbridled imagination.

THIS PAGE

This platinum necklace from the Gallop collection is set with round-, princess- and baguette-cut diamonds (13.38 carats), providing an elegant counterpoint for the 18-karat white-gold Gallop earrings, which are set with round-, princess- and baguette-cut diamonds (4.00 carats).

FACING PAGE

These white- and yellow-gold earrings from the Gallop collection are set with fancy intense yellow diamonds (3.18 carats) and white round-, princess- and baguette-cut diamonds (3.65 carats).

Gumuchian

In the world of fine jewelry, the question "What do women want?" always involves another, less-pondered query: "What will women wear?" As skilled, inventive designers and jewelry aficionados who wear nothing but their own creations, Myriam and Patricia Gumuchian work with their mother Anita to carry on a family legacy that is now in its fourth generation of providing women with beautiful, exceptionally versatile jewelry that can take a woman from day to night, from ring to bracelet, from thrilling event to cherished memory.

TOP AND BOTTOM

This 18-karat pink-gold daisy ring
from the Ring Cycle collection
boasts pavé-set petals with round-
cut diamonds (0.72 carats)... which
add extra sparkle when the ring
unfolds into a bracelet.

CENTER

Set with a central round-cut
diamond (0.05 carat), this
understated 18-karat pink-
gold daisy hides a clasp
that facilitates the ring's
transformation into a bracelet.

Gumuchian

RING CYCLE

Richard Wagner's Ring Cycle is one of the world's most esteemed operas, full of heroic deeds, golden apples and, naturally, some irresistible jewelry. Gumuchian's own Ring Cycle line might not be quite as epic in scope, but it is as alluring as the Ring of the Nibelung, and there is certainly more than meets the eye in the collection's various components. One overriding concept guides the line, that of versatility. At first glance, each ring seems to have a simple design: that of an 18-karat yellow, white or rose gold flower perched upon an unusually generous hoop. A closer look, however, reveals the secret hidden within: far from being a homogenous component, the ring's hoop actually consists of several bands, hinged together and edged with a petal motif. Another hidden clasp behind the central flower and voilà!—the simple ring has become a delicate daisy chain of a bracelet. In a further nod to the varied needs of the modern woman, the central flower is available with either a single diamond at the center, or flamboyant full-pavé petals

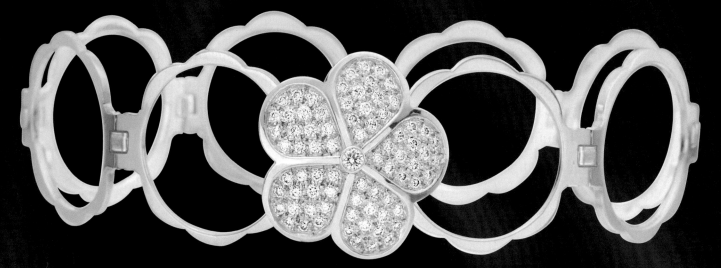

LEFT
A dramatic 5-row structure dominates this Harem ring from the Nutmeg collection, alternating 18-karat pink-gold bands with bezels set with 14 round-cut diamonds (0.50 carat).

RIGHT
Crafted in warm 18-karat pink gold, these Nutmeg earrings intersperse the spice motif with 6 round-cut diamonds (0.26 carat).

443

NUTMEG

With its Nutmeg collection, Gumuchian reminds us that at one time, spices were even more highly valued than gold. In bangles, hoop earrings and simple rings, the round, distinctively "veiny" shape of the seed crops up as a recurring motif, interspersed with the high-quality diamonds Gumuchian uses in all its collections. Once thought to protect its consumer from the plague, nutmeg loans its mystical medicinal properties to fine jewels— which, throughout history, have also been credited with curing or preventing disease. Gumuchian's Harem rings, which comprise part of the Nutmeg collection, take the powerful spice—which has hallucinogenic effects when consumed in extreme quantities—and turns up the volume. The familiar nutmeg motif is now combined with diamond bands in alternating precious stripes, though always in uneven numbers, as is all but required practice for wearing multiple bangles or rings.

This 3-row Harem ring from the Nutmeg collection includes a line of 7 round-cut diamonds (0.25 carat) between the 18-karat pink-gold nutmeg motifs.

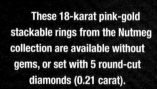

These 18-karat pink-gold stackable rings from the Nutmeg collection are available without gems, or set with 5 round-cut diamonds (0.21 carat).

BOWLERO

Seizing upon the
grace and whimsy
of fluttering ribbons
as an emblem of carefree
femininity, Gumuchian combines
them with the enchanting rhythms of Spanish
dance for the Bowlero collection. Crafted in platinum,
encrusted with diamonds, the bows of Bowlero abound

TOP
Crafted in platinum, these
charming Bowlero stud earrings
scintillate with round-cut
diamonds (0.73 carat).

CENTER
This charming Bowlero necklace
sparkles with an assortment
of round-cut and marquise-cut
diamonds (7.25 carats).

in playful loops, and
diamond-set chains
that drip from a pair
of earrings capture the
glittering, sensual magic
of ribbons flying freely in the
breeze. The line's necklaces explore
the possibilities of this motif even more extensively,
incorporating not only multiple diamond chains, but strands
that seem to twist and form smaller bows of their own.

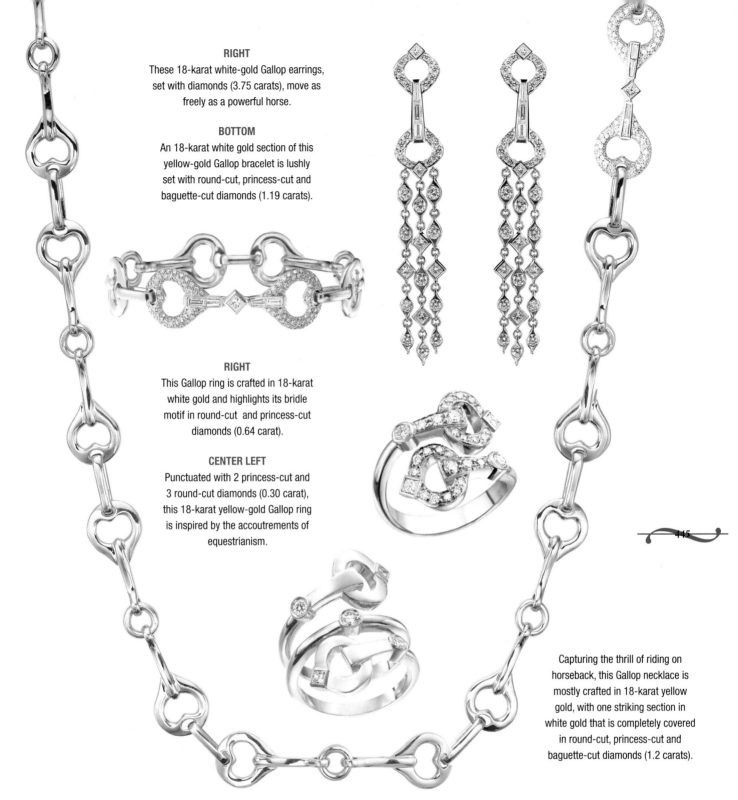

RIGHT

These 18-karat white-gold Gallop earrings, set with diamonds (3.75 carats), move as freely as a powerful horse.

BOTTOM

An 18-karat white gold section of this yellow-gold Gallop bracelet is lushly set with round-cut, princess-cut and baguette-cut diamonds (1.19 carats).

RIGHT

This Gallop ring is crafted in 18-karat white gold and highlights its bridle motif in round-cut and princess-cut diamonds (0.64 carat).

CENTER LEFT

Punctuated with 2 princess-cut and 3 round-cut diamonds (0.30 carat), this 18-karat yellow-gold Gallop ring is inspired by the accoutrements of equestrianism.

445

Capturing the thrill of riding on horseback, this Gallop necklace is mostly crafted in 18-karat yellow gold, with one striking section in white gold that is completely covered in round-cut, princess-cut and baguette-cut diamonds (1.2 carats).

GALLOP

The Gallop necklace is also supremely flexible, with hidden clasps that subtly hook and unhook to provide a plethora of options for the busy modern woman. A sense of power and movement pervades the entire collection, stemming from Gumuchian's equestrian inspiration. The visual motifs of bridle and reins infiltrate each piece in its own way, crafting the icons in 18-karat white, yellow or rose gold and adding a classic touch of femininity. The collection strides around wrists, curls around fingers, dangles from the ears like a pair of stirrups, and puts the iconic necklace through its paces.

Round-cut diamonds in their centers (0.04 carat) make these yellow-gold Floating Daisy stud earrings sparkle with life.

This charming, open Floating Daisy ring features diamond pavé (0.90 carat) on its flowers' petals.

Combining a yellow-gold chain and a white-gold daisy motif, this G Boutique pendant glimmers with white diamonds (0.28 carat).

G BOUTIQUE

The clean lines of the petals on these Floating Lotus frame round-cut diamonds (1.18 carats).

In its quest to provide a range of options for every jewelry lover, the Gumuchian women expand the palette with their G Boutique line, honing the jeweler's distinctive look to the essentials. A sophisticated, understated garden awaits the cognoscenti, with cheerful floral pieces that brighten fingers, wrists, ears and necks.

White-gold lotus flowers dazzle with round-cut diamond pavé (0.70 carat) on this G Boutique Floating Lotus ring.

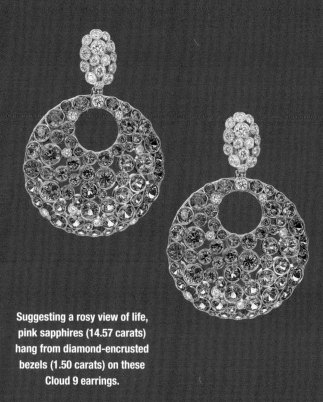

As blue as the heavens, these 18-karat white-gold Cloud 9 earrings are set with round-cut diamonds (1.50 carats) and sapphires (14.90 carats).

Suggesting a rosy view of life, pink sapphires (14.57 carats) hang from diamond-encrusted bezels (1.50 carats) on these Cloud 9 earrings.

Set with white diamonds (1.50 carats) and yellow sapphires (14.68 carats), these Cloud 9 earrings capture the golden light of pure pleasure.

One hundred sixty-six round-cut white diamonds (13.08 carats) shine from every inch of these white-gold Cloud 9 earrings, conveying the purity of bliss.

CLOUD 9

Crafted in billowing waves of colored sapphires and white diamonds, the Cloud 9 collection offers just that: a soothing tide of elation for women who love jewelry with a visual impact. Earrings link diamond clusters to sophisticated, chic hoop-inspired shapes whose outlines are filled by lacy mosaics of white diamonds or sapphires in blue, pink or yellow. Three-dimensional rings offer a similar aesthetic oomph, limning each stone in platinum or 18-karat yellow, white or rose gold. The resulting effect is that of solid, all but unscratchable precious stones transformed into an airy, ethereal ornament.

THIS PAGE
This flower-inspired ring is set with 15.25 carats
of vivid yellow diamonds.

FACING PAGE
Guy Ellia's spectacular diamond selection shines
to perfection on this vivid yellow diamond set,
which comprises a rivière necklace (70.26 carats)
and floral-inspired ring (15.25 carats).

Guy Ellia

A rare but documented physiological phenomenon, Stendhal syndrome causes its victims to feel dizzy or even faint when faced with overwhelming or extreme beauty. To elicit this reaction in those who see Guy Ellia's jewelry collections is the founder's declared objective, and many would agree that these bold, exuberant jewels have the potential to—at the very least—make one see stars. A purity of vision shines from these pieces, whose utterly refined silhouettes scintillate with the most precious materials. One fancy yellow diamond rivière necklace expresses this philosophy perfectly, creating a strong visual impact with an elemental shape and perfect harmony of shape, size, color and line.

449

Guy Ellia pieces draw life from the world itself—not just the materials that give physical presence to their elegant contours, but the bristling energy of street art, the extravagant perspectives of haute couture, the serendipity of natural beauty and the subtle details that often pass unnoticed. From this constantly bubbling pot of inspiration, Guy Ellia emerges with designs that find the eternal in the ephemeral, creating essential collections for passionate women. A set in multi-colored diamonds embodies this imaginative diversity: the organic-looking arrangement of the precious gemstones evokes the spontaneous unfurling of a flower, the fleeting moments of a fireworks display or the youthful impudence of a hastily scribbled graffito.

The use of different shades of diamonds is also characteristic of Guy Ellia's jewelry, treating the variety of hues as a nearly endless palette of possibilities, as well as an intriguing technical puzzle. Creating an entire set, matching size to size and shade to shade, is an undertaking that only the most confident jewelers carry off with ease.

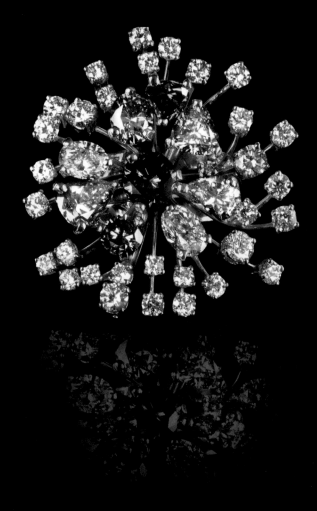

ABOVE
The Bollywood at Sunset pendant captures the fiery intensity of the sun with multi-colored diamonds in a white-gold setting.

RIGHT
The Soleiado ring bursts with energy, using white gold to hold multi-colored diamonds in a radiant design.

The Soleidao ring, in white gold with white, yellow and brown diamonds, makes an exquisite partner to Guy Ellia's Douze watch in white gold, whose bezel and crown are set with diamonds.

452

Located at 16 Place Vendôme, Guy Ellia translates that historic setting into jewels that tell a story steeped in tradition, as well as a constant infusion of fresh creativity and vivacity. The spirit of the place and the beauty of Guy Ellia's reception area permeate each piece, with the sparkle of the chandeliers, the delicacy of the architectural bas-relief and the curve of the alcove finding expression in diamonds—a favorite material of the House—and other materials, such as pearls, mother-of-pearl and white opal.

A diamond-set bird with an emerald eye perches on a true treasure—an intense yellow VS1 diamond (52.12 carats)—on the Milan Royal brooch.

Featuring a wide array of approaches—from simple, minimalist pieces to the most opulent one-of-a-kind creations—Guy Ellia's jewels sparkle with possibility. They invite women to explore the possibilities inherent in themselves as well; this may be why Guy Ellia collections are so beloved by contemporary women—confident women who pride themselves on taking charge of their lives, lighting up rooms with the force of their personalities and not just their impeccable adornments.

Suspended from delicate interlocking filigrees set with 664 baguette-cut diamonds, the Himalaya necklace stars a DFL Golconda diamond at its heart (20.16 carats).

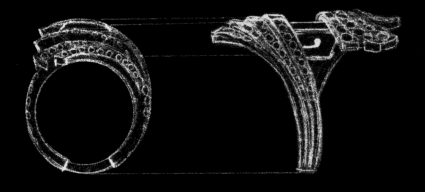

Sketches for the Sparkling Lady ring and the Dazzling Lady watch and bracelet reveal the keen artistic mind at work in the jewelry-making process.

Moving beyond rings and necklaces, Guy Ellia applies the slippery complexities of the bracelet to the jeweler's extensive watch collection. Whatever their size, Guy Ellia's watch bracelets fit like a second skin, regardless of the number of carats or the richness of the design. The ingenious, luxurious bracelets correspond perfectly with the timepieces they support, which range from minimalist dials to highly complicated masterpieces with diameters of 50mm or more.

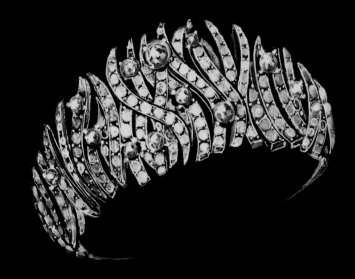

The platinum and white-gold Dazzling Lady secret watch, from Guy Ellia's Collection Haute-Joaillerie, hides a simple, square, mother-of pearl dial, and behind it the Jaeger-LeCoultre 601 caliber. Interlacing flames, paved with 448 brilliant-cut diamonds, are accented with diamonds up to 1 carat in size for a total of 33.32 carats. With this exceptional piece, Guy Ellia joins the company's expertise in haute horology and haute jewelry.

455

The Les Boules collection includes a classic 40-inch 18-karat white-gold lariat necklace with full- and rose-cut diamond boules and matching 18-karat white-gold earrings with full- and rose-cut diamond boules, worn here with a pair of striking diamond-pavé bangles with black onyx, one with scalloped edges and the other in a cushion shape, an outrageous bombé-shaped onyx and diamond cuff in 18-karat white gold and a chic oval rose-cut diamond bangle in 18-karat white gold.

FACING PAGE

A match made in heaven: a platinum pendant with a Deco dream of diamonds embracing an impressive 17.35-carat blue sapphire meets a platinum ring featuring an opulent blue sapphire (7.15 carats) surrounded by perfectly symmetrical diamond baguettes.

Hammerman Brothers

A family business for 75 years, Hammerman Brothers upholds the tradition upon which it has built its reputation: creating jewels of such high quality that they become instant heirlooms. Eschewing the recent trend of outsourcing production, the brother and sister team behind Hammerman continues to design and fabricate the brand's jewelry in house, in its New York City atelier. This allows Hammerman to maintain strict control over all phases of production, ensuring an exceptionally high level of quality. This meticulous creation process lies behind the guarantee of the house's motto: "Hammerman Made – American Made."

RIGHT
This striking Medallion pendant in 18-karat yellow gold features diamond-laden swirls in a finely designed pattern.

LEFT
This Sunburst Medallion earring in 18-karat yellow gold sparkles with an intricate setting of cognac and white diamonds.

The Hammerman name stands for heritage, for hand-craftsmanship—and for happiness. It is known as "the house behind the houses," due to its history of producing haute jewelry for prestigious companies such as Tiffany & Co. In a landscape of fleeting trends, finding stunning jewelry with craftsmanship to match is a rare joy. Unless, that is, one is familiar with Hammerman's finely wrought pieces, which combine artisanal expertise with inventive, eclectic designs in collections that use a vast array of precious materials to interpret an even more diverse range of inspiration. Combining their talents, Brett and Darcy Hammerman can conceptualize a piece, sketch out a design, source exceptional stones that bring it to life, construct it to last a lifetime and interpret it in new and unexpected ways, with uniquely conceived precious materials.

RIGHT
This 18-karat rose-gold cuff
features a celebration of rose-cut
diamonds.

BOTTOM
A singular sensation, this 18-karat
yellow-gold ring uses a bed of
white diamonds to accent a central
orange sapphire (12.5 carats).

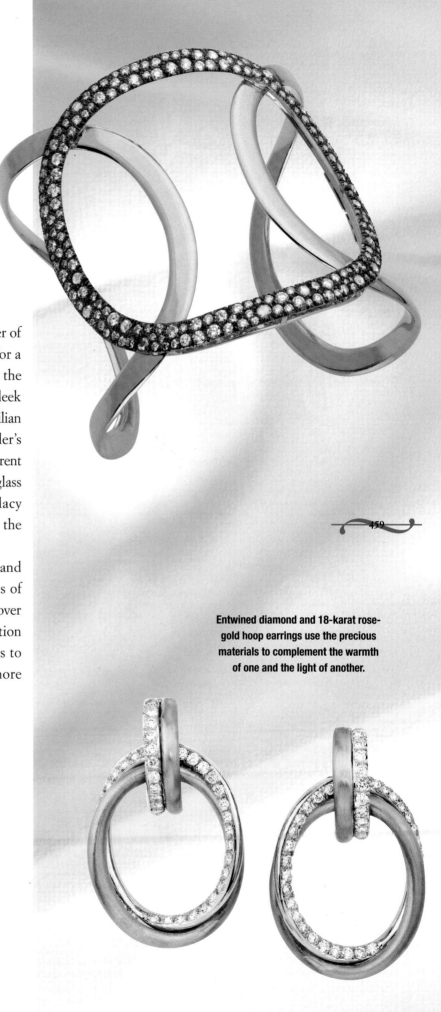

The design process can begin from any number of starting points. Sometimes a stone will spark an idea for a one-of-a-kind piece. For example, a stunning ring in the form of a snake provides the slithering animal with a sleek black opal body, whose natural shape suggested the reptilian form to Brett. A popular collection, such as the jeweler's Flowers necklaces, might beg to be reinterpreted in different colors of gold and gemstones, or the legendary stained glass windows of Notre Dame Cathedral might inspire lacy pendant medallions whose intricate designs speak to the quality of its fabrication.

"We stand for better product, better design and better quality," says Brett. These are the main tenets of Hammerman's design philosophy, which ranges widely over styles and approaches. The company's diverse collection encompasses everything from necklaces and earrings to watches and cufflinks, from a $1 million ring to a more casual look that is still refined and elegant.

459

Entwined diamond and 18-karat rose-gold hoop earrings use the precious materials to complement the warmth of one and the light of another.

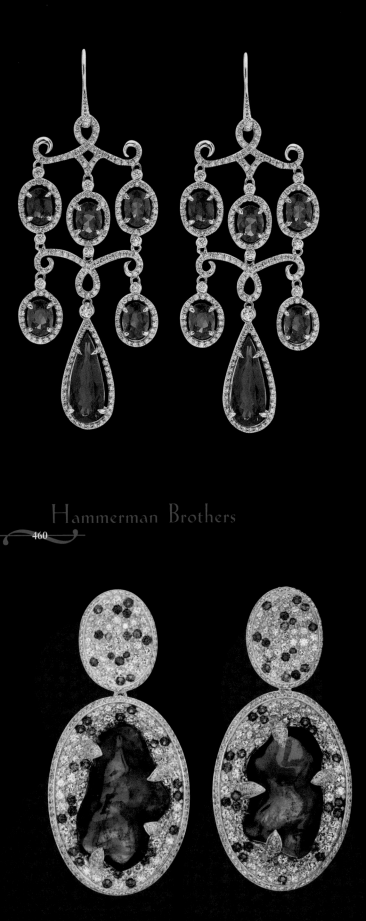

TOP

These superb rubellite and diamond micro-pavé fringe chandelier earrings in 18-karat white gold lend a tinge of effortless elegance to any wardrobe.

ABOVE

These exuberant 18-karat white-gold earrings capture an explosion of rubellites and pink sapphires against a backdrop of diamonds.

TOP RIGHT

A spectacular serpent uncoils from this 18-karat white-gold ring, set with black opal, emeralds, sapphires and diamonds.

BOTTOM RIGHT

Crystal briolettes in a diamond sling lend an icy flair to these 18-karat white-gold earrings, which also feature surmounts of diamond balls.

Hammerman's collections exemplify this comprehensive approach to design, sometimes in more ways than one. The Amorphous collection features naturally shaped stones on an oval pavé-set background, and contains interpretations that range from candy-colored pink tourmaline to an austere yet opulent field of white diamonds. Les Boules is a line of earrings and necklaces

characterized by three-dimensional, rounded, pavé-set teardrop shapes that can be affixed or removed at will using invisible screws, providing the luxury of versatility. Also versatile is a limited edition collection of *objets d'art* that appear to be miniature Grecian urns, complete with classical scenes in golden relief. The urns can also be worn as brooches.

TOP
Platinum and diamonds chime in perfect harmony on these geometric earrings.

CENTER
A triple strand of diamonds (28 carats) scintillates several times over on this Art Deco-inspired 18-karat white-gold necklace.

RIGHT
This spectacular chandelier pendant necklace boasts diamonds and azure blue sapphires (23 carats) in 18-karat white gold.

One aspect of Hammerman's collections that makes them so popular is the range of options they provide. Interpreting an idea in several different arrays of gemstones and precious metal offers a range of price points to the jewelry aficionado. Noting the rise in popularity of pink and blue diamonds, exceptionally rare gems that can sell for millions of dollars—per carat—Brett fashioned 100 unique pieces using high-quality aquamarine and kunzite as central

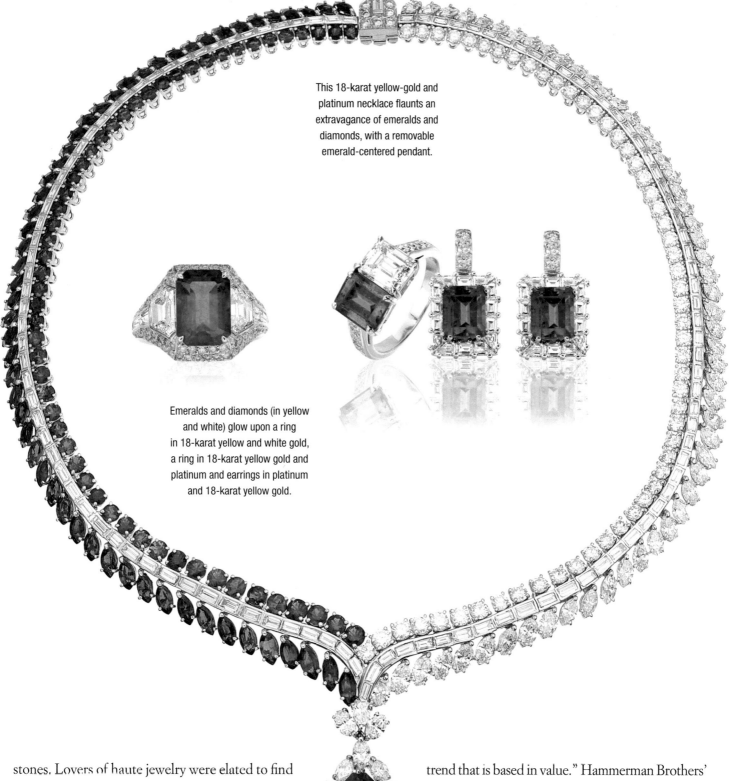

This 18-karat yellow-gold and platinum necklace flaunts an extravagance of emeralds and diamonds, with a removable emerald-centered pendant.

Emeralds and diamonds (in yellow and white) glow upon a ring in 18-karat yellow and white gold, a ring in 18-karat yellow gold and platinum and earrings in platinum and 18-karat yellow gold.

stones. Lovers of haute jewelry were elated to find a look that went for five figures instead of eight, with exquisite craftsmanship to boot.

The jeweler's focus on painstakingly wrought, high-quality fine jewelry has set Hammerman Brothers outside the rush and flow of passing fashion. "We can't make pieces fast enough to follow the trends," explains Brett. "We *create* trends—we create a feeling and a trend that is based in value." Hammerman Brothers' collections are fashionable, true, but they have a foundation of deep jewelry expertise that surpasses fleeting vogues and roots each piece firmly in the realm of the timeless. These are investment pieces for the discerning jewelry connoisseur, whom Brett succinctly describes as, "a woman who is aware of trends but unique in her style."

THIS PAGE
Madonna wears Jacob & Co.'s diamond mesh glove from the Rare Touch collection, which is crafted in 18-karat white gold and set with 17.88 carats of round brilliant-cut diamonds.

FACING PAGE
Flaunting the jeweler's sumptuous collection of colored diamonds, this white-gold cocktail ring features a yellow oval-cut diamond (16.12 carats) flanked by two matching yellow oval-cut diamonds (16.06 carats), with the centerpiece surrounded by pear-shape white diamonds (5.59 carats) and pavé-set round brilliant-cut white and yellow diamonds (3.06 carats).

Jacob & Co.

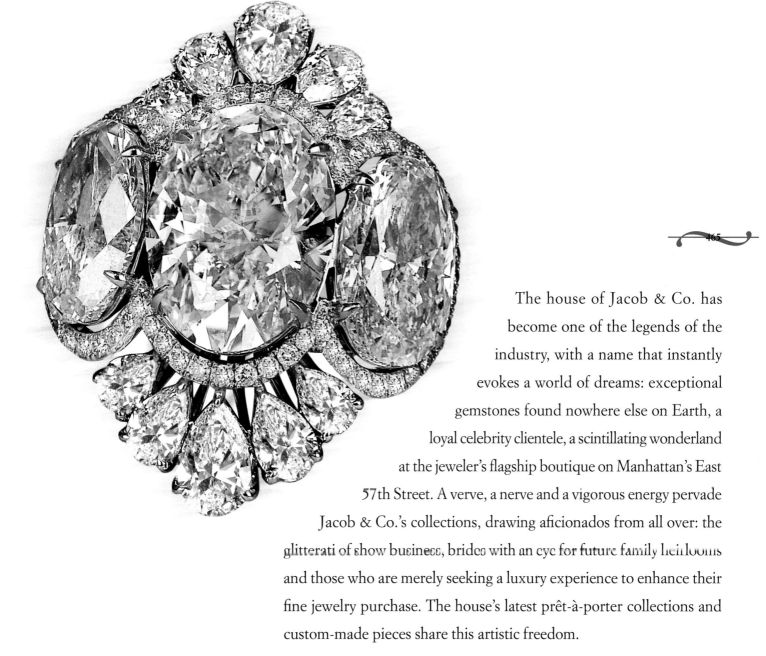

The house of Jacob & Co. has become one of the legends of the industry, with a name that instantly evokes a world of dreams: exceptional gemstones found nowhere else on Earth, a loyal celebrity clientele, a scintillating wonderland at the jeweler's flagship boutique on Manhattan's East 57th Street. A verve, a nerve and a vigorous energy pervade Jacob & Co.'s collections, drawing aficionados from all over: the glitterati of show business, brides with an eye for future family heirlooms and those who are merely seeking a luxury experience to enhance their fine jewelry purchase. The house's latest prêt-à-porter collections and custom-made pieces share this artistic freedom.

40TH ANNIVER
ERICAN MUSIC A
2

0TH ANNIVERS
CAN MUSIC AWA
2

VERSA
AWAR
201

Carrie Underwood
wears Jacob & Co. jewelry.

The fan-inspired Abanico collection
includes an 18-karat rose-gold pendant
set with round brilliant-cut white
diamonds (3.94 carats) and 18-karat
rose-gold earrings featuring round
brilliant-cut white diamonds
(7.78 carats).

Once an essential feminine accessory, the fan has
been relegated to the same status as nosegays and evening
gloves, its flirtatious flutter all but forgotten. With its new
Abanico collection, however, Jacob & Co. revives the
lacy, delicate allure of times gone by, with a thoroughly
modern design. Abanico is the Spanish word for fan, and
the collection boasts a definite Iberian flair, with earrings
and a necklace that abstract a familiar shape in a dozen
slightly different ways, creating something entirely new with

Jezebel chandelier earrings, crafted in palladium, create a dynamic dangling effect with round brilliant-cut diamonds (26.12 carats).

confident sweeps of white diamonds and rose gold. A third piece blurs the lines between different forms of jewelry—its central ornament perches upon the finger, but a diamond-studded chain extends down to embrace the wrist as well, creating an imaginative piece that is wholly sui generis.

For the jeweler's Jezebel collection, Jacob & Co. explores the power and fascination of statement jewelry. In this context, the name of Jezebel evokes a strong woman, one who does what she likes—and wears what she loves. Diamond strewn tassels dangle like flowering vines, chiming softly with a woman's every movement, and the collection seems to draw on some ancient ideas and motifs the high arch and Greek key that support the tassel, the "hanging garden" effect—with an up-to-the-minute feel. Observant connoisseurs will notice a highly stylized Jacob & Co. logo worked into the design—just one more wink to the cognoscenti.

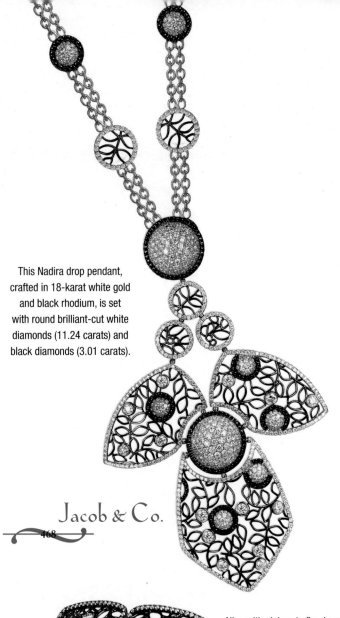

This Nadira drop pendant, crafted in 18-karat white gold and black rhodium, is set with round brilliant-cut white diamonds (11.24 carats) and black diamonds (3.01 carats).

Jacob & Co.

468

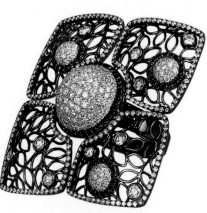

Alive with elaborate floral motifs, the Nadira collection features a square cocktail ring set with round brilliant-cut white diamonds (3.76 carats) and black diamonds (0.66 carat), as well as a bracelet with round brilliant-cut white diamonds (16.50 carats) and black diamonds (2.72 carats). Both pieces continue the monochrome theme with 18-karat white gold and black rhodium.

Diane Kruger wears Jacob & Co.'s palladium "wing" clip-on earrings, which sparkle with 314 black diamonds (6.69 carats) and 86 white diamonds (1.47 carats).

The Nadira line, which draws its title from an Arabic name meaning "rare," is just that. Bold, chunky designs populate the collection with an aesthetic that is both imposing and delicate. The main focus of each piece is the diamond-pavé orb that acts as the jewel's center of gravity. Around it grows a fantastical, modernist garden in black and white diamonds, white gold and black rhodium. The overall effect is that of balance between opposing forces—black and white, simplicity and complexity—an easily upset equilibrium that is familiar to any modern woman.

With brighter colors and a more whimsical focus, the Papillon collection uses a light touch and colorful stones to depict several fanciful butterflies in precious and semiprecious colored stones and—of course—white

These 18-karat white-gold earrings from the Papillon collection flaunt a fun feminine flair, with pink tourmalines (12.68 carats) dropped from surmounts set with pink tourmaline (10.99 carats) and round brilliant-cut white diamonds (6.07 carats).

diamonds. The earring is the perfect choice of jewelry to depict this shy, delicate creature, as the slightest movement of the woman wearing these coy pieces will cause them to flutter like a butterfly ready to take off for the next flower.

Playing on a cunning juxtaposition of meticulous craftsmanship and apparent effortlessness, the Cascata collection takes as its foundational motif the classic solitaire engagement ring. Diamond-set ovals, many set with an eye-catching "extra" stone, seem to tumble from their confines in a scintillating splash. Catching the light like the droplets spraying from a waterfall, Cascata's diamonds capture the liberating beauty of nature.

Sparkling with a spray of diamonds, the Cascata collection encompasses 18-karat white-gold earrings with pavé-set white diamonds (11.05 carats) and a stunning wristlet-ring hyrbid pavé-set with white diamonds (6.26 carats).

469

Actress Debra Messing wears Jacob & Co.'s Cascata collection.

Jacob & Co.'s most remarkable pieces, however, do not fit within the aesthetic confines of a fully realized collection. Renowned for collecting extraordinary gemstones, the jeweler will often design a unique piece to highlight the qualities of an exceptional diamond, emerald, ruby or sapphire. A particular passion for colored diamonds threads through many of these pieces, such as the Splendors of Nature necklace, which features not only two enormous white diamonds of over 18 and 44 carats, but yellow, blue and pink diamonds of 3.94 carats, 5 carats and 10.09 carats respectively. The number of 10-carat

pink diamonds in the world is vanishingly small: over two and a half centuries, world-famous auction house Christie's has sold fewer than twenty. To combine one with two other extremely rare colored diamonds acts as a stunning example of the brio and flair with which Jacob & Co. creates designs. Other astonishingly large colored diamonds also star—alone or in conjunction—in pieces throughout Jacob & Co.'s superlative selection.

Many brides looking for the chance to be queen for a day come to Jacob & Co. to explore the house's exquisite line of bridal jewelry, or to select an outspoken diamond

ring that declares their love. For clients with something unique in mind, Jacob & Co. can realize any vision, providing a vast palette of stones to choose from, or reimagining a woman's own jeweled pieces.

This comprehensive approach to jewelry—vibrant, imaginative collections, unique pieces with magnificent gemstones and completely bespoke jewels—explains why

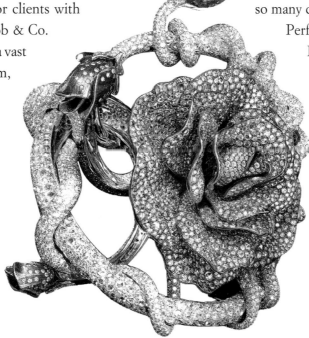

so many celebrities have chosen Jacob & Co. Performers such as Madonna, Jennifer Lawrence, Anna Paquin, Jennifer Hudson, Carrie Underwood, Freida Pinto, Diane Kruger, Morena Baccarin, Emilia Clarke, Kelly Osbourne and Julianne Hough have all recently appeared on the red carpet sporting knockout jewelry to complement their charismatic presence.

Jewelmer Joaillerie

473

Enamored of the seductive golden South Sea pearl, Jewelmer Joaillerie has built an artistic empire upon its gleaming foundation. Always beginning with the rich, nearly decadent "queen of gems," Jewelmer Joaillerie creates a setting in which the pearl can realize its individual beauty, framing it with silky swoops of 18-karat gold and glittering diamond pavé accents. Each piece represents a fully formed idea of what the pearl signifies, from the serendipitous beauty that nature provides in the most unexpected places, to an aesthetic experience of unparalleled perfection and joy, to a conduit for more complex motions about the world around us.

Jewelmer Joaillerie

The ancient Greeks considered the sphere
to be the perfect shape, and the lustrous golden
orbs that animate Jewelmer Joaillerie'spieces
make manifest the truth of this notion. Like
small gleaming suns, Jewelmer's pearls seem to
illuminate all that surrounds them, imbuing the
skin of the women who wear them with a
warm, golden glow. The age-old tradition
of sculpture in the round permeates the
way in which Jewelmer Joaillerie creates
pearl jewelry—it is designed to be worn,
not just seen, and great care has been given to

Necklaces from the Charleston collection create a festive atmosphere, particularly on the runway at the Jewelmer Gala.

every aspect of the jewelry's three dimensions. Diamond-set leaves or flower petals gently cradle the central pearl in necklaces, bracelets and rings that recreate the wonder of the natural world. More abstract pieces maintain the focus on the physicality of the pearl.

Gaëlle Branellec, Creative Director of Jewelmer Joaillerie, sees the House's identity as transcending the usual jeweler's role. "We are beyond jewelers," she explains. "We are sculptors: we concretize volume, movement and life." All begins with the pearl, a nacreous wonder of the ocean that represents, in the philosophy of Jewelmer, a harmonious partnership between humanity and nature.

Regarding its pieces as a tribute to the many splendors of life, Jewelmer Joaillerie's designers pick up on the atmosphere and fleeting moments of a changing world, capturing them in unique, artistic jewelry creations. Each jewel is inextricably bound up with twenty-first century style, guiding trends even as it insists upon its own individuality.

Born of a partnership between a French pearl farmer and a Filipino entrepreneur, Jewelmer—whose name includes the French word for "sea"— uses techniques honed by Place Vendôme jewelers and puts them at the service of the South Sea's unmatched bounty. A stunning combination of Southeast Asian provenance and French influence, Jewelmer Joaillerie's creations end up adorning ears,

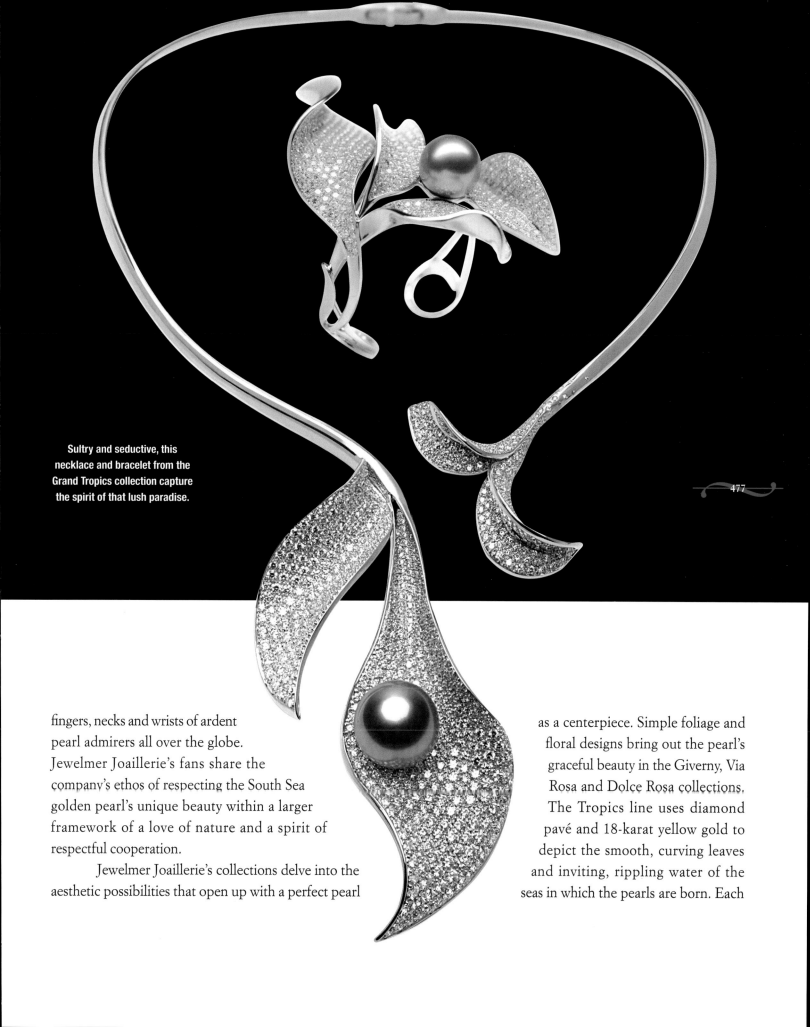

477

fingers, necks and wrists of ardent
pearl admirers all over the globe.
Jewelmer Joaillerie's fans share the
company's ethos of respecting the South Sea
golden pearl's unique beauty within a larger
framework of a love of nature and a spirit of
respectful cooperation.

Jewelmer Joaillerie's collections delve into the
aesthetic possibilities that open up with a perfect pearl

as a centerpiece. Simple foliage and
floral designs bring out the pearl's
graceful beauty in the Giverny, Via
Rosa and Dolce Rosa collections.
The Tropics line uses diamond
pavé and 18-karat yellow gold to
depict the smooth, curving leaves
and inviting, rippling water of the
seas in which the pearls are born. Each

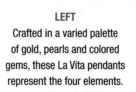

RIGHT
These Zen rings from the Lautitia collection use slightly off-kilter geometry to highlight the natural beauty of their materials.

LEFT
Crafted in a varied palette of gold, pearls and colored gems, these La Vita pendants represent the four elements.

BOTTOM LEFT
This C'est La Vie cuff injects a devil-may-care attitude into haute jewelry with overlapping rings of colored gemstones centered around golden South Sea pearls.

BOTTOM RIGHT
Effloro rings from the Lautitia collection transform simple, unassuming flowers into works of precious art.

element—fire, water, earth and air—receives its due in another collection, called La Vita The lines that are inspired by art and philosophy—Zen, Toccata, Vitta—also underscore the essential simplicity of the pearl, in shape and color, using gold and diamonds with restraint and impeccable taste to tell a story or express an idea. Explains Gaëlle, "We always begin a creation by first defining an aesthetic idea where each jewelry type can find its place naturally. Our process of creation is a global view of a certain style, which can then be cascaded from a single masterpiece to an everyday jewel."

479

True to its name, Jewelmer has made protecting the seas a crucial part of its mission. Oysters are among the first creatures to suffer from pollution, ocean acidity and rising temperatures, so any creator—or wearer—of pearl jewelry has an interest in protecting the environment. Jewelmer is involved with the Save Palawan Seas Foundation, and makes protecting the ocean one of its priorities. Says Gaëlle, "The pearl comes from a pure, pristine environment and we would like to see humanity take an active role in preserving this delicate ecology, giving us the possibility of continuing our dream of producing the rare Golden South Sea pearl in harmony with nature."

Combining bold geometric shapes with a soft, flexible construction, the Silk earrings from Messika's Fine Jewelry collection sparkle with white gold and diamonds (19.90 carats).

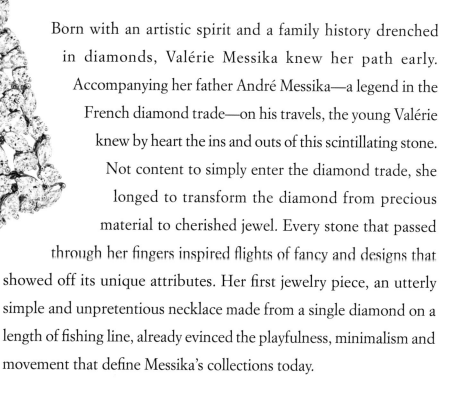

Messika

Born with an artistic spirit and a family history drenched in diamonds, Valérie Messika knew her path early. Accompanying her father André Messika—a legend in the French diamond trade—on his travels, the young Valérie knew by heart the ins and outs of this scintillating stone. Not content to simply enter the diamond trade, she longed to transform the diamond from precious material to cherished jewel. Every stone that passed through her fingers inspired flights of fancy and designs that showed off its unique attributes. Her first jewelry piece, an utterly simple and unpretentious necklace made from a single diamond on a length of fishing line, already evinced the playfulness, minimalism and movement that define Messika's collections today.

Valérie Messika.

These Ovale earrings delineate clear geometric forms in white gold and diamonds (6.40 carats).

This deep background informs every piece in Messika's Fine Jewelry collection. This haute jewelry family consists of 50 unique pieces, each of which requires particular jewelmaking expertise. The creation of these exceptional necklaces, earrings, rings and bracelets envelops Messika's Parisian atelier for hundreds of hours at a time. Like skillful couturiers creating a stunning gown, Messika's artisans work to realize shimmering sculptures, like sparkling stones inscribed within a defining framework, or arranged upon the ear as if to fly away.

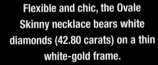

Crafted in white gold, these Silk earrings bristle with diamonds (10.20 carats).

Flexible and chic, the Ovale Skinny necklace bears white diamonds (42.80 carats) on a thin white-gold frame.

BELOW
Meticulously crafted to be soft and forgiving, the unique Silk necklace sparkles with a stunning 95 carats of diamonds, cut in a variety of shapes: marquise, pear, oval and brilliant.

RIGHT
Vahina Giocante wears Messika's Silk necklace at the 2011 Cannes Film Festival.

One feat accomplished by Valérie's team is the transubstantiation of crystalline gemstones into a precious fabric that drapes like silk. The Silk necklace is one such unique piece from the Fine Jewelry collection. Taking eight months to create, the Silk necklace is jewelry reimagined. Because each diamond is set independently from the rest, the flexibility of the piece is unparalleled, fitting any woman perfectly as it drapes across the clavicle like a fine scarf. The necklace brings a sexy vibe to effortless comfort, acting as a second skin for the lucky woman who wears it.

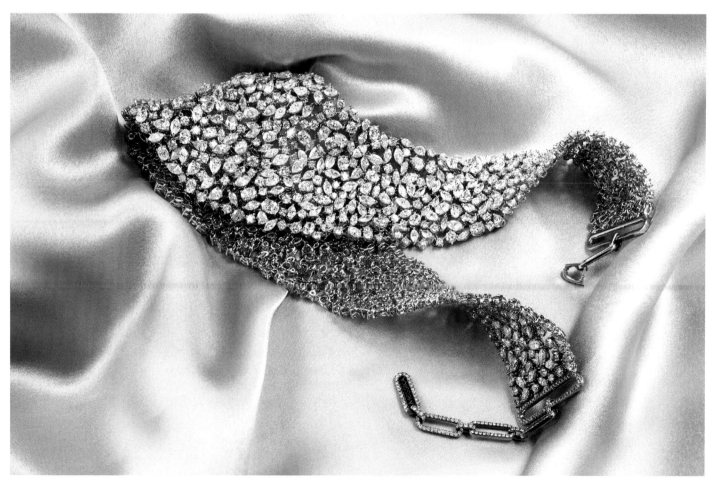

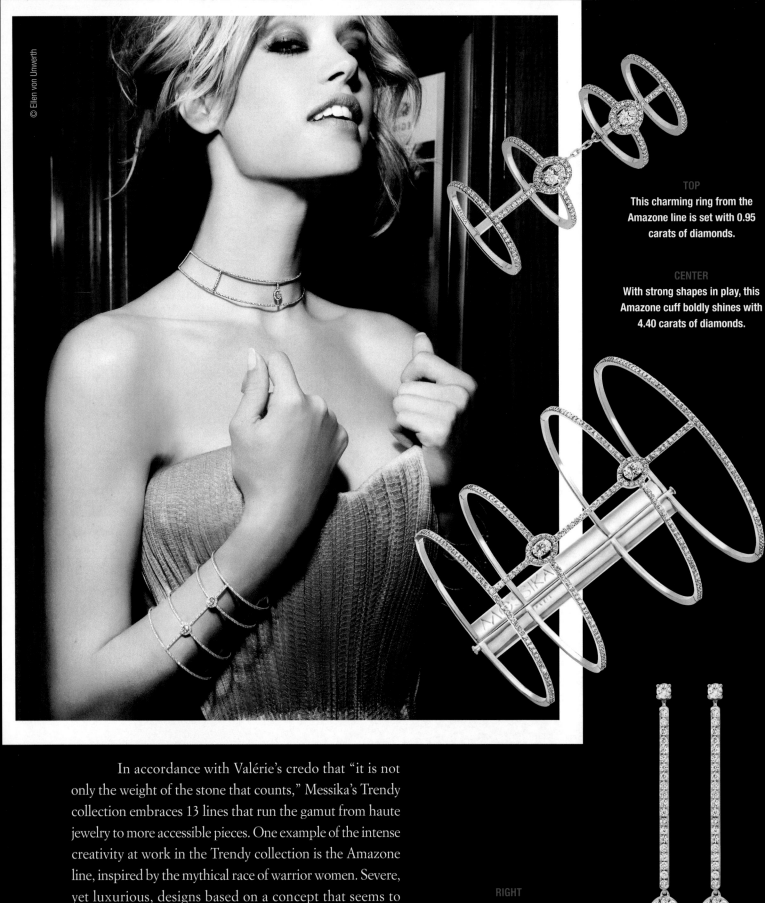

TOP

This charming ring from the Amazone line is set with 0.95 carats of diamonds.

CENTER

With strong shapes in play, this Amazone cuff boldly shines with 4.40 carats of diamonds.

RIGHT

Direct, minimalist white-gold Amazone earrings catch the light with 1.30 carats of diamonds.

In accordance with Valérie's credo that "it is not only the weight of the stone that counts," Messika's Trendy collection embraces 13 lines that run the gamut from haute jewelry to more accessible pieces. One example of the intense creativity at work in the Trendy collection is the Amazone line, inspired by the mythical race of warrior women. Severe, yet luxurious, designs based on a concept that seems to protect as it reveals, the Amazone jewelry brings out the strength and femininity that is the birthright of every woman.

The Eden line takes us back to a time of innocence, using a lattice of lace-like diamonds in a girlish floral motif. The stones' subtle gradations in size emphasize the lightness of the abstract floral filigree, and the design flirts with the contrast between transparency—the negative space in the motif—and the perpetual motion of light.

RIGHT AND TOP RIGHT
Eden earrings capture a delicate spirit in lacy white gold and diamonds (3.50 carats).

This white-gold Eden hairpin sports a feminine filigree in diamonds (1.10 carats).

Adorning the central flower with a bed of leafy motifs, the Eden tiara elegantly gleams with 6.60 carats of diamonds.

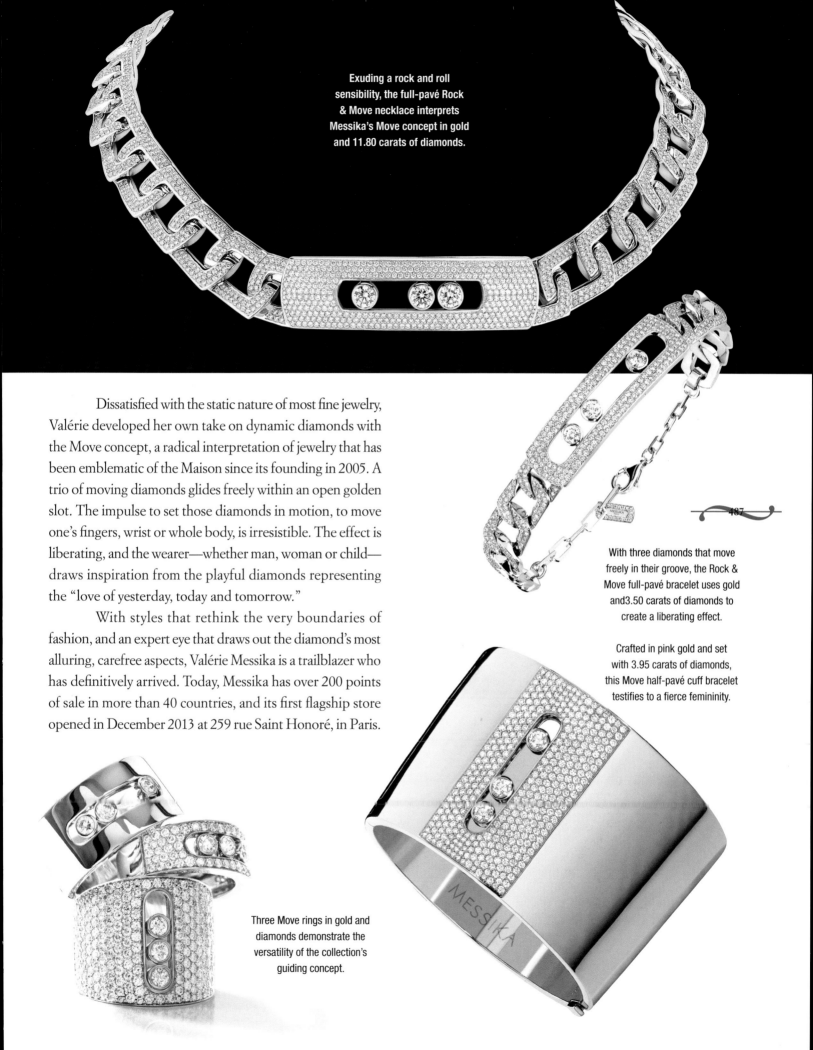

Dissatisfied with the static nature of most fine jewelry, Valérie developed her own take on dynamic diamonds with the Move concept, a radical interpretation of jewelry that has been emblematic of the Maison since its founding in 2005. A trio of moving diamonds glides freely within an open golden slot. The impulse to set those diamonds in motion, to move one's fingers, wrist or whole body, is irresistible. The effect is liberating, and the wearer—whether man, woman or child— draws inspiration from the playful diamonds representing the "love of yesterday, today and tomorrow."

With styles that rethink the very boundaries of fashion, and an expert eye that draws out the diamond's most alluring, carefree aspects, Valérie Messika is a trailblazer who has definitively arrived. Today, Messika has over 200 points of sale in more than 40 countries, and its first flagship store opened in December 2013 at 259 rue Saint Honoré, in Paris.

With three diamonds that move freely in their groove, the Rock & Move full-pavé bracelet uses gold and 3.50 carats of diamonds to create a liberating effect.

Crafted in pink gold and set with 3.95 carats of diamonds, this Move half-pavé cuff bracelet testifies to a fierce femininity.

Three Move rings in gold and diamonds demonstrate the versatility of the collection's guiding concept.

Piaget

Long admired for its sophisticated take on haute jewelry as well as haute horology, Piaget understands that a narrowly focused inspiration can be a liberating endeavor. Drawing on a deep connection with the world of roses—and one rose in particular—Piaget has released a jewelry collection with pieces that play all roles, from a grace note of chic understatement to a vivid, even ecstatic, look in its own right. Each jewel explores a different aspect of the rose, examining, with playfulness and passion, just why it exerts such an enchantment on the human psyche.

TOP
White gold and diamonds curl up
in floral vines on these earrings set
with 164 brilliant-cut diamonds
(approximately 1.29 carat).

RIGHT
A rose garland graces this 18-karat
white-gold pendant, set with
110 brilliant-cut diamonds
(approximately 0.61 carat).

Capturing both the exuberant shape
and distinctive hue of the Yves
Piaget rose, this ring in 18-karat
white gold is set with 39 brilliant-cut
diamonds (approximately 0.44 carat)
and 1 tourmaline (approximately
2.86 carats).

Delicate, fragrant, lushly petaled and richly hued, roses speak a near-universal language of tenderness, generosity and a sensual approach to life. Yves Piaget, President of Piaget, is tremendously fond of roses, and a glorious variety—the 1982 winner of the Geneva International Competition of New Roses—was in fact named for him. Combining a deep pink hue with a strong fragrance and an exuberant abundance of petals, the Yves Piaget rose is a jaw-dropping, eye-popping, show-stopping marvel, even by the standards of the elite floral world.

Yves reflected on his longstanding affection for the blossom when he wrote, "For me, roses speak of childhood and I well remember my first thrill of love for the wild flowers known as sweet briar or Eglantine roses, growing in complete freedom at an altitude of 1,100 meters." Coveted by gardeners, admired by botanists, the Piaget rose reaches a new audience of aesthetes with its latest incarnation: a fine jewelry collection that interprets the bloom in a variety of precious materials.

This stunning necklace, crafted in 18-karat white gold, depicts blooming roses in 52 brilliant-cut diamonds (approximately 0.74 carat) and 2 tourmalines (approximately 2.82 carats).

These perky earrings in 18-karat white gold sparkle with 72 brilliant-cut diamonds (approximately 0.45 carat) and 2 tourmalines (approximately 2.80 carats).

This necklace and earring set from Piaget Couture Précieuse collection lives up to its name with brilliant-cut and square-cut diamonds set in 18-karat white gold.

A flamboyant depiction of a rose in full bloom graces each piece in the collection, taking a form so expertly realized that the scent of attar seems to fill the air. One theme at play is an abstracted monochrome representation: necklaces, earrings, rings and bracelets in 18-karat white gold bear blossoms whose every petal—and there are many—is pavé set with white diamonds. Pink tourmalines also adorn some of the jewels, bringing their bright, sensual color to bear as a concrete reminder of the similarly hued Piaget Rose. Some designs insist on the idea of the plant as a whole, incorporating vines and leaves—but not thorns—into a flowing motif.

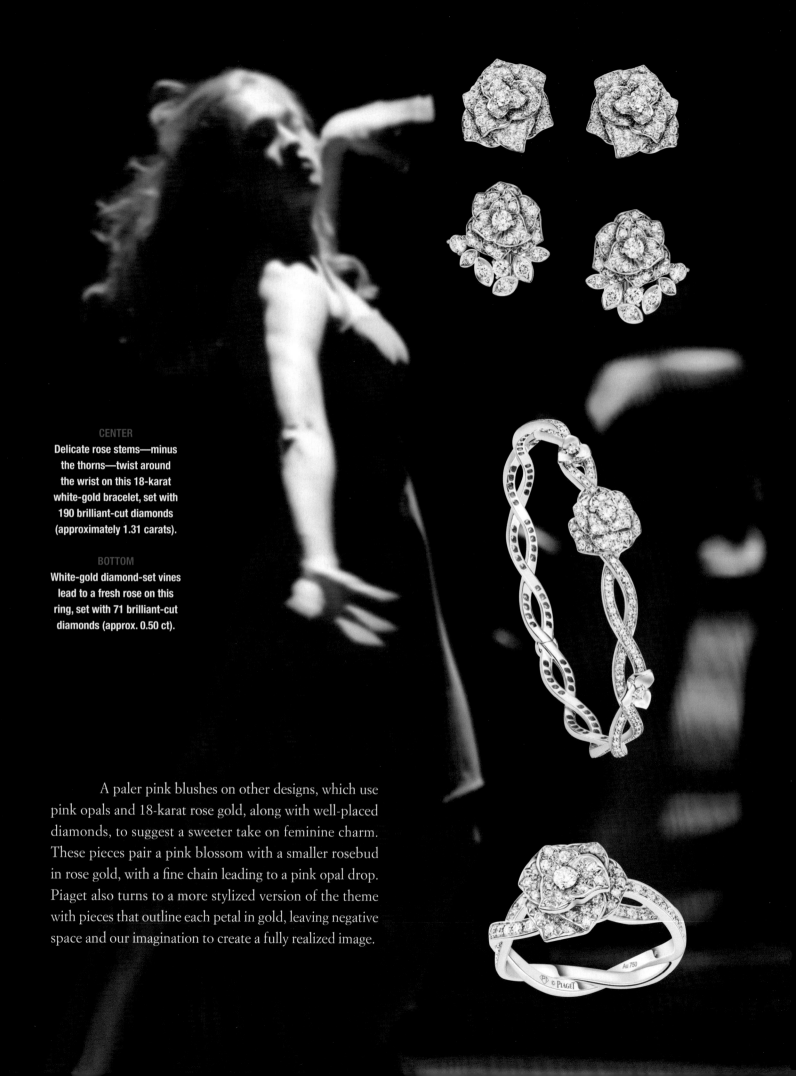

CENTER

Delicate rose stems—minus
the thorns—twist around
the wrist on this 18-karat
white-gold bracelet, set with
190 brilliant-cut diamonds
(approximately 1.31 carats).

BOTTOM

White-gold diamond-set vines
lead to a fresh rose on this
ring, set with 71 brilliant-cut
diamonds (approx. 0.50 ct).

A paler pink blushes on other designs, which use
pink opals and 18-karat rose gold, along with well-placed
diamonds, to suggest a sweeter take on feminine charm.
These pieces pair a pink blossom with a smaller rosebud
in rose gold, with a fine chain leading to a pink opal drop.
Piaget also turns to a more stylized version of the theme
with pieces that outline each petal in gold, leaving negative
space and our imagination to create a fully realized image.

FACING PAGE
TOP LEFT
Roses burst into full bloom on these 18-karat white-gold earrings, set with 178 brilliant-cut diamonds (approximately 2.8 carats).

BOTTOM LEFT
These 18-karat white-gold earrings use 92 brilliant-cut diamonds (approximately 1.44 carats) to depict leaves and petals of two glorious roses.

RIGHT
Dripping with diamond dewdrops, this 18-karat white-gold necklace uses 60 brilliant-cut diamonds (approximately 1.38 carats) to paint a winning picture.

Piaget's Couture Précieuse collection shines with diamonds in supremely elegant array.

June is the month when roses burst out in the fullness of their bloom, and June 13 is a signal day for jewelry lovers—in 2013, Piaget celebrated the date as the first ever "Piaget Rose Day." In events throughout the world, Piaget paid tribute to the luscious flower and the collection it inspired—in New York, the jeweler planted special Piaget Rose bushes in the New York Botanical Garden's famous Peggy Rockefeller Rose Garden. In Paris, the jeweler reopened its flagship store on the Place Vendôme, marking the occasion with a private concert by singer Melody Gardot, who is also a Piaget ambassador. The highlight of the show was—what else?—her rendition of "La Vie en rose."

CENTER
A passionate necklace in 18-karat rose gold glints with 19 brilliant-cut diamonds (approximately 0.28 carat).

RIGHT
Pieces from Piaget's Couture Précieuse collection gleamed on the runway at the collection's launch in Beijing.

ABOVE
Vines and blossoms in 18-karat rose gold frame a charming bloom whose petals are set with 40 brilliant-cut diamonds (approximately 0.48 carat).

RIGHT
This elegant 18-karat rose-gold bracelet decorates its center link with 19 brilliant-cut diamonds (approximately 0.27 carat).

Melody Gardot is far from the only prominent artist to favor Piaget Rose jewelry. Talented actresses such as Zoe Saldana, Teri Hatcher, Rose McGowan, Paula Patton, Emmy Rossum and Taraji P. Henson have all been spotted sporting the precious blooms. In iterations that range from subtle to sumptuous, and monochromatic to explosions of color, the Piaget Rose collection graces women the world over, from every walk of life, who have just one thing in common: a fondness for the flower that effortlessly inspires a wealth of artistic creation.

POIRAY

In the year 1975, the august Place Vendôme welcomed a fresh young vision to its stately setting: Maison POIRAY. Barely had the new jeweler opened its doors when it began to shake things up in the highly traditional world of haute jewelry, using fine stones in cuts such as pear, cabochon and marquise—shapes that had previously been reserved for diamonds. This initial daring on the part of Place Vendôme's "jeune fille" evolved into POIRAY's emblematic style. Precious and playful, luxurious and lighthearted, POIRAY's collections express the fundamental harmony between sophistication and sensuality. The jewelry of POIRAY is recognized, known and loved for the color of its stones, its playful structure, and the fluidity of its geometrical forms, which all contribute to the transformation of each carefully constructed piece. POIRAY becomes a synonym for ornament, opulence, sensuality, intimacy: the very subjects of jewelry's art.

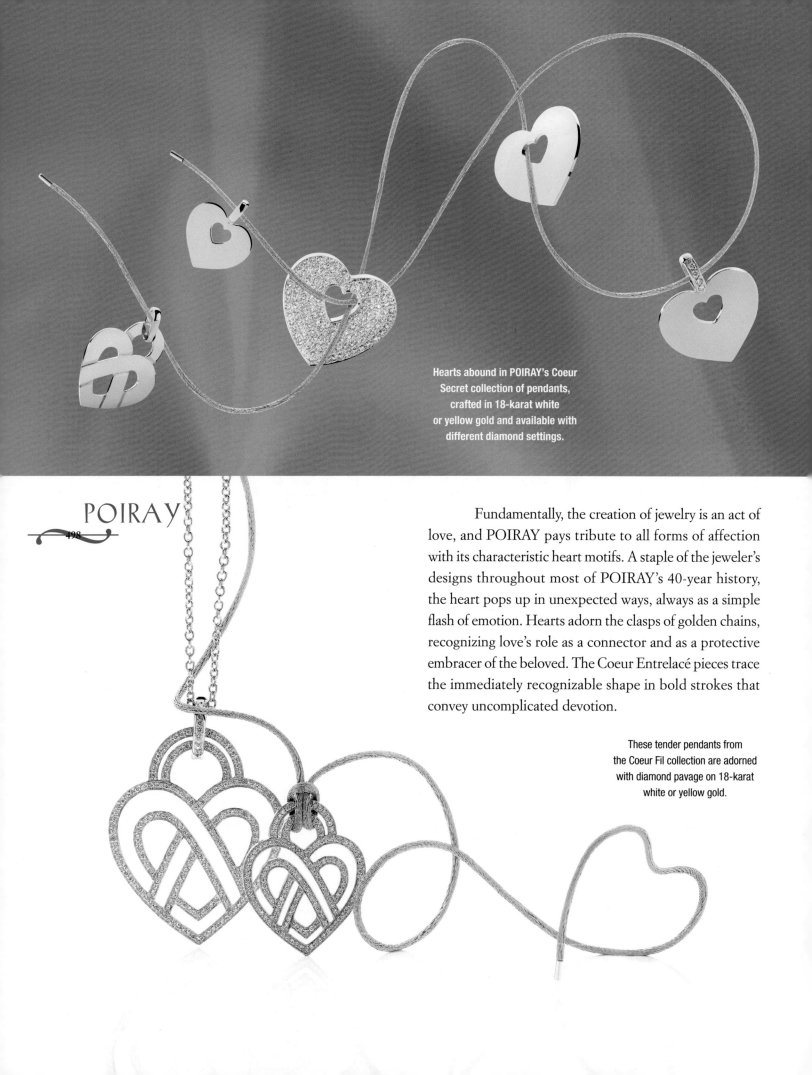

Hearts abound in POIRAY's Coeur Secret collection of pendants, crafted in 18-karat white or yellow gold and available with different diamond settings.

Fundamentally, the creation of jewelry is an act of love, and POIRAY pays tribute to all forms of affection with its characteristic heart motifs. A staple of the jeweler's designs throughout most of POIRAY's 40-year history, the heart pops up in unexpected ways, always as a simple flash of emotion. Hearts adorn the clasps of golden chains, recognizing love's role as a connector and as a protective embracer of the beloved. The Coeur Entrelacé pieces trace the immediately recognizable shape in bold strokes that convey uncomplicated devotion.

These tender pendants from the Coeur Fil collection are adorned with diamond pavage on 18-karat white or yellow gold.

LEFT AND BELOW
The Coeur Entrelacé pendant in
18-karat yellow gold makes a
bold, stylized statement of love.

The flowing silhouettes of the Coeur Fil collection add a layer of abstraction, presenting the form in designs that evoke a butterfly's delicate wings or even the vigorous energy of action painting. The Coeur Secret shape nestles one heart inside another, using precious metal, diamonds and open space to suggest the famous lines by the poet e.e. cummings: "i carry your heart with me(i carry it in / my heart)." Whether intertwined, outlined or secret, hearts bring an unmistakable feel to a POIRAY piece, which may explain why they capture the hearts of women with a magnetism that irresistibly draws like to like.

499

The Coeur Fil shape brings
a geometric shape to this
yellow-gold semi-cuff.

Featuring a design with two hearts
that just barely kiss, this Coeur
Papillon ring is set with diamonds
and crafted in 8.70g of white gold.

This Indrani ring is crafted in rose gold (16g) and set with a central rose quartz (10 carats).

POIRAY also uses jewelry design to express the intensity of love in another fashion: with its Tresse rings, the Maison creates one beautiful jewel from the union of two separate strands intertwined with each other. Whether pavé-set with black or white diamonds, or smooth and glossy in yellow, white or black gold, the Tresse rings use sleek simplicity to convey the idea that a relationship is greater than the sum of its parts. The name of the collection—which is French for "braid"—is also evocative of an almost-forgotten part of jewelry history. During the Victorian era, people would make and wear hair jewelry meticulously crafted from the hair of their loved ones. POIRAY's Tresse rings draw upon that kind of love, and the need to always have near a token of the beloved, but transform the gesture from earthly and ephemeral to eternal simply by using changeless precious materials to realize the vision.

The Indrani collection is inspired by an even older jewelry trend, that of the signet ring. In pre-literate societies, the signet ring would serve as a person's signature, and POIRAY's Indrani rings possess a highly individual flair.

Tresse rings are available in four colors of gold: rose, yellow, white and black.

The rings in the Indrani collection are made of 4 distinct parts for a unique contemporary style. According to a woman's preference, the ring can be enhanced with a white diamond ribbon (0.26 carat) that outlines the central stone.

POIRAY's Cabaret ring collection features large, signet-style rings with brilliant-cut gems surrounding the central cabochon.

Chunky and bold, the Indrani pieces make a fresh statement about the use of jewels in today's society. Crafted in rose or white gold, the setting welcomes generously proportioned, faceted fine gemstones such as amethyst, milky aquamarine and rose quartz, adorning some models with a ribbon of white diamonds. Transposing a traditionally male style of jewelry into an unambiguously feminine register, POIRAY reaffirms its willingness to shake up conventions.

A lighthearted use of color is key in the Cabaret collection, in which rings surround candy-colored cabochon-cut fine stones with a bed of pavé-set gems in contrasting shades. The freewheeling aesthetic at work here emphasizes the joy to be found in serendipity and the beauty that flashes out at us from unexpected relationship.

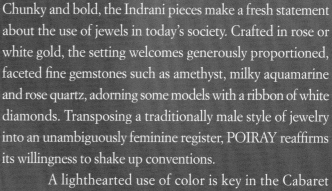

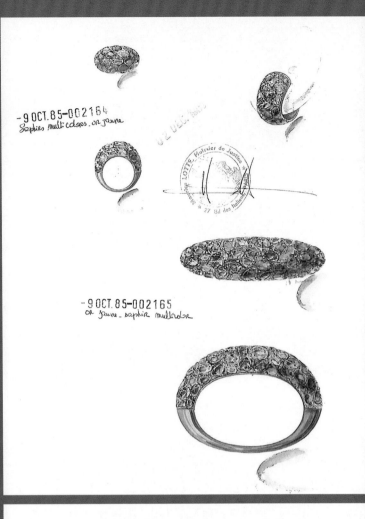

- 9 OCT. 85-002164
Saphirs multicolores. or jaune

- 9 OCT. 85-002165
or jaune - saphir multicolor

19 FEV 85-J00008

19 FEV 85-000302

grises - or jaune - nacre

19 FEV. 85-000303

000449

000450

FACING PAGE
Designs from POIRAY's
archives testify to the House's
rich creativity and deft touch
with jewels.

POIRAY's Ma Première watch collection includes bracelets
in pink tourmaline (far left) and garnet (left), as well as the
Ma Première Gold & Diamonds (above), in 18-karat yellow gold
(19.5g), set with diamonds (1.71 carats). With a sapphire crystal
to protect the diamond-set dial, the Ma Première is powered
by a Swiss Made quartz mechanism.

The world of watchmaking was also shaken up by POIRAY's fresh outlook and willingness to toy with convention. The iconic Ma Première watch remains a startlingly modern statement: its square case mitigates its shape with rounded corners, while the gadroon bezel conveys the strength inherent in right angles and forceful lines. The innovation of presenting the watch with interchangeable straps was liberating for a generation of timepiece aficionados—suddenly, the same piece could go from iconic and classic to iconoclastic in a matter of seconds. The many materials available to mount the watch upon the wrist include straps in alligator, ostrich, lizard, teju, matte or glossy leather, quilted lambskin or techno satin; bracelets in gemstones, jewelry, pearls or even metal, with 75g of yellow gold. Mounted on exotic animal skins, elegant metals or chic fabrics, the discreet pieces may also be shown off against rows of pearls or semiprecious stones such as peridot and garnet.

THIS PAGE
Model Elena Alekseïevna Lenina wears a Robert Wan Tahiti Pearl strand, strung with 27 multicolor round AAA pearls (15mm and above) and fastened with an 18-karat white-gold round ball clasp that is pavé-set with round brilliant-cut diamonds (2.98 carats). The look is completed by a white-gold ring from the Robert Wan Gold Collection, set with an AAA Tahitian pearl (15mm) and diamonds, and earrings set with diamonds and drop Tahitian pearls (16mm).

FACING PAGE
Named for the diamond motifs in its setting, the Heart ring, crafted in 18-karat white gold, uses diamonds in the shape of hearts and leaves, as well as round-cut diamonds, to accent a round Tahitian pearl (14mm).

Robert Wan

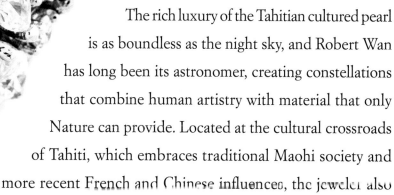

The rich luxury of the Tahitian cultured pearl is as boundless as the night sky, and Robert Wan has long been its astronomer, creating constellations that combine human artistry with material that only Nature can provide. Located at the cultural crossroads of Tahiti, which embraces traditional Maohi society and more recent French and Chinese influences, the jeweler also draws upon a personal history of blended cultures: Robert himself has French nationality, Chinese ancestry and Tahitian roots. Robert Wan's creations provide us with a new way of looking at the sea and its bounty, with extravagant, simple, opulent jewels that express a coherent aesthetic vision with assured longevity.

The jeweler recently celebrated its 40th anniversary, with much ceremony and attendant fanfare. Among the new projects embarked upon in honor of the Tahitian cultured pearl was the first Robert Wan Design Award, an opportunity for local jewelry designers to riff on the theme of "the pearl in all its forms." The jewelry creations of the eight finalists were brought to stunning life in Robert Wan's workshops, and each took a turn in the spotlight at the 40th anniversary gala evening, and the three

TOP

The delicate Butterfly set includes a pendant, earrings and ring, all set with precious stones and semi-round and drop-shaped Tahitian pearls (14-15mm). It is accented here by a sumptuous sautoir of round Tahitian pearls (15-18mm) from the Robert Wan Tahiti Connoisseur Collection, which draws on the crème de la crème of Tahitian pearls.

CENTER RIGHT

This unique ring, crafted by Philippe Tournaire, boasts a total of 9 exceptional, perfectly round and multicolor Tahitian pearls, a lucky number in Chinese cosmology.

BOTTOM RIGHT

This pearl-themed lighter was crafted by Maison S.T. Dupont Place Vendôme to celebrate Robert Wan's 40th anniversary.

This necklace from the Robert Wan Connoisseur collection is strung with green and cherry Tahitian pearls (15-16mm) and a gold clasp with inlaid diamonds and sapphires.

CENTER

This aquatic-themed necklace makes waves with 51 semi-round AA-AAA pearls (14-18mm), adorned with frolicking dolphins in blue sapphires and diamonds.

RIGHT

This mermaid pen was conceived by S.T. Dupont, and realized in 18-karat gold and mother-of-pearl crowned by a 15mm round Tahitian pearl. The theme is the universe of Mr. Robert Wan: an emperor of the sea, pearls and power...

BOTTOM

This white-gold Dolphin ring boasts a Tahitian pearl (14mm) among dolphins and waves represented by blue sapphires and diamonds.

finalists had the chance to see their creations on display at Robert Wan's Musée de la Perle in Tahiti.

A breathtaking element in the 40th anniversary celebration was the jeweler's collection The King of Pearl, the culmination of the jeweler's partnership with Maison S.T. Dupont Place Vendôme, a manufacturer of luxury accessories. The King of Pearl collection features an 18-karat gold-plated pen and a lighter, each engraved with a Polynesian-inspired pattern, topped with tridents, adorned with mermaids and crowned by a

perfect 15mm Tahitian cultured pearl. These pieces, which playfully capture the essence of the sea's bounty, were also given a venue at the Musée de la Perle.

Another Place Vendôme artist, Philippe Tournaire, took the opportunity to fête Robert Wan with an extraordinary ring. Set with nine flawless Tahitian pearls and 90 diamonds, the ring draws upon the Chinese symbolism of the numeral—nine stands for eternity in Chinese culture—to signify the impressive longevity of the Robert Wan vision.

The Desert Rose set blooms with a necklace that bears 55 dark cherry round AAA pearls (7-12mm), white diamonds (10.7 carats) and fancy pink diamonds (1.58 carats); earrings set with 8 dark cherry round AAA pearls (7-10mm), white diamonds (2.75 carats) and pink diamonds (0.4 carat); and a ring with 1 dark cherry round AAA pearl (11mm) and diamonds (1.3 carats), all crafted in 18-karat white and pink gold (87.8g for the necklace, 17.9g for the earrings and 7.64g for the ring).

Though the Tahitian pearl possesses an inherent beauty, Robert Wan has developed a novel way to enhance and adorn a perfect gem. With the Ariake Pearls, Robert Wan weaves a connection between the Tahitian and Japanese cultures by using an intricate Japanese art with the Tahitian pearl as its base. Trained artisans, using a fine brush dipped in powder of silver or 24-karat gold, transform the pearl into a setting for a gleaming surmount. Over three years, the addition gradually settles into permanence, eventually reaching a hardness of 5 Mohs. Just one of these sublime

509

Ariake pieces takes an entire week to finish; it is fitting that the process is slow and steady, as the name "Ariake," in Japanese, means "the moon at dawn." A pale orb lingering in the morning as light comes to wake up the world…

The Tatoo collection follows the same train of thought, but after an even more painstaking fashion; the artisan paints delicate designs upon the pearl, leaving a mark like the image of ink on living skin.

Tahiti exists in a paradise by the sea, but the vast, arid desert also sparks Robert Wan's imagination. With its Desert Rose set, the jeweler creates an immense landscape of Tahitian pearls, interspersing them with details in white and pink gold, set with white and fancy pink diamonds, sparkling like sand that stretches out in every direction. A necklace, ring and pair of earrings each affirm the fact of beauty in every spot on Earth, and the way in which life persists even in the most inhospitable climates. The stunning Rose des Sables ring seems to depict an impossible wonder rising from the arid dunes, playing with our perceptions and expectations of desert and sea.

Robert Wan

510

Because the pearl is organic, living material, pearls should be worn as often as possible, making them the perfect finishing touch to any outfit. However, some pearl creations are so exceptional, so dramatic, that they provide an opportunity for once-in-a-lifetime glamour, and that outfit that they accent so exquisitely… is a wedding dress. The Robert Wan Bridal Collection uses

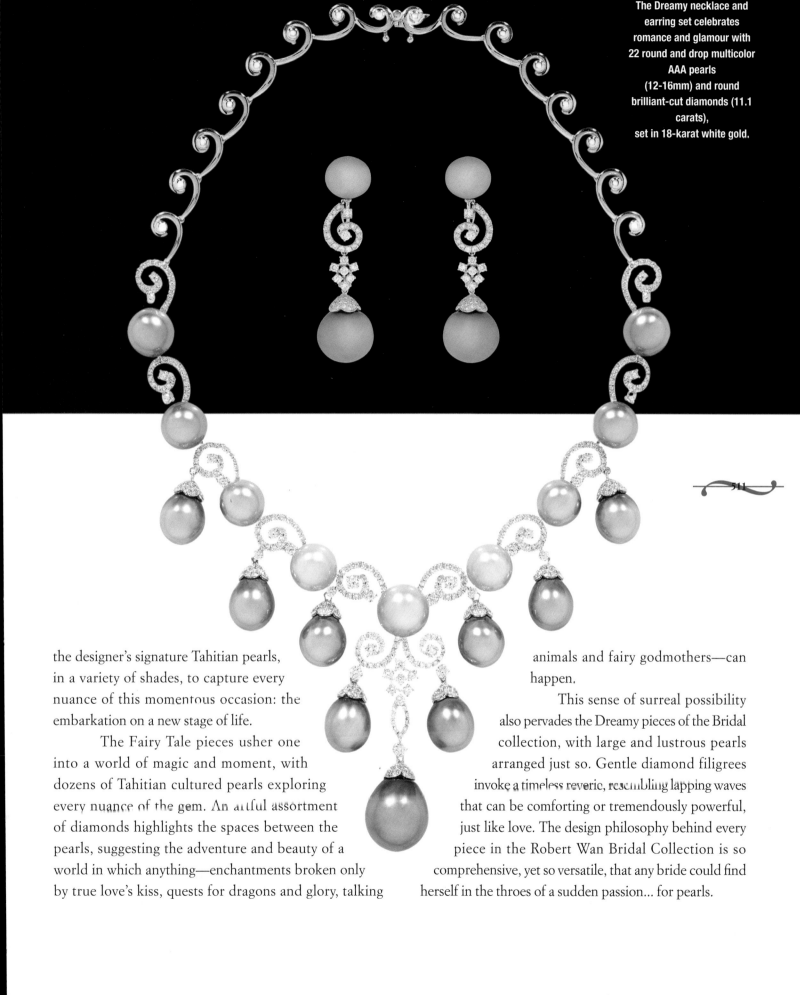

The Dreamy necklace and earring set celebrates romance and glamour with 22 round and drop multicolor AAA pearls (12-16mm) and round brilliant-cut diamonds (11.1 carats), set in 18-karat white gold.

the designer's signature Tahitian pearls, in a variety of shades, to capture every nuance of this momentous occasion: the embarkation on a new stage of life.

The Fairy Tale pieces usher one into a world of magic and moment, with dozens of Tahitian cultured pearls exploring every nuance of the gem. An artful assortment of diamonds highlights the spaces between the pearls, suggesting the adventure and beauty of a world in which anything—enchantments broken only by true love's kiss, quests for dragons and glory, talking animals and fairy godmothers—can happen.

This sense of surreal possibility also pervades the Dreamy pieces of the Bridal collection, with large and lustrous pearls arranged just so. Gentle diamond filigrees invoke a timeless reverie, resembling lapping waves that can be comforting or tremendously powerful, just like love. The design philosophy behind every piece in the Robert Wan Bridal Collection is so comprehensive, yet so versatile, that any bride could find herself in the throes of a sudden passion... for pearls.

Sutra
512

Sutra

"She has a flair for fashion," says Arpita Navlakha, designer of Sutra Jewels, "and she's not afraid to stand out." She is describing the woman she pictures as she designs Sutra's stunning, one-of-a-kind pieces, replete with exotic gemstones, eclectic design influences and an unerring sense of individual style. "Every woman is special and unique, just like our jewelry, so it's only fitting!"

These cascading drop earrings get their cool fire from electric blue Paraiba tourmalines (35 carats).

RIGHT
Singer Taylor Swift wears Sutra earrings set with agate slices, blue sapphires and diamonds.

CENTER
A sinuous snake cuff shines with blue sapphires (13.5 carats) and rose-cut diamonds (5 carats).

BOTTOM
Fifteen carats of electric blue Paraiba tourmaline take center stage on this striking ring, which is accented with rose-cut diamonds (5 carats).

The founding of Sutra Jewels seems to have been both foreordained and inspired by a completely fortuitous turn of events. Arpita and Divyanshu Navlakha, the married couple at the heart of the company, both grew up surrounded by gemstones, learning their secrets as a first language. Chance—or was it fate?—stepped in to bring them together at GIA, just ten days before Arpita's graduation with a degree in jewelry design. With Divyanshu's expertise in fine gemstones, and Arpita's boundless creative spirit, they formed Sutra.

The family relationship influences all aspects of the business. Divyanshu travels all over the world for the finest gemstones, armed with his highly trained eye and a shopping list from Arpita of the materials she wants to work with next. One of Sutra's collections shines with the cerulean glow of astounding Paraiba tourmalines—the exact color, Arpita declares, of the ocean in the Maldive Islands. Divyanshu's brother and sister have joined Sutra, and the couple's young daughter, Samaira, has also developed a fascination with jewels. "One of the first things she ever said," describes Arpita, "was

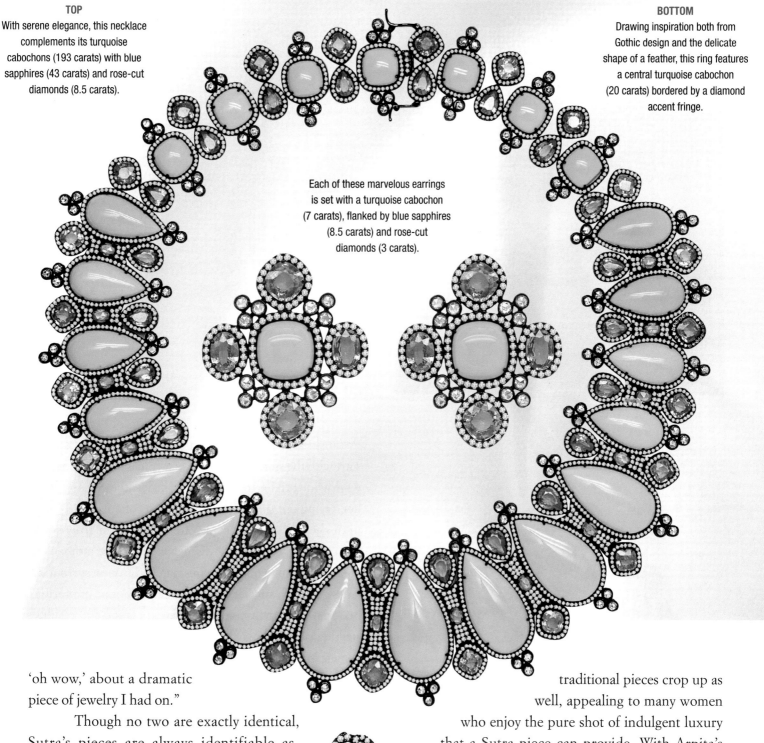

'oh wow,' about a dramatic piece of jewelry I had on."

Though no two are exactly identical, Sutra's pieces are always identifiable as springing from the same artistic vision. Many pieces have a Gothic feel, with motifs of gem-studded spikes and stars that evoke the centuries-old churches that still dot the European landscape. Arpita also crafts feminine pieces that seem to have grown organically, full of nature-inspired shapes such as flowers that intimately caress the body. More

traditional pieces crop up as well, appealing to many women who enjoy the pure shot of indulgent luxury that a Sutra piece can provide. With Arpita's distinctive vision guiding such a wide range of possibilities, it is no wonder that Sutra is sold all over the world. The collection has been seen on celebrities and socialites including First Lady Michelle Obama, Halle Berry, Mila Kunis, Rihanna, Taylor Swift and many more, who can also attest to the appeal of Sutra's one-of-a-kind aesthetic.

Sutra literally means collection of sacred verses in Sanskrit, so it is an apt name for the line. Most designs start with the stones that arrive at Arpita's atelier from their worldwide origins. In the studio, she lets the gems speak to her, trying out different combinations of color and shape until she has crafted an idea for a piece that truly sings. All rules are completely disregarded in that moment of creation—Arpita might use mismatched stones, surround a large gem with smaller ones, or create a mosaic of precious materials. The only thing that matters is the end result, a striking piece that is always wholly unique. "I want to do something new, something exciting, something different

BOTTOM
Thirty-two carats of rubies exude fiery glamour on this stunning pendant.

TOP LEFT
Actress Catherine Zeta-Jones wears Sutra diamond drop earrings (25 carats) with rose-cut diamond accents.

TOP RIGHT
Flirty and feminine, these earrings feature floating pink coral cabochon droplets (52 carats) with delicate haloes of diamonds (9 carats).

RIGHT
These impressive drop earrings are set with 51 carats of rubies.

TOP
Floral-inspired stud earrings shine with 22 carats of rubies.

RIGHT
Actress Mila Kunis wears Sutra earrings set with ruby slices (96 carats) and diamond accents.

CENTER
This bold yet sweet ring sports a central pink coral dome cabochon (11 carats), set off by a fringe of rose-cut diamonds and diamond accents (12 carats).

every day," she says, elaborating on her affection for the endlessly varied cuts, shapes and colors of her raw material.

And what raw material it is! Sutra's voracious appetite for gems of the highest caliber is evident in every piece of the jeweler's collection. "Every colored stone is different," explains Arpita. "For instance, red is very sensual." She embraces the individuality inherent in colored gems. Many of the emeralds in Sutra's jewels are purposely cut to reveal the matrix, the stone material that surrounds

The central ruby (7 carats) on this architectural ring is framed by a geometric border with diamond accents.

emerald in its natural state. "Imperfections make the stone special," says Arpita, describing how the personality of each piece comes from the balance of refinement and the individuality of each stone. The importance of imperfections as design elements becomes undeniably clear when a pair of earrings shows as not only a theoretical matched set, but a perfect one—most earrings are cut from the same stone as their mates, so any inclusions on one show up as a mirror image on the other.

TOP LEFT
Actress Jennifer Hudson wears Sutra drop earrings set with opals (41 carats), blue sapphires (5 carats) and rose-cut diamonds.

BOTTOM
These delicate, flexible earrings, inspired by the elegant shape of a peacock feather, feature emeralds (25 carats), green tourmalines (2 carats) and rose-cut diamonds (6 carats).

TOP RIGHT
Blue sapphires (9 carats) and rose-cut diamonds (4 carats) highlight the cool tones of the central opals (25 carats) on these feather earrings.

This show-stopping bracelet is mounted with opals (46 carats) bordered by rose-cut diamonds (3 carats).

Singer Katy Perry wears Sutra earrings set with black and rose-cut diamonds.

Sutra brings out the romance in these sometimes avant-garde pieces by using the rose cut, a many-faceted cut that gives a piece a classic, antique feel. "The rose cut is a Sutra trademark," says Arpita. "It's different, subtle, not too in-your-face." The mix of stones on any given Sutra piece is such that rose-cut accents of diamonds and sapphires might sparkle upon a uniquely cut turquoise piece. Each Sutra piece—whatever the cut of its stones—combines tradition and ingenuity, precious and semiprecious, romance and revolution in a jewel like no other.

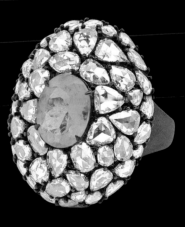

This spectacular haute jewelry set includes a white-gold necklace set with 11 round-cut Zambian emeralds, set off by round-cut diamonds (22.53 carats) and baguette-cut diamonds (22.07 carats).

TAKAT

The jewelry a woman wears communicates a great deal about her personality and taste. Many of the most fortunate and discerning women turn to TAKAT for expressive jewelry that is sheer poetry in mineral form. Each of TAKAT's richly evocative pieces makes a statement without words, and transforms any event into the grandest of occasions. The high-quality colored stones for which the jeweler is known bring wonderful depth and beauty to every piece, with combinations of emeralds, rubies, sapphires, tanzanites, paraiba tourmalines, alexandrites and tsavorites set off with a thick smattering of sparkle from delicious diamonds. The TAKAT signature style incorporates timeless elegance in a wide selection of distinctive jewelry designed in daring combinations of color, precious metals, gemstones and innovative materials.

Trillion-cut tanzanites (13.24 and 12.59 carats) lend their distinctive sparkle to these white-gold earrings, which are also set with round diamonds (4.17 carats) and marquise-cut and pear-shape diamonds (3.87 carats).

Rich blue earrings show off 2 pear-shape cabochon tanzanites (35.45 and 30.52 carats) in a glittering framework of baguette-cut diamonds (3.90 carats) and round-cut diamonds (2.91 carats).

TAKAT started as a family business in 1955, and originally focused on loose gemstones. Rayaz Ahmed Takat is a member of the family's third generation of jewelers. From the beginning, his goal was to expand the family business to include the creation of exclusive, high-end jewelry with the trade in gemstones. In 2005, Rayaz made his first step toward realizing his dream: he opened a design studio in New York, changing the TAKAT family strategy and its very raison d'être. From that point forward, Rayaz Takat has created unique fine jewelry pieces. He knew there was a niche out there: women who thirsted for a jewelry experience that he could provide. The rest of the family was skeptical, but Rayaz had experience following his instincts. "As a jeweler and a designer, I always have ideas for creative jewelry that no one else has," he explains, "and so other people might think I'm a dreamer."

This mesmerizing ring shines with a tanzanite (48.12 carats) bordered by baguette-cut diamonds (4.03 carats) and round-cut diamonds (1.79 carats).

This extraordinary pendant is set with an enormous tanzanite (74.80 carats), framing it with baguette-cut diamonds (3.87 carats) and round-cut diamonds (2.77 carats).

The design codes of Art Deco permeate earrings set with 2 octagonal tanzanites (30.14 carats), round diamonds (0.38 carat) and baguette-cut diamonds (4.21 carats).

Over the years, his passion for creating exclusive jewelry lines has grown, leading him to a boundless evolution and development of his artistic vision. Rayaz falls in love with every piece in TAKAT's collection, referring to them as his "children." Passion alone, however, does not a successful jewelry house build, and Rayaz also credits his jeweler's skills and head for business. He praises TAKAT's talented workforce as another key competitive advantage. As the company has grown and expanded throughout the world, its workforce has become increasingly diverse. Rayaz Takat believes that each person makes a valuable contribution to the company's success, and he treats each worker with the same courtesy that he showers on TAKAT's customers.

A cushion cabochon tanzanite (95.04 carats) sits upon a white-gold framework of round-cut diamonds (3.21 carats) and oval-cut diamonds (5.38 carats) in this extraordinary ring.

Round-cut diamonds (5.58 carats) and trillion-cut diamonds (3.59 carats) provide a chic framework to support a cushion-cut tanzanite (84.57 carats).

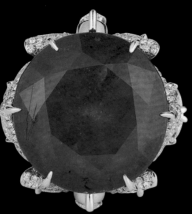

This white-gold ring with yellow-gold prongs is set with round-cut diamonds (2.75 carats) and fancy-cut diamonds (1.75 carats), supporting an extraordinary round-cut Zambian emerald (28.99 carats).

CENTER
Upon a white-gold hoop set with round-cut diamonds (1.73 carats), an octagonal emerald (16.82 carats) enjoys a frame of pear-shape diamonds (4.27 carats).

TAKAT

Rayaz's philosophy is touchingly universal: "Beautiful pieces bring us closer together, no matter what the culture or tradition." Eschewing mass production, TAKAT creates one-of-a-kind pieces that explore the possibilities inherent in the whole spectrum of light. Rayaz counts emeralds and tanzanites among his favorite gemstones, but the jeweler's color range also extends into the startling brightness of paraiba tourmaline and the cool green of tsavorite, as well as the chameleon-like color shift of rare alexandrite. The care taken when hand-selecting these precious stones, and the ardor poured into the designs that eventually guide their final form, shines through every piece.

Rayaz describes TAKAT's signature as a "touch of refinement and luxury," but TAKAT's sumptuous jewels are refined and luxurious from start to finish. The jeweler starts with an exceptional stone in a hard-to-find shade. The gem then becomes the focus of a unique design accented with remarkable diamonds and arranged with an adventurous eye. This mix of colored and white stones is a hallmark of TAKAT collections. Rayaz enjoys a special relationship with his materials, saying, "You have to let the stones talk to you." Rayaz also discusses the creative process with the women who wear these jewels,

A trillion-cut emerald (11.07 carats) sits in splendor among round-cut diamonds (1.65 carats).

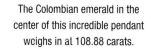

The Colombian emerald in the center of this incredible pendant weighs in at 108.88 carats.

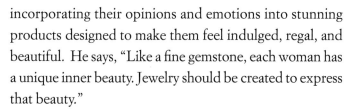

incorporating their opinions and emotions into stunning products designed to make them feel indulged, regal, and beautiful. He says, "Like a fine gemstone, each woman has a unique inner beauty. Jewelry should be created to express that beauty."

TAKAT's original designs feature stones that demand attention, by virtue of their size, rarity, and quality. One show-stopping pendant stars a Colombian emerald that weighs an astonishing 108.88 carats. Gübelin and GIA have both certified the stone, which is set among 25.25 carats of round, marquise, and pear cut diamonds, also GIA-certified. The chain supporting this exceptional pendant is impressive as well, with 47.02 carats of round and marquise cut diamonds. This necklace reflects all that is noteworthy about this remarkable jeweler.

BOTTOM
This white-gold ring, set with round-cut diamonds (2.94 carats) and pear-shape and marquise-cut diamonds (2.74 carats), uses yellow-gold prongs for its octagonal central emerald (15.15 carats).

ABOVE
An extraordinary cushion-cut Colombian emerald (58.27 carats) boasts a mount accented with round-cut diamonds (2.89 carats) and pear-shape and marquise-cut diamonds (2.05 carats).

Round cabochon emeralds (8.35 carats) dominate these white-gold cufflinks, encircled by round-cut diamonds (1.35 carats).

Nine emeralds (24.43 carats) appeal to the eye on this remarkable white- and yellow-gold bracelet, which is also set with round-cut diamonds (0.51 carat) and marquise-cut diamonds (14.22 carats).

A gorgeous octagonal emerald (32.77 carats) is the central stone on this white-gold ring, set with round-cut diamonds (3.09 carats) and fancy-cut diamonds (2.68 carats).

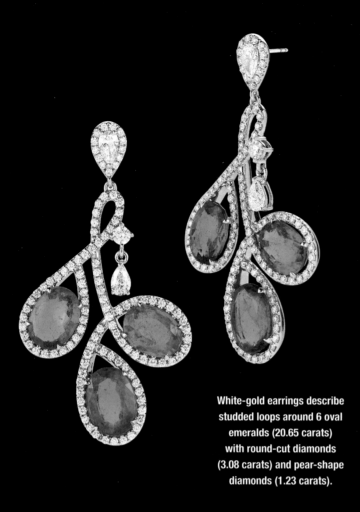

White-gold earrings describe studded loops around 6 oval emeralds (20.65 carats) with round-cut diamonds (3.08 carats) and pear-shape diamonds (1.23 carats).

White-gold prongs set with round-cut diamonds (1.51 carats) and marquise-cut diamonds (1.15 carats) hold this ring's oval emerald (16.19 carats) in all its glory.

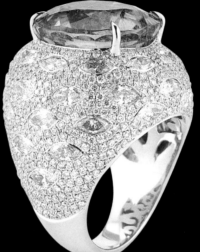

LEFT
An impeccable paraiba tourmaline (15.70 carats) sits upon a white-gold bed of round-cut diamonds (3.65 carats) and marquise-cut diamonds (3.84 carats) on this sparkle-filled ring.

527

RAYAZ TAKAT – IN HIS OWN WORDS

While we are proud of our accomplishments, we are dedicated to building a better future for our customers and employees. We are truly honored that many of the world's finest jewelers and most discerning end users rely on us, and we work every day to earn their confidence and business. TAKAT is focused on providing the highest level of quality and customer service in creating and marketing exceptional jewelry. Our goal is always to meet the needs of our customers and to exceed their expectations. We will continue to pursue our goal through hard work, excellent service, materials of exceptional quality and beauty, meticulous attention to craftsmanship, creative design, and adherence to business practices based on the values of our founder TAKAT believes in treating all people with respect and dignity. We strive to create and foster a supportive and understanding environment in which all individuals realize their maximum potential within the company. Our business success is a reflection of the quality and skill of our people and our overall commitment to diversity.

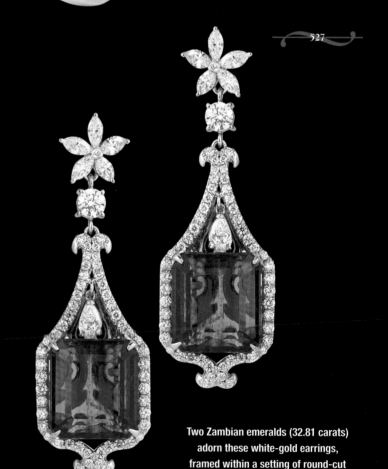

Two Zambian emeralds (32.81 carats) adorn these white-gold earrings, framed within a setting of round-cut diamonds (2.85 carats) and fancy-cut diamonds (1.65 carats).

Listing

Listing

528

ANDREOLI
PAGE 376
Tutti Frutti necklace.

ANDREOLI
PAGE 376
Tutti Frutti earrings.

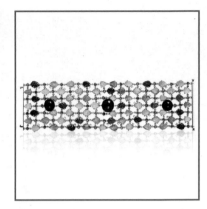

ANDREOLI
PAGE 377
Rose-gold bracelet with rubies, emeralds and sapphires.

ANDREOLI
PAGE 378
Multi-colored sapphire necklace.

ANDREOLI
PAGE 378
Multi-colored sapphire earrings.

ANDREOLI
PAGE 378
Multi-colored sapphire ring.

ANDREOLI
PAGE 378
Smoky topaz ring.

ANDREOLI
PAGE 378
Rose-gold and onyx earrings.

ANDREOLI
PAGE 379
Necklace with white diamonds and yellow sapphires.

ANDREOLI
PAGE 379
Diamond necklace and earring set.

ANDREOLI
PAGE 379
Yellow jade ring.

ANDREOLI
PAGE 379
Brown diamond ring.

ANDREOLI
PAGE 380
Ruby and diamond necklace and earring set.

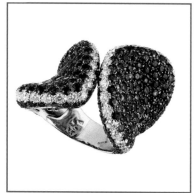

ANDREOLI
PAGE 380
Sapphire ring.

ANDREOLI
PAGE 380
Sapphire ring.

ANDREOLI
PAGE 381
Diamond earrings.

ANDREOLI
PAGE 381
Coral and emerald necklace.

ANDREOLI
PAGE 381
Coral and emerald earrings.

ANDREOLI
PAGE 381
Coral and black diamond earrings.

ANDREOLI
PAGE 381
Pearl rings.

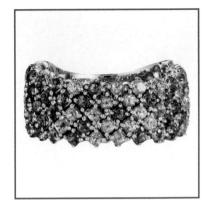

ANDREOLI
PAGE 382
Multi-colored sapphire ring.

Listing

530

ANDREOLI
PAGE 382
Turquoise earrings.

ANDREOLI
PAGE 382
Turquoise necklace.

ANDREOLI
PAGE 382
Turquoise and black diamond earrings.

ANDREOLI
PAGE 383
Emerald ring.

ANDREOLI
PAGE 383
Emerald earrings.

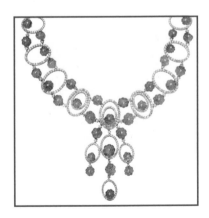

ANDREOLI
PAGE 383
Emerald necklace.

ASSAEL
PAGE 384
Pearl necklace.

ASSAEL
PAGE 384
Pearl earrings.

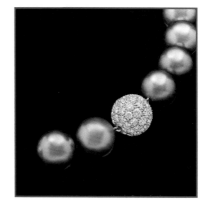

ASSAEL
PAGE 385
Pearl necklace.

ASSAEL
PAGE 386
Pearl earrings.

ASSAEL
PAGE 386
Pearl necklace.

ASSAEL
PAGE 387
Pearl necklace.

ASSAEL
PAGE 387
Diamond ring.

ASSAEL
PAGE 388
Pearl ring.

ASSAEL
PAGE 388
Pearl earrings.

ASSAEL
PAGE 388
Pearl and diamond necklace.

ASSAEL
PAGE 389
Sapphire ring.

ASSAEL
PAGE 389
Pearl necklace.

Listing
532

ASSAEL
PAGE 390
Pearl necklace.

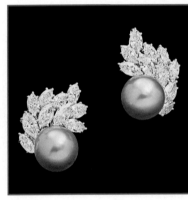

ASSAEL
PAGE 390
Pearl earrings.

ASSAEL
PAGE 391
Pearl necklaces.

ASSAEL
PAGE 391
Pearl brooch.

BAYCO
PAGE 392
Ruby ring.

BAYCO
PAGE 393
Ruby bracelet.

BAYCO
PAGE 394
Sapphire earrings.

BAYCO
PAGE 394
Sapphire jewelry.

BAYCO
PAGE 395
Sapphire necklace.

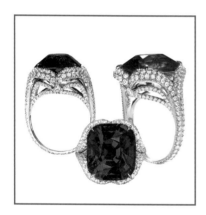

BAYCO
PAGE 395
Sapphire rings.

BAYCO
PAGE 395
Diamond ring.

BAYCO
PAGE 397
Diamond ring.

BAYCO
PAGE 397
Ruby earrings.

BAYCO
PAGE 397
Ruby ring.

BAYCO
PAGE 397
Ruby earrings.

BAYCO
PAGE 398
Diamond ring.

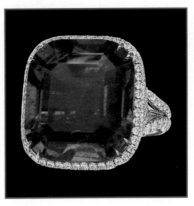

BAYCO
PAGE 398
Emerald ring.

BAYCO
PAGE 398
Diamond earrings.

BAYCO
PAGE 398
Emerald earrings.

BOUCHERON
PAGE 400
Cypris earrings.

BOUCHERON
PAGE 401
Cypris ring.

BOUCHERON
PAGE 402
Goutte de Lumière ring.

BOUCHERON
PAGE 402
Soleil Radiant ring.

BOUCHERON
PAGE 402
Soleil Radiant necklace.

BOUCHERON
PAGE 403
Lierre de Paris ring.

BOUCHERON
PAGE 403
Caméléon brooch.

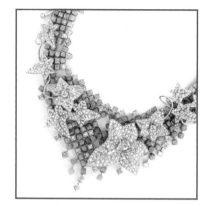

BOUCHERON
PAGE 403
Lierre de Paris necklace.

BOUCHERON
PAGE 404
Serpent Bohème brooch.

BOUCHERON
PAGE 404
Serpent Bohème ring.

BOUCHERON
PAGE 404
Adam bracelet.

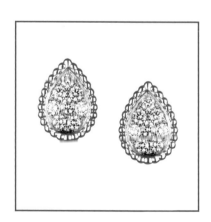

BOUCHERON
PAGE 405
Serpent Bohème earrings.

BOUCHERON
PAGE 405
Hera ring.

BOUCHERON
PAGE 405
Serpent Opalescent earrings.

BOUCHERON
PAGE 405
Caméléon Perle au Trésor brooch.

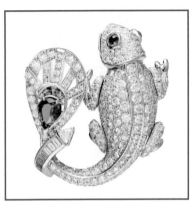

BOUCHERON
PAGE 405
Caméléon Plume de Paon brooch.

BOUCHERON
PAGE 405
Grace necklace and Ava earrings.

Listing
536

BOUCHERON
PAGE 406
Quatre Radiant Edition ring.

BOUCHERON
PAGE 406
Quatre Black Edition ring.

BOUCHERON
PAGE 406
Quatre pendant.

BOUCHERON
PAGE 406
Quatre White Edition ring.

BOUCHERON
PAGE 406
Quatre Lumière earrings.

BOUCHERON
PAGE 407
Delilah bracelet.

BOUCHERON
PAGE 407
Halo Delilah ring.

BOUCHERON
PAGE 407
Diamond bracelet.

CARTIER
PAGE 409
Diamond tiara.

CARTIER
PAGE 410
Odyssée – Parcours d'un style ring.

CARTIER
PAGE 410
Odyssée – Parcours d'un style necklace.

CARTIER
PAGE 411
Odyssée – Parcours d'un style necklace.

CARTIER
PAGE 411
Odyssée – Parcours d'un style bracelet.

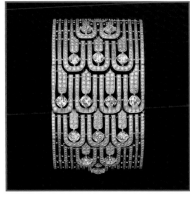

CARTIER
PAGE 411
Odyssée – Parcours d'un style bracelet.

CARTIER
PAGE 412
Sapphire necklace.

CARTIER
PAGE 412
Diamond ring.

CARTIER
PAGE 412
Diamond ring.

CARTIER
PAGE 413
Pearl and padparadscha sapphire ring.

Listing
538

CARTIER
PAGE 413
Multicolored diamond bracelet.

CARTIER
PAGE 414
Aquamarine bracelet.

CARTIER
PAGE 414
Opal and emerald bracelet.

CARTIER
PAGE 415
Green tourmaline ring.

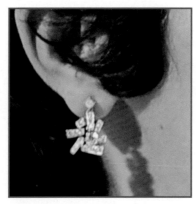

CHAUMET
PAGE 416
Diamond earrings.

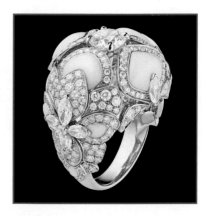

CHAUMET
PAGE 417
Chaumet Hortensia ring.

CHAUMET
PAGE 418
Chaumet Hortensia necklace.

CHAUMET
PAGE 418
Chaumet Hortensia earrings.

CHAUMET
PAGE 418
Chaumet Hortensia ring.

CHAUMET
PAGE 419
Chaumet Hortensia earrings.

CHAUMET
PAGE 419
Chaumet Hortensia bracelet.

CHAUMET
PAGE 419
Chaumet Hortensia necklace.

CHAUMET
PAGE 419
Chaumet Hortensia ring.

CHAUMET
PAGE 419
Chaumet Hortensia ring.

CHAUMET
PAGE 419
Chaumet Hortensia ring.

CHAUMET
PAGE 420
Chaumet Hortensia necklace.

CHAUMET
PAGE 420
Chaumet Hortensia earrings.

CHAUMET
PAGE 421
Chaumet Hortensia watch.

Listing
540

CHAUMET
PAGE 421
Chaumet Hortensia ring.

CHAUMET
PAGE 421
Chaumet Hortensia ring.

CHAUMET
PAGE 421
Yellow-gold and diamond earrings.

CHAUMET
PAGE 422
Chaumet Liens ring.

CHAUMET
PAGE 422
Chaumet Liens ring.

CHAUMET
PAGE 422
Chaumet Liens ring.

CHAUMET
PAGE 423
Attrape-Moi... Si Tu M'Aimes watch.

CHAUMET
PAGE 423
Attrape-Moi... Si Tu M'Aimes watch.

CHAUMET
PAGE 423
Attrape-Moi... Si Tu M'Aimes watch.

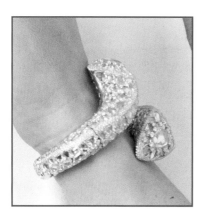

CHOPARD
PAGE 424
Diamond bracelet.

CHOPARD
PAGE 425
Red Carpet Collection necklace.

CHOPARD
PAGE 426
Red Carpet Collection ring.

CHOPARD
PAGE 427
Red Carpet Collection necklace.

CHOPARD
PAGE 427
Red Carpet Collection earrings.

CHOPARD
PAGE 427
Red Carpet Collection ring.

CHOPARD
PAGE 428
Red Carpet Collection earrings.

CHOPARD
PAGE 428
Red Carpet Collection ring.

CHOPARD
PAGE 429
Red Carpet Collection ring.

Listing
544

CHOPARD
PAGE 429
Red Carpet Collection necklace.

CHOPARD
PAGE 429
Red Carpet Collection bracelet.

CHOPARD
PAGE 429
Red Carpet Collection necklace.

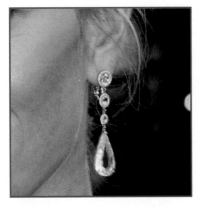

CHOPARD
PAGE 430
Red Carpet Collection earrings.

CHOPARD
PAGE 430
Red Carpet Collection earrings.

CHOPARD
PAGE 430
Red Carpet Collection earrings.

CHOPARD
PAGE 430
Red Carpet Collection watch.

CHOPARD
PAGE 430
Red Carpet Collection ring.

CHOPARD
PAGE 430
Red Carpet Collection ring.

CHOPARD
PAGE 430
Red Carpet Collection ring.

CHOPARD
PAGE 431
Diamond ring.

CHOPARD
PAGE 431
Diamond earrings.

CHOPARD
PAGE 431
Red Carpet Collection necklace.

CHOPARD
PAGE 431
Diamond earrings.

CHOPARD
PAGE 431
Diamond earrings.

CHOPARD
PAGE 431
Diamond necklace.

DE GRISOGONO
PAGE 433
Emerald and diamond necklace.

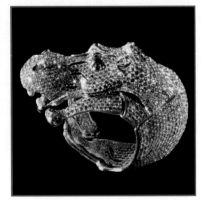

DE GRISOGONO
PAGE 434
Brown diamond bracelet.

Listing
544

DE GRISOGONO
PAGE 435
Brown diamond necklace.

DE GRISOGONO
PAGE 435
Coral earrings.

DE GRISOGONO
PAGE 436
Diamond earrings.

DE GRISOGONO
PAGE 436
Diamond ring.

DE GRISOGONO
PAGE 437
Diamond ring.

DE GRISOGONO
PAGE 437
Black diamond earrings.

DE GRISOGONO
PAGE 437
Diamond earrings.

DE GRISOGONO
PAGE 438
Emerald and yellow diamond earrings.

DE GRISOGONO
PAGE 438
Emerald and yellow diamond ring.

DE GRISOGONO
PAGE 439
Diamond earrings.

DE GRISOGONO
PAGE 439
Diamond bracelet.

GUMUCHIAN
PAGE 440
Gallop earrings.

GUMUCHIAN
PAGE 440
Gallop necklace.

GUMUCHIAN
PAGE 441
Gallop earrings.

GUMUCHIAN
PAGE 442
Ring Cycle ring/bracelet.

GUMUCHIAN
PAGE 442
Ring Cycle ring/bracelet.

GUMUCHIAN
PAGE 442
Ring Cycle ring/bracelet.

GUMUCHIAN
PAGE 443
Harem ring.

Listing
546

GUMUCHIAN
PAGE 443
Harem ring.

GUMUCHIAN
PAGE 443
Nutmeg earrings.

GUMUCHIAN
PAGE 443
Nutmeg ring.

GUMUCHIAN
PAGE 443
Nutmeg ring.

GUMUCHIAN
PAGE 444
Bowlero earrings.

GUMUCHIAN
PAGE 444
Bowlero earrings.

GUMUCHIAN
PAGE 444
Bowlero necklace.

GUMUCHIAN
PAGE 445
Gallop necklace.

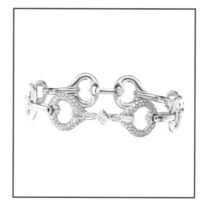

GUMUCHIAN
PAGE 445
Gallop bracelet.

GUMUCHIAN
PAGE 445
Gallop earrings.

GUMUCHIAN
PAGE 445
Gallop ring.

GUMUCHIAN
PAGE 445
Gallop ring.

GUMUCHIAN
PAGE 446
Floating Daisy earrings.

GUMUCHIAN
PAGE 446
Floating Lotus ring.

GUMUCHIAN
PAGE 446
Floating Daisy ring.

GUMUCHIAN
PAGE 446
G Boutique necklace.

GUMUCHIAN
PAGE 446
Floating Lotus earrings.

GUMUCHIAN
PAGE 447
Cloud 9 earrings.

Listing
548

GUMUCHIAN
PAGE 447
Cloud 9 earrings.

GUMUCHIAN
PAGE 447
Cloud 9 earrings.

GUMUCHIAN
PAGE 447
Cloud 9 earrings.

GUY ELLIA
PAGE 448
Yellow diamond ring.

GUY ELLIA
PAGE 449
Yellow diamond ring.

GUY ELLIA
PAGE 449
Yellow diamond necklace.

GUY ELLIA
PAGE 450
Bollywood at Sunset pendant.

GUY ELLIA
PAGE 450
Soleiado ring.

GUY ELLIA
PAGE 451
Douze watch.

GUY ELLIA
PAGE 452
Milan Royal brooch.

GUY ELLIA
PAGE 453
Himalaya necklace.

GUY ELLIA
PAGE 454
Sparkling Lady ring.

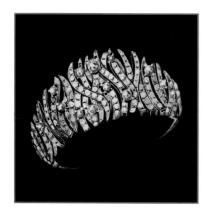

GUY ELLIA
PAGE 454
Dazzling Lady bracelet.

GUY ELLIA
PAGE 454
Dazzling Lady watch.

GUY ELLIA
PAGE 455
Dazzling Lady watch.

HAMMERMAN BROTHERS
PAGE 456
Onyx and diamond bangles.

HAMMERMAN BROTHERS
PAGE 456
Les Boules earrings.

HAMMERMAN BROTHERS
PAGE 456
Les Boules necklace.

Listing
550

HAMMERMAN BROTHERS
PAGE 457
Sapphire necklace.

HAMMERMAN BROTHERS
PAGE 457
Sapphire ring.

HAMMERMAN BROTHERS
PAGE 458
Sunburst Medallion earrings.

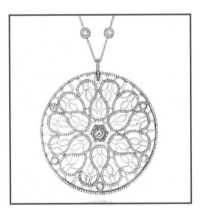

HAMMERMAN BROTHERS
PAGE 458
Medallion pendant.

HAMMERMAN BROTHERS
PAGE 459
Orange sapphire ring.

HAMMERMAN BROTHERS
PAGE 459
Diamond hoop earrings.

HAMMERMAN BROTHERS
PAGE 459
Diamond cuff.

HAMMERMAN BROTHERS
PAGE 460
Rubellite earrings.

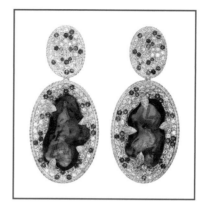

HAMMERMAN BROTHERS
PAGE 460
Rubellite earrings.

HAMMERMAN BROTHERS
PAGE 460
Black opal ring.

HAMMERMAN BROTHERS
PAGE 460
Crystal and diamond earrings.

HAMMERMAN BROTHERS
PAGE 461
Tourmaline and diamond earrings.

HAMMERMAN BROTHERS
PAGE 461
Turquoise and diamond earrings.

HAMMERMAN BROTHERS
PAGE 461
Aquamarine earrings.

HAMMERMAN BROTHERS
PAGE 461
Aquamarine pendant.

HAMMERMAN BROTHERS
PAGE 462
Diamond earrings.

HAMMERMAN BROTHERS
PAGE 462
Diamond necklace.

HAMMERMAN BROTHERS
PAGE 462
Sapphire necklace.

Listing

HAMMERMAN BROTHERS
PAGE 463
Emerald and diamond necklace.

HAMMERMAN BROTHERS
PAGE 463
Emerald and diamond ring.

HAMMERMAN BROTHERS
PAGE 463
Emerald and diamond earrings.

HAMMERMAN BROTHERS
PAGE 463
Emerald and diamond ring.

JACOB & CO.
PAGE 464
Rare Touch diamond mesh glove.

JACOB & CO.
PAGE 465
Yellow diamond ring.

JACOB & CO.
PAGE 466
Lace earrings.

JACOB & CO.
PAGE 466
Abanico earrings.

JACOB & CO.
PAGE 466
Abanico pendant.

JACOB & CO.
PAGE 467
Jezebel earrings.

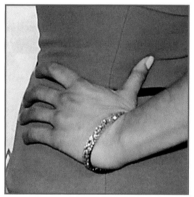

JACOB & CO.
PAGE 467
Diamond bracelet.

JACOB & CO.
PAGE 467
Yellow diamond neclace.

JACOB & CO.
PAGE 468
Nadira ring.

JACOB & CO.
PAGE 468
Nadira pendant.

JACOB & CO.
PAGE 468
Nadira bracelet.

JACOB & CO.
PAGE 468
White and black diamond clip-on earrings.

JACOB & CO.
PAGE 469
Papillon earrings.

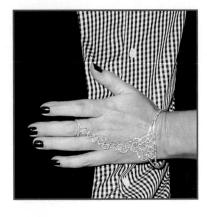

JACOB & CO.
PAGE 469
Cascata bracelet.

Listing
554

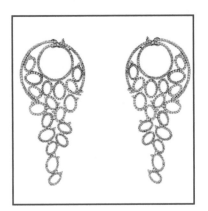

JACOB & CO.
PAGE 469
Cascata earrings.

JACOB & CO.
PAGE 470
Pink diamond ring.

JACOB & CO.
PAGE 470
Blue diamond ring.

JACOB & CO.
PAGE 470
Diamond necklace.

JACOB & CO.
PAGE 471
Titanium and diamond bracelet.

JACOB & CO.
PAGE 471
Pearl and emerald tassel necklace.

JACOB & CO.
PAGE 471
Diamond bangles.

JEWELMER JOAILLERIE
PAGE 472
Charleston collection.

JEWELMER JOAILLERIE
PAGE 473
Vitta ring.

JEWELMER JOAILLERIE
PAGE 474
Madame de Pompadour earrings.

JEWELMER JOAILLERIE
PAGE 474
Madame de Pompadour bracelet.

JEWELMER JOAILLERIE
PAGE 474
Goldenberry ring.

JEWELMER JOAILLERIE
PAGE 474
Goldenberry necklace.

JEWELMER JOAILLERIE
PAGE 475
Charleston necklace.

JEWELMER JOAILLERIE
PAGE 475
Charleston collection.

JEWELMER JOAILLERIE
PAGE 476
Dolce Rosa ring.

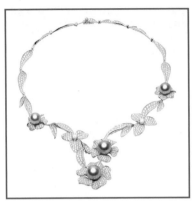

JEWELMER JOAILLERIE
PAGE 476
Dolce Rosa necklace.

JEWELMER JOAILLERIE
PAGE 477
Grand Tropics bracelet.

Listing

556

JEWELMER JOAILLERIE
PAGE 477
Grand Tropics necklace.

JEWELMER JOAILLERIE
PAGE 478
La Vita pendants.

JEWELMER JOAILLERIE
PAGE 478
C'est La Vie cuff.

JEWELMER JOAILLERIE
PAGE 478
Effloro rings.

JEWELMER JOAILLERIE
PAGE 478
Zen ring.

JEWELMER JOAILLERIE
PAGE 478
Zen ring.

JEWELMER JOAILLERIE
PAGE 478
Zen ring.

JEWELMER JOAILLERIE
PAGE 479
Giverny necklace.

JEWELMER JOAILLERIE
PAGE 479
Giverny bracelet.

JEWELMER JOAILLERIE
PAGE 479
Guimard collection.

MESSIKA
PAGE 481
Silk earrings.

MESSIKA
PAGE 482
Diamond bracelet.

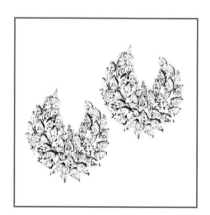

MESSIKA
PAGE 482
Silk earrings.

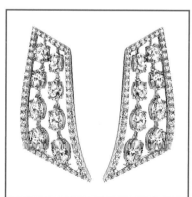

MESSIKA
PAGE 482
Ovale earrings.

MESSIKA
PAGE 482
Ovale Skinny necklace.

MESSIKA
PAGE 483
Silk necklace.

MESSIKA
PAGE 484
Amazone earrings.

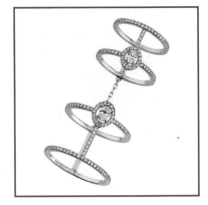

MESSIKA
PAGE 484
Amazone ring.

Listing
558

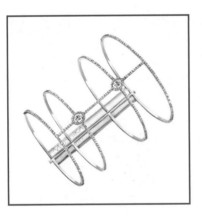

MESSIKA
PAGE 484
Amazone cuff.

MESSIKA
PAGE 484
Amazone necklace.

MESSIKA
PAGE 485
Eden hairpin.

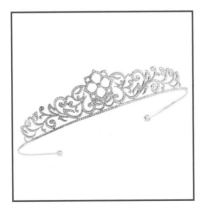

MESSIKA
PAGE 485
Eden tiara.

MESSIKA
PAGE 485
Eden earrings.

MESSIKA
PAGE 486
Move bracelets.

MESSIKA
PAGE 487
Move rings.

MESSIKA
PAGE 487
Rock & Move necklace.

MESSIKA
PAGE 487
Move cuff.

MESSIKA
PAGE 487
Rock & Move bracelet.

PIAGET
PAGE 488
Couture Précieuse ring.

PIAGET
PAGE 488
Couture Précieuse necklace.

PIAGET
PAGE 488
Couture Précieuse earrings.

PIAGET
PAGE 489
Piaget Rose necklace.

PIAGET
PAGE 489
Piaget Rose ring.

PIAGET
PAGE 490
Piaget Rose necklace.

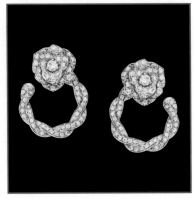

PIAGET
PAGE 490
Piaget Rose earrings.

PIAGET
PAGE 490
Piaget Rose ring.

PIAGET
PAGE 491
Piaget Rose necklace.

PIAGET
PAGE 491
Piaget Rose earrings.

PIAGET
PAGE 491
Couture Précieuse earrings.

PIAGET
PAGE 491
Couture Précieuse necklace.

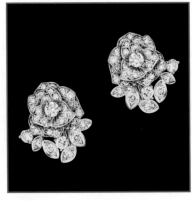

PIAGET
PAGE 492
Piaget Rose earrings.

PIAGET
PAGE 492
Piaget Rose earrings.

PIAGET
PAGE 492
Piaget Rose ring.

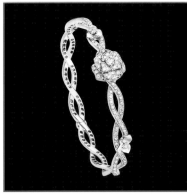

PIAGET
PAGE 492
Piaget Rose bracelet.

PIAGET
PAGE 493
Piaget Rose necklace.

PIAGET
PAGE 410
Couture Précieuse necklace.

PIAGET
PAGE 493
Limelight Couture Précieuse watch.

PIAGET
PAGE 494
Piaget Rose ring.

PIAGET
PAGE 494
Couture Précieuse earrings.

PIAGET
PAGE 494
Couture Précieuse necklace.

PIAGET
PAGE 494
Piaget Rose earrings.

PIAGET
PAGE 495
Couture Précieuse earrings.

PIAGET
PAGE 495
Couture Précieuse necklace.

PIAGET
PAGE 495
Possession bracelet.

Listing

562

PIAGET
PAGE 495
Possession necklace.

PIAGET
PAGE 495
Piaget Rose bracelet.

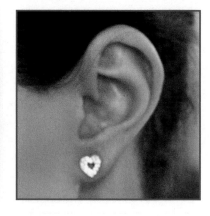

POIRAY
PAGE 496
Coeur Secret earrings.

POIRAY
PAGE 496
Coeur Fil pendant.

POIRAY
PAGE 497
Coeur Fil cuff bracelet.

POIRAY
PAGE 498
Coeur Secret pendants.

POIRAY
PAGE 498
Coeur Fil pendants.

POIRAY
PAGE 499
Coeur Entrelacé pendant.

POIRAY
PAGE 499
Coeur Entrelacé pendant.

POIRAY
PAGE 499
Coeur Fil bracelet.

POIRAY
PAGE 499
Coeur Papillon ring.

POIRAY
PAGE 500
Tresse ring.

POIRAY
PAGE 500
Indrani ring.

POIRAY
PAGE 500
Tresse ring.

POIRAY
PAGE 500
Tresse ring.

POIRAY
PAGE 501
Indrani ring.

POIRAY
PAGE 501
Cabaret rings.

POIRAY
PAGE 501
Indrani rings.

Listing
564

POIRAY
PAGE 503
Ma Première watch.

POIRAY
PAGE 503
Ma Première watch.

ROBERT WAN
PAGE 504
Robert Wan Tahiti Pearl necklace.

ROBERT WAN
PAGE 505
Heart ring.

ROBERT WAN
PAGE 506
Multi-colored pearl ring.

ROBERT WAN
PAGE 506
Pearl-themed lighter.

ROBERT WAN
PAGE 506
Robert Wan Connoisseur necklace.

ROBERT WAN
PAGE 507
Mermaid-themed pearl pen.

ROBERT WAN
PAGE 507
Dolphin ring.

ROBERT WAN
PAGE 507
Dolphin necklace.

ROBERT WAN
PAGE 508
Desert Rose set.

ROBERT WAN
PAGE 509
Tatoo ring.

ROBERT WAN
PAGE 509
Ariake earrings.

ROBERT WAN
PAGE 509
Ariake pendant.

ROBERT WAN
PAGE 509
Rose des Sables ring.

ROBERT WAN
PAGE 510
Butterfly necklace.

ROBERT WAN
PAGE 510
Fairy Tale necklace.

ROBERT WAN
PAGE 511
Dreamy necklace.

Listing
566

SUTRA
PAGE 512
Diamond and sapphire earrings.

SUTRA
PAGE 513
Ruby earrings.

SUTRA
PAGE 513
Ruby necklace.

SUTRA
PAGE 514
Paraiba tourmaline earrings.

SUTRA
PAGE 514
Sapphire bracelet.

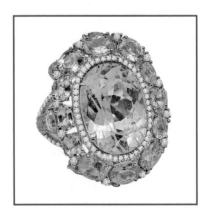

SUTRA
PAGE 514
Paraiba tourmaline ring.

SUTRA
PAGE 514
Agate earrings.

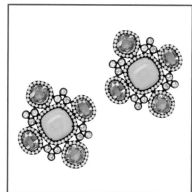

SUTRA
PAGE 515
Turquoise earrings.

SUTRA
PAGE 515
Turquoise necklace.

SUTRA
PAGE 515
Turquoise ring.

SUTRA
PAGE 516
Ruby pendant.

SUTRA
PAGE 516
Ruby earrings.

SUTRA
PAGE 516
Diamond drop earrings.

SUTRA
PAGE 516
Coral earrings.

SUTRA
PAGE 517
Ruby earrings.

SUTRA
PAGE 517
Coral ring.

SUTRA
PAGE 517
Ruby earrings.

SUTRA
PAGE 517
Ruby ring.

Listing
568

SUTRA
PAGE 518
Black opal bracelet.

SUTRA
PAGE 518
Black opal earrings.

SUTRA
PAGE 518
Emerald earrings.

SUTRA
PAGE 519
Emerald earrings.

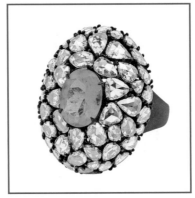

SUTRA
PAGE 519
Emerald and diamond ring.

SUTRA
PAGE 519
Emerald and diamond ring.

SUTRA
PAGE 519
Emerald and diamond bracelet.

TAKAT
PAGE 520
Emerald earrings.

TAKAT
PAGE 520
Emerald ring.

TAKAT
PAGE 521
Emerald necklace.

TAKAT
PAGE 522
Tanzanite earrings.

TAKAT
PAGE 522
Tanzanite earrings.

TAKAT
PAGE 522
Tanzanite pendant.

TAKAT
PAGE 522
Tanzanite ring.

TAKAT
PAGE 523
Tanzanite earrings.

TAKAT
PAGE 523
Tanzanite ring.

TAKAT
PAGE 523
Tanzanite ring.

TAKAT
PAGE 523
Tanzanite ring.

Listing
570

TAKAT
PAGE 523
Tanzanite necklace.

TAKAT
PAGE 524
Emerald ring.

TAKAT
PAGE 524
Emerald ring.

TAKAT
PAGE 525
Emerald ring.

TAKAT
PAGE 525
Emerald necklace.

TAKAT
PAGE 525
Emerald ring.

TAKAT
PAGE 525
Emerald ring.

TAKAT
PAGE 525
Emerald cufflinks.

TAKAT
PAGE 526
Emerald ring.

TAKAT
PAGE 526
Emerald bracelet.

TAKAT
PAGE 526
Emerald earrings.

TAKAT
PAGE 527
Emerald earrings.

TAKAT
PAGE 527
Emerald ring.

TAKAT
PAGE 527
Paraiba tourmaline ring.

TAKAT
PAGE 528
Emerald earrings.

PHOTO CREDITS

BIBLIOGRAPHY

Becker, Vivienne. "The secret watch: Time for a hint of fantasy." *Financial Times*. London: January 20, 2013.

Belcher, David. "Wrist Watches: From Battlefield to Fashion Accessory." *The New York Times*. New York: October 22, 2013.

Bennett, David, and Daniela Mascetti. *Celebrating Jewellery: Exceptional Jewels of the Nineteenth and Twentieth Centuries*. Antique Collectors' Club Ltd.: Woodbridge, Suffolk, 2012.

Bradner, Liesl. "Madeleine Albright's brooches tell a story at Bowers Museum." *Los Angeles Times*. Los Angeles: October 15, 2012.

Church, Rachel. *Rings*. V & A Publishing: London, 2011.

Corbett, Patricia. *Verdura: The life and work of a master jeweler*. Thames & Hudson: London, 2002.

Falk, Fritz. *Serpentina: Snake Jewelry from around the World*. Arnoldsche: Stuttgart, 2011.

Geoffroy-Schneiter, Bérénice. *Asian Jewellery: Ethnic Rings, Bracelets, Necklaces, Earrings, Belts, Head Ornaments*. Skire Editore: Milan, 2011.

Geoffroy-Schneiter, Bérénice. *Ethnic Style: History and Fashion*. Assouline: New York, 2001.

Loring, John. *Louis Comfort Tiffany at Tiffany & Co.* Harry N. Abrams, Inc.: New York, 2002.

Loring, John. *Tiffany Jewels*. Harry N. Abrams, Inc.: New York, 1999.

Markowitz, Yvonne J. *Artful Adornments: Jewelry from the Museum of Fine Arts, Boston*. MFA Publications: Boston, 2011.

Mascetti, Diana, and Amanda Triossi. *Earrings from Antiquity to the Present*. Thames & Hudson: London, 1990.

Mascetti, Daniela and Amanda Triossi. *The Necklace: From Antiquity to the Present*. Harry N. Abrams, Inc.: New York, 1997.

Mouillefarine, Laurence, and Évelyne Possémé. *Art Deco Jewelry*. Thames & Hudson: New York, 2009.

Munn, Geoffrey. *Tiaras: Past and Present*. V&A Publishing: London, 2002.

Peltason, Ruth. *Jewelry from Nature*. Thames & Hudson: London, 2010.

Safire, William. "On Language; Broaching the Telltale Brooch." *The New York Times*. New York: March 8, 1998.

Scarisbruck, Diana. *Rings: Jewelry of Power, Love and Loyalty*. Thames & Hudson: London, 2007.

St. John, James Augustus. *The Hellenes: The History of the Manners of the Ancient Greeks*. R. Bentley: London, 1844.

Stierlin, Henri. *The Gold of the Pharaohs*. Paris: Éditions Pierre Terrail, 2003.

Zapata, Janet, Carol Woolton and David Warren. *Anna Hu: Symphony of Jewels, Opus 1*. Thames & Hudson: London, 2012.

THIS PAGE: Gumuchian necklace.